# MOBILE AND WIRELESS COMMUNICATIONS

# MOBILE AND WIRELESS COMMUNICATIONS: AN INTRODUCTION

**Gordon A. Gow and Richard K. Smith**

Open University Press

Open University Press
McGraw-Hill Education
McGraw-Hill House
Shoppenhangers Road
Maidenhead
Berkshire
England
SL6 2QL

email: enquiries@openup.co.uk
world wide web: www.openup.co.uk

and Two Penn Plaza, New York, NY 10121–2289, USA

First published 2006

A catalogue record of this book is available from the British Library

ISBN 10: 0335 217 613 (pb) 0335 217 621 (hb)
ISBN 13: 978 0 335 217 618 (pb) 9780 335 217 625 (hb)

Library of Congress Cataloging-in-Publication Data
CIP data applied for

Typeset by YHT Ltd, London
Printed in Poland by OZ Graf. S.A.
www.polskabook.pl

# Dedication

To Davis – for whom this will all seem like ancient history.
To Deborah – who indulges my fascination for mobile gadgets.

Dedication

# Contents

# List of figures and tables

## Figures

## Tables

The authors and the Publisher would like to thank the following for their contribution and permission to use the following images and illustrations:

**Figure 2.1** *Electromagnetic Spectrum*, courtesy of Hatem Zayed, 2006
**Figure 2.4** *ITU World Regions*, courtesy of Hatem Zayed, 2006
**Figure 3.1** *Mobile Telephones in the 1960s*, reproduced with permission from Geoff Fors
**Figure 3.2** *Radio Cells in a typical configuration for Bell AMPA system*, courtesy of Hatem Zayed, 2006
**Figure 3.3** *A typical antenna mast at a cell-site base station*, courtesy of Tod Klassy
**Figure 3.4** *Three segments of a mobile phone network*, courtesy of Hatem Zayed, 2006
**Figure 3.5** *A mobile phone from the 1980s*, reproduced with permission from Tom Farley
**Figure 3.6** *The Carterfone*, reproduced with permission from www.sandman.com
**Figure 4.1** *The last mile of a mobile phone network*, courtesy of Hatem Zayed, 2006
**Figure 4.2** *Illustration of the TDMA concept*, courtesy of Hatem Zayed, 2006
**Figure 4.3** *Illustration of the CDMA concept*, courtesy of Hatem Zayed, 2006
**Figure 4.4** *Nokia phones from the 1990s*, reproduced with permission from Nokia
**Figure 4.6** *SMS use worldwide*, courtesy of Hatem Zayed, 2006
**Figure 4.7** *Zed Phillipines portal*, courtesy of zed (http://smart.zed.com)
**Figure 5.1** *The Fixed-Mobile continuum*, courtesy of Hatem Zayed, 2006
**Figure 5.2** *The fixed-portable-mobile continuum*, courtesy of Hatem Zayed, 2006
**Figure 5.4** *Mobile data network architecture*, courtesy of Hatem Zayed, 2006
**Figure 6.1** *An early IMT-2000 concept*, courtesy of Hatem Zayed, 2006
**Figure 8.1** *Ofcom's proposal for liberalizing its spectrum management policy*, courtesy of Hatem Zayed, 2006
**Figure 8.2** *Spectrum use in the PCS and Wi-Fi bands*, courtesy of Hatem Zayed, 2006
**Figure 8.3** *A full mesh network concept*, courtesy of Hatem Zayed, 2006
**Figure 8.4** *Comparison of narrowband versus spread spectrum systems*, courtesy of Hatem Zayed, 2006
**Figure 9.1** *RFID Transponder*, reproduced courtesy of Wikipedia
**Figure 9.2** *Mobile TV*, courtesy of DVB Online

Every effort has been made to trace the copyright holders but if any have been inadvertently overlooked the publisher will be pleased to make the necessary arrangement at the first opportunity.

# Acknowledgements

The authors would like to thank all those who have contributed to this effort, including those students who agreed to read and comment on chapter drafts. In particular we wish to thank Rob McTavish from the Centre for Distance Education at Simon Fraser University for allowing us to develop the course that has resulted in this book. Julie Simonsen provided much needed assistance in preparing the manuscript and helping to maintain 'WiBo', the Plone-based content management system that helped to span the gap between London and Vancouver while we collaborated on this project. We would especially like to acknowledge Chris Cudmore from Open University Press/McGraw-Hill Education for taking an initial interest in the proposal and for his ongoing support throughout the review and publishing process. We would also like to extend our appreciation to the efforts of those reviewers whose comments have led to significant improvements in a number of key areas of the book.

# 1 Introduction

One of the very first books published on the social impact of the mobile phone was Timo Kopomaa's *The City in Your Pocket: Birth of the Mobile Information Society*. The book, published in 2000, was based on research that Kopomaa had undertaken for Nokia and Sonera as part of his doctoral studies in the Centre for Urban and Regional Studies at the Helsinki University of Technology. The first line he writes in the book is peculiar: 'Mobile communication is not a serious matter'. By this, we assume he is referring to a view of the world that would regard the mobile phone as little more than an unremarkable fact of everyday life – a simple plaything for the young, or a productivity tool for the business executive and busy parent. Kopomaa then proceeds to summarize the findings of his research, concluding that the mobile phone has in fact altered in some profound ways the urban landscape and pace of city living in northern European cities like Helsinki, suggesting in a McLuhanesque way that, 'the compass and the sounder of the urban nomad is the mobile phone'.

Then, in the closing passage of his preface he deliberately contradicts his opening remark, suggesting that the apparently mundane aspects of the mobile are indispensable for understanding this new communications medium:

> The mobile phone is already one of the world's most popular electronic devices. The crucial question in the future evolution of the mobile phone is, will it still be steered by the choices of the users, or will the social aspect be replaced by the demands of technological convergence? It seems that mobile telecommunication is, after all, a serious business.[2]

A serious business it would certainly prove to be in the years immediately following the publication of Kopomaa's trail blazing effort. On the one hand, mobile phones were quickly becoming one of the world's most popular electronic consumer items with global subscriber numbers topping one billion in 2003, and exceeding total fixed line telephone connections. On the other hand, shortly after the publication of Kopomaa's book, in 2001–02, the European mobile telecom industry teetered on the brink of financial ruin following the outrageous spending sprees for licences to build third generation mobile phone networks.

In the academy, social scientists also began to take a growing interest in the everyday life of the mobile phone and its social impact. To be more precise, the social aspects of mobile communications had been integral to the industrial design strategy of companies like Nokia for some time prior to 2001 but it was not until 2002 that the first general collection of scholarly research made its way to the bookshelf. James Katz and Mark Aakhus (2002) edited an international collection of papers in their book *Perpetual Contact: Mobile Communication, Private Talk, Public Performance*. Popular interest in mobile communications was also sparked in 2002 with Howard Rheingold's (2002) book *Smart Mobs*, which brought the world of

**3G** and **Wi-Fi** out of the engineering labs and into the street, and prompted a generation of students to wonder about this new way of communicating and its impact on our lives.

While this growing body of scholarly literature has been a tremendous asset for teaching the social impact of mobile communications, we realized quite early on that a well rounded intellectual engagement with this topic would require that students have a firm grounding in the key technical terms and concepts. In the summer of 2001 we first introduced an undergraduate course on the social impact of the mobile phone at Simon Fraser University in Vancouver, Canada. The limited selection of books and articles available at that time was helpful but we also wanted to explain to our students how the devices functioned and why these seemingly mundane technical details are important for social studies. We also found that students were often hindered in discussions on topics such as text messaging culture, the role of **GSM** in European politics, and the policy implications of 3G, simply because they lacked the confidence that a basic grounding in technical matters would have given them. Moreover, our students wanted to know where these developments had come from, how these technologies work, why they have given rise to certain social issues, and where wireless networks might be headed in the near future.

Our quest to locate suitable readings to fulfil this demand proved to be a greater challenge than we initially expected, mostly because the large amount of technical material available was located in specialized business and engineering publications. In fact, we could not find a suitable source able to provide our students with an integrated overview and basic grounding in the key terms and concepts of this emerging field. On the contrary, we often found very good material spread across a range of technically detailed or otherwise narrowly focused books and reports. Undaunted, we began to gather and sift through the range of materials in order to compile our own guide suitable for classroom teaching.

That compilation has since become this book, with the philosophy behind it reflecting our initial experience in the classroom: a firm grounding in basic technical terms and concepts is an important prerequisite for an informed, critical engagement with current social issues in mobile and wireless communications. In following this core idea we have assembled a reasonably self-contained introduction to the field of mobile communications and designed it specifically as a course 'primer' or supplement to other discipline-specific readings that explore the issues in greater detail.

This book is intended primarily as a resource for college and university courses across a range of social scientific disciplines, including media and communications, sociology, public policy and management studies. However, we also believe this book will appeal to academics and professional researchers in the social sciences who are looking for a quick introduction to the field of mobile and wireless communications. We hope that a number of features of the book will appeal to this broad readership.

First, it provides a single source point for key technical terms and concepts for the otherwise non-technical reader. While there is a generous selection of technical material on the market, much of it is spread across a wide number of publications that are written for engineers or upper-level management students. The content of this book has been gathered from across this range of materials and revised for a non-technical audience. We have tried wherever possible to integrate these details into a set of narrative structures that will helps students to perceive their relevance in the wider social and industry context.

Second, it offers a socially relevant perspective on the technical foundations of mobile and wireless communications. This perspective draws attention to the institutional, regulatory and cultural influences over the past several decades rather than simply dealing with pure technical details. Each chapter attempts to highlight the pervasive influence of social factors on major developments in the field and how these inform new public policy issues, stimulate emergent cultural practices and to reinforce competing visions for mobile communications networks.

Third, it aims to be global in coverage and reasonably comprehensive in scope. This book covers major developments and emerging aspects of the North American, European and Asia Pacific markets. We have included a diverse range of mobile communications technology and services including voice and data services, wireless **LAN**s, and emerging data applications such as third generation (3G) mobile telecommunications.

The book is divided into nine chapters, including this Introduction. The remaining chapters progress from radio basics into more complex subject matter and are intended to provide readers with an opportunity to first learn and then to encounter key terms and concepts in use. As a result, the writing style may at times feel somewhat repetitive. This is deliberate effort on our part to provide readers with the opportunity to refresh their new vocabulary and knowledge.

We begin, in Chapter 2 with the basic terms and concepts relevant to **radio spectrum**. Spectrum is the foundation for mobile communications and much of the significant social, economic, and political aspects of the wireless sector are rooted in these technical dimensions of radio systems. This chapter provides a basic vocabulary and perspective on **spectrum management** on which much of the rest of the book then builds.

Chapter 3 describes the early history of mobile radiotelephony, drawing out the impetus behind the development of **cellular network design** and the key innovations that made possible the first handheld mobile phones. In Chapter 4, we discuss the second generation (2G) digital mobile phones of the 1990s and how they led to a personal communications revolution. In this chapter we also introduce a range of technical terms and innovations that remain of vital importance in today's mobile communications sector.

Chapter 5 expands on the terms and concepts to present the so-called 2.5G innovations that have transformed the mobile phone into a multipurpose gadget for imaging and entertainment. The movement toward third generation (3G) mobile phones is covered in Chapter 6, where we introduce the early **IMT–2000** vision of a 'virtual home environment' that was radically transformed by the advent of the Internet in the mid-1990s to become today's vision of a Wireless Web technology for mobile broadband. Chapter 7 turns to examine a potential competitor to 3G in the form of Wi-Fi in its various permutations.

Chapter 8 returns to the subject of radio spectrum, explaining how new technologies and network design concepts are raising fundamental questions about spectrum management practices that have been around for nearly a century. Finally, in Chapter 9, we discuss the advent of the wireless **Personal Area Network (PAN)** enabled by **Bluetooth** technology and then cast our gaze ahead to see what might be over the horizon both in terms of technological change and emerging social issues. At the end of each chapter we have included a set of recommended readings to encourage further exploration of these topics.

For those students who will enter the world of communications policy analysis or research, or perhaps media production, a good working knowledge of the terms and concepts of mobile communications is a definite asset. Such knowledge will give them the ability to negotiate the maze of acronyms found in the trade press and government reports. It will also help to clarify some of the confusion and inaccuracies that often appear in the popular press. For those not so inclined, we believe that a technical foundation in mobile communications can contribute to a diverse repertoire of knowledge that will provide students with the confidence to ask critical questions and to prompt further exploration into the social origins, present day influence and future possibilities of this remarkable medium of communication.

# 2 Radio basics

The frequency spectrum is technology, industry, money, culture, and power.
(J.D. Bedin in Struzak 2000)

## 2.1 Introduction

A world with mobile phones would not be possible without the one resource essential to all wireless communications: electromagnetic energy. It is electromagnetic energy that enables us to broadcast radio signals over the air. It exists everywhere in the universe, it is invisible and it works in ways that are still something of a mystery to scientists. In historical terms, humans harnessed it only very recently – within the past one hundred years or so – for the transmission of human intelligence, and yet the social impact of this new medium of communication has been nothing less than phenomenal. Some say the historical impact of wireless communications will seem as revolutionary for the world as Gutenberg's moveable type was in the 15th century.

Radio communications technology is derived from the knowledge and ability to build devices that can transmit and receive electromagnetic energy without the use of wires or other cables. This technology, in effect, uses electromagnetic energy – also known as the *radio spectrum* – as a medium of communication. It is important to remember that the radio spectrum is a naturally occurring resource, much like air or water, and it is here where the possibilities for radio communications begin and end. For this reason it is important to understand something about electromagnetic energy and the radio spectrum, if only because this is the foundation of mobile and cellular telephone systems.

The aim of this chapter is to present some of the basic terms and concepts relevant to radio spectrum and a public policy activity known as spectrum management. These terms and concepts are important if you are to grasp the technology of radio in some of its more significant social, economic and political aspects. The chapter also includes a brief casestudy intended to illustrate key steps in the policymaking process for spectrum management and to provide a starting point for international comparison. One commentator has observed that the radio spectrum is a resource that supports a high stakes game of 'technology, industry, money, culture, and power'. Over the past century this has always been true, but today it is more so than ever before.

## 2.2    Radio basics

The 'radio spectrum' is a term that scientists, engineers and policymakers use to classify a vast and otherwise undifferentiated swath of electromagnetic energy that exists in the universe. This form of energy makes possible the development and use of technologies such as broadcast radio and TV, garage door openers, remote controlled toy airplanes, geographic positioning systems (GPS) and mobile phones. In fact, none of these technologies would be possible without the pioneering work of people like the French mathematician Jean-Baptiste Fourier (1768–1830), who first theorized an idea of radio spectrum or the entrepreneurship of Guglielmo Marconi (1874–1937) who is credited with the first successful experiments in wireless telegraphy in the late 19th century.

With a growing stock of theoretical and practical knowledge in the technique of wireless transmission, entrepreneurs in the early 20th century developed the first reliable radio systems and the spectrum (sometimes called 'RF' for radio frequency) quickly became recognized as a radically new means by which human beings could communicate. This recognition would bring immense changes to maritime communications and military strategy; it would also inspire the birth of new forms of entertainment, revolutionize industrial techniques and inaugurate a major globalization initiative to coordinate its use within and across international borders.

In the early years there was comparatively little need to differentiate between various sections of the radio spectrum because there was relatively modest demand for access to it. At that time anybody could build and operate a radio system. Soon, however, the growing popularity of amateur and broadcast radio stations created interference problems and led to political pressure to manage this resource so that it could meet growing demand, particularly for commercial interests in an emerging broadcasting industry. Over the past century, nationally and internationally supervised spectrum management programmes have become the means by which access to the radio spectrum is controlled. At the heart of these programmes is a system for dividing radio spectrum into discrete bands of frequencies, and then allocating those frequencies for specific types of use.

One reason for dividing the radio spectrum into discrete bands is because radio energy possesses both electrical and magnetic properties, which makes different portions of the spectrum suitable for different purposes. In fact, it is the interaction of the electrical and magnetic properties of radio energy combined with changing social demands for particular kinds of radio communications systems that makes spectrum management a *socio-technical* undertaking, often of considerable complexity and controversy.

### 2.2.1    Electromagnetic energy

To begin to understand how radio energy is harnessed for human communication it is helpful to start with a simple rule of physics: when materials vibrate they transfer energy to their surroundings. This transference of energy can take the form of either 'compressional' waves or *transverse* waves. Sound is transmitted through the air by means of compressional waves like, for example, when we speak and our mouth expels air from our lungs. These waves travel through the air and eventually to a listener's ears. The air acts as a medium that enables these compressional waves to propagate from one place to another. Sound waves can also travel through other media, such as water, oil, concrete, wood or many other physical materials. However, the specific properties of a material will have an influence on the propagation of compressional waves: sound waves moving through the air will be affected by altitude and temperature. At sea level, with a temperature of 15 degrees centigrade, the speed of sound waves is about 340 metres per second, which is the equivalent of 1225 Km/h or 761 Mph. At higher altitudes or different temperatures this velocity will change. The velocity will also change depending on the type of medium. For example, sound waves tend to travel more quickly through water than through the air.

Radio energy, however, is quite different from sound energy because it consists of transverse waves. Compared with sound energy, radio waves travel at an extremely high velocity – at the speed of light (about 300,000,000 metres per second) – and radio waves can travel in a vacuum where there is no air or other apparent physical entity to act as a medium. All electromagnetic energy consists of transverse waves. For instance, the visible light reflected from this page reaches your eyes by way of transverse waves, so does the electrical energy that powers your reading lamp and so does the radio signal that is transmitted and received by a mobile phone. In fact, as far as most physicists are concerned, visible light, electricity and radio waves are all part of the same extended family of energy:

> light is part of what is called the electromagnetic spectrum, which includes infrared radiation, radio waves, gamma rays, X-rays, ultraviolet radiation, and so on. All of these are a form of light; they just have energies that differ from the visible light that our eyes can see. Thus, these forms of electromagnetic radiation all travel at the speed of light too.[1]

It is perhaps remarkable to realize that if we consider light as belonging to the extended family of radio energy, then our eyes are a kind of radio receiver! Our ears, on the other hand, are 'acoustic' receivers, designed for the compressional waves of natural sound but not the transverse waves generated by electromagnetic energy.

In many cases radio technologies use *both* compressional and transverse waves to support human communication. For example, in the case of radio dispatch for a taxi service, it is necessary to convert the natural sound energy (compressional waves) created by the dispatcher's speech into electromagnetic energy (transverse waves) in order for it to be transmitted by the radio system. This is done using a

## The Electromagnetic Spectrum

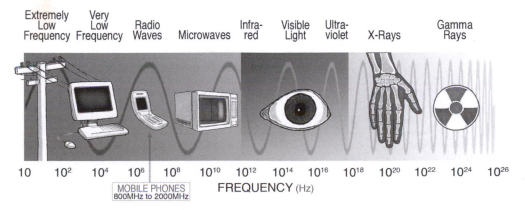

**Figure 2.1**   Electromagnetic spectrum

'transducer', which is a device more commonly known as a microphone. Once converted into the transverse waves of electromagnetic energy, the spoken word can then be transmitted 'over the air' to be received by the taxi fleet. Radios installed in the taxis then convert the electromagnetic energy back into acoustic compressional waves so that the taxi driver can hear the dispatcher's voice through a speaker (another type of 'transducer'). This process of conversion from one type of energy into another, and back again, is known as **modulation** and **demodulation**, and is very important in mobile communications systems. In fact, 'modem' comes from the conjugation of terms *modulation-demodulation* and describes a device for computers that converts sound energy into electromagnetic energy.

Another reason to make this distinction between natural sound and electromagnetic energy is that many of the same terms and concepts – such as **frequency** and **wavelength** – are used to describe both types of energy, even though compressional and transverse waves have very different properties. It is important to recognize that *radio waves are not the same form of energy as sound waves*. Radio waves travel at the speed of light and can pass through a vacuum, such as outer space. Sound waves move much, much slower and require a physical medium such as air or water in order to propagate from one place to another.

Recalling that basic rule of physics – when materials vibrate they transfer energy to their surroundings – is also helpful in understanding the terms and concepts used to measure and classify radio energy. Radio waves are the result of a 'vibrating' magnetic field that is created by a pulsating electrical signal – hence they are a form of electro-magnetic energy. The function of an antenna on a radio is to concentrate and direct these vibrations in a particular direction – either from the radio into its surrounding environment (transmission) or from the surrounding environment into the radio (reception). The tempo at which the electromagnetic field vibrates determines whether the transverse waves are longer or shorter and, in turn, dictates the portion of the spectrum that a radio system will occupy. As you might imagine, this relationship between wavelength and spectrum is a primary consideration in the design and regulation of all radiocommunications technologies, including mobile phone networks.

### 2.2.2  Frequency and wavelength

The length of a radio wave is a property that allows us to classify the radio spectrum according to *frequency*. During transmission or reception, the number of energy vibrations reaching an antenna each second is measured as the frequency of the signal. One vibration per second is known by the term '**Hertz**' (Hz), named after Heinrich Rudolf Hertz (1847–94) the German physicist who is credited with being the very first person to send and receive radio waves in the laboratory. The range of electromagnetic energy designated specifically as 'the radio spectrum' is measured in thousands, millions or billions of vibrations per second. Table 2.1 shows the correct terms and abbreviations for each range of frequencies.

**Table 2.1**  Radio waves measured as frequencies

| Vibrations per second | Term | Abbreviation |
| --- | --- | --- |
| 1 | hertz | Hz |
| 1 000 | kilohertz | kHz |
| 1 000 000 | megahertz | MHz |
| 1 000 000 000 | gigahertz | GHz |

The frequency of a radio wave will determine whether it is longer or shorter, which provides another measure known as *wavelength*. As a rule, the longer the wavelength, the lower the frequency; and the shorter the wavelength, the higher the frequency. We can work out this relationship more specifically with simple mathematics. Recalling that radio waves travel at the speed of light, we can divide that by the number of waves measured per second (Hertz) to arrive at a calculation for wavelength.

$$\text{wavelength (measured in metres)} = \frac{\text{speed of light (measured in metres per second)}}{\text{frequency (measured in waves per second)}}$$

**Figure 2.2**   Wavelength equation (Part 1)

Most mobile phones in North America operate at a frequency of 1.9GHz, which means they transmit and receive radio waves at almost *two billion vibrations per second*. If it were possible to take a ruler and measure the length of each individual wave, you would find it to be about 16cm (6 inches) in length. If the frequency were increased then the wavelength would become shorter. If the frequency were decreased then the wavelength would become longer.

$$\text{wavelength (measured in metres)} = \frac{\text{300 000 000 metres per second (speed of light)}}{\text{1 900 000 000 waves per second (frequency)}}$$

$$\text{wavelength (measured in metres)} = \text{0.1579 metres (about 16cm, or 6 inches)}$$

**Figure 2.3**   Wavelength equation (Parts 2 and 3)

Wavelength is an important measure because it tells us something about the useful value of any frequency being considered for radiocommunications. For instance, shorter wavelengths (higher frequencies) have difficulty passing through solid objects. If the wavelength is very, very short then the presence of rain or fog might create interference to transmission or reception because water droplets suspended in the air can cause the radio waves to be absorbed or scattered. Direct to home (DTH) satellite television (operating frequency about 12GHz) is a case in point, where trees or heavy rain may cause interference to the signal being received at the television (in the case of rain this is sometimes called 'rain fade'). Higher frequencies therefore tend to be most useful for 'line of sight' radiocommunications, where there is a low likelihood of objects standing in the way of the transmission path.

On the other hand, longer wavelengths have quite different propagation properties and in some instances can travel great distances without suffering interference. It is therefore the lower frequencies that tend to be used in very long range communications, such as short wave radio (3000kHz to 30MHz) or for military submarines operating in the deep ocean (40 to 80Hz).

In most countries around the world, it has been agreed that the portion of the electromagnetic spectrum generally used for radiocommunications is the range of frequencies between 9kHz to 275GHz. This classification is based on a long-standing arrangement established through the International Telecommunications Union and is referred to formally as 'the radio spectrum' in order to differentiate it from other types of electromagnetic energy such as visible light or X-rays.

The radio spectrum itself is then divided into eight separate **frequency bands** that are in turn subdivided into smaller groupings of frequencies according to the purpose for which they are intended to be used. Most of the radio spectrum allocated to mobile telephone service falls within the **Ultra High Frequency (UHF)** band. By contrast, satellite and fixed wireless services tend to fall within the Super High Frequency (SHF) band. AM radio broadcast is located within the Medium Frequency (MF) band and FM radio broadcast radio is located within the Very High Frequency (VHF) band.

## 2.3    Spectrum management

While people have long known about electromagnetic energy and have experimented with its effects, it is only within the last century or so that it has come to be thoroughly exploited by humans as a naturally occurring resource for communication and other purposes. We use it in our homes in the form of commercial electricity to run our dishwashers, vacuum cleaners and other appliances (alternating current (AC) in North America has a frequency of 60Hz). We also use radio energy to cook food directly in our microwave ovens (microwave energy in the 2GHz band), to open our garage doors (40MHz), and for playing with remote controlled cars and model airplanes (75MHz). With so many different types of devices using the radio spectrum, the problem of unwanted interference needs to be managed. You may have experienced unwanted radio interference, perhaps when watching television and somebody in another room starts up the vacuum cleaner or a power tool. The disruption to the signal on the TV is interference, and in some cases it could be more than a minor nuisance when, for instance, it interrupts radiocommunications for emergency services dispatch such as police, fire or ambulance.

Radio interference is a problem related to both the physical properties of the radio spectrum and to the equipment used to transmit and receive radio signals. Together, these combined factors place constraints on how effectively spectrum can be shared among different users. Based on the current understanding and accepted practice, the radio spectrum is widely considered a finite natural resource that is infinitely renewable. In other words, it is possible to run out of usable frequencies in the spectrum because of congestion and interference from many users making demands for it. This possibility leads to a situation of **spectrum scarcity**. Unlike some other natural resources, however, the radio spectrum will never be depleted over the course of time because the moment a radio system stops transmitting, that frequency becomes available for someone else to use it. The radio spectrum is a therefore renewable resource, and this possibility of **frequency sharing** or **frequency re-use** is very important for the design of mobile phone networks and for the prospects of future radio technologies, as will be discussed later in the book.

### 2.3.1    Managing a natural resource

Like other natural resources, the radio spectrum has an influence over the daily lives of all of us, and its proper management is an important factor in balancing the social and economic needs of a modern society. First and foremost, the radio spectrum is a central factor in maintaining national sovereignty and security, and governments ultimately retain the right to control access to it. In fact a considerable amount of radio spectrum is allocated for government purposes, in large part to support radiocommunications for national security and public safety activities. In the United States, for example, it is estimated that there are some 270,000 frequency assignments to federal agencies.[2] In addition to government services, the radio spectrum supports a wide range of scientific research activities, such as wildlife radio-collar tracking or radio astronomy.

In the private sector, the radio spectrum supports a wide range of businesses, such as mobile telephony or radio dispatch. It also enables the dissemination of culture through broadcast radio and television and drives a multibillion dollar industry in the form of communications equipment manufacturing. Some of the more commonly known manufacturers of radio equipment around the world include Motorola (USA), Nortel (Canada), Sony Ericsson (Sweden), Nokia (Finland) and Fujitsu (Japan).

Consumers and industry organizations are all counting on well managed radio spectrum to give them confidence to invest in research and development efforts in wireless systems. In fact, it may be useful to think of the radio spectrum as the 'real estate' of the wireless communications sector – every service provider requires a plot of frequencies on which to build a network. Without timely management of this valuable property there would likely be no mobile phone service today. This situation has led to some important debates about how the radio spectrum should be managed, what kinds of principles spectrum management should follow and what objectives it should seek to achieve in a world where radio is more important to the global economy than ever.

### 2.3.2 Allocation, allotment, assignment

In virtually all countries around the world, the radio spectrum is considered a public resource, meaning that no one single person can own it. Governments *license* the use of it to private firms or public groups, but no single company or individual person can claim an inalienable right to the radio spectrum or any portion of it.

Spectrum management generally involves a three-step process of allocation, allotment and assignment. First, the radio spectrum must be divided up into frequency bands that are *allocated* to various categories of services, such as broadcasting, navigation or mobile telecommunications. Second, specific blocks of frequencies are then *allotted* within each band according to a specific type of service and its unique technical requirements. Finally, allotments are then *assigned* to a specific type of service, such as a direct to home satellite TV provider or a mobile phone carrier. This is usually done by means of a government-led licensing or authorization process. Licenses are often limited to specific geographical areas and usually must be renewed after a certain period of time has expired.

Each step in this process of allocation, allotment and assignment must take into account competing interests in economic, technical and public policy. Engineers and planners involved in spectrum management refer to the importance of balancing economic and technical efficiency, while taking into account public interest obligations. Striking a balance between technical and economic efficiency means achieving the most effective use of spectrum without creating unwanted interference, while ensuring that it is allocated and assigned in a way that will also meet the needs of those who will provide the greatest value from it. However, these efficiencies must be counter-balanced with public policy goals that in some instances may override both technical and economic considerations. Public policy goals might include the provision of radio communications for public safety, national defence and public service broadcasting.

In recent years the challenge of achieving this balance of objectives has become more difficult than ever for a number of reasons. First, the demand for access to the radio spectrum in the past decade has been greater than in the entire preceding history of radio. This growth in demand is partly a result of the worldwide explosion of mobile phones and other wireless communications technologies. Another factor in the growing demand for access to spectrum is the wave of regulatory reform in the telecommunications sector that has taken place starting in the mid-1980s, and which had led to increased competition in the supply of both radio equipment and in demand for wireless services from businesses and individual consumers. The appearance of new technologies, such as the Geographic Positioning System (GPS) and Radio Frequency Identification Tags (RFID) have been instrumental in creating new demand for access to the radio spectrum.[3]

In most countries the responsibility for balancing these priorities falls under national government jurisdiction and usually within the portfolio of a department that is also responsible for other communications concerns, such as radio and TV licensing, and perhaps telecommunications.[4]

## 2.4   The ITU and world radio conferences

While each country is ultimately responsible for managing spectrum within its own borders, radio waves do not behave in such a politically correct manner. As a result, the process of spectrum management is also an international issue that requires countries to come together to coordinate spectrum use on a multilateral basis. The **International Telecommunications Union (ITU)**, under the auspices of the United Nations (UN) system headquartered in Geneva, is where the worldwide coordination of spectrum and the creation of radio regulations begins. The ITU is one of the oldest international organizations, founded in 1865 by 20 European states initially to coordinate telegraph communications across national borders. Today the ITU has expanded its work to encompass three main sectors of activity in telecommunications:

* Radiocommunication (ITU-R)
* Telecom Standardization (ITU-T)
* Telecom Development (ITU-D)

Of these three branches of the ITU the Radiocommunication Sector (ITU-R) is mandated to address radio spectrum management in a number of areas. It is important to note that its mandate includes satellite orbits as well as terrestrial radio systems:

> [ITU-R shall] effect allocation of bands of the radio frequency spectrum, the allotment of radio frequencies and the registration of radio frequency assignments and of any associated orbital position in the geostationary satellite orbit in order to avoid harmful interference between radio stations of different countries.[5]

Among its many activities, the ITU-R sponsors the **World Administrative Radio Conference (WRC)**, which is convened every two or three years. The previous two were held in Istanbul in 2000 and Geneva in 2003 respectively, and the 2007 conference is also planned for Geneva. The general scope of the agenda for the conferences is set well in advance (typically four to five years in advance), and offers a glimpse at some of the developments one might expect to see taking place in radio systems in the forthcoming years.

What happens at a WRC and why is it important? The WRC is the place where spectrum management issues are addressed at a worldwide level. In particular, the WRC may revise international radio regulations as well as any associated frequency allocation and allotment plans. It is the event where international policy is made with respect to the future of radio spectrum. For instance, an important accomplishment from WRC in 2000 included increasing the available spectrum for third generation (3G) mobile phone services in order to cope with the unanticipated growth in demand that followed the initial allocation of 3G spectrum at the 1992 WRC.

An important objective and difficult challenge within the WRC is the requirement to balance international standards with regional flexibility. International standards are important to enable countries to make their own plans for assigning and licensing spectrum while reducing interference problems across their borders, to create a stable context for equipment manufacturers to invest in research and development for new radio technologies, and to create economies of scale for network equipment and handsets in order to make them more affordable for consumers. If each country arbitrarily decided its own spectrum allocation for mobile phones, for instance, the result might be highly fragmented markets, with high barriers to entry due to the complicated roaming requirements in handsets and network equipment that would result.

International coordination of spectrum allocation is an essential starting point, but each region may have different industry requirements, national regulations and historical issues, and therefore must be permitted some flexibility when deciding on when and how to allocate and assign radio spectrum. At WRC-2000 when additional spectrum was allocated for mobile phone services, the final decision had to balance between allowing individual countries to accommodate national priorities while establishing a reasonable degree of international cooperation to encourage investment in new technology. A statement from that WRC summarizes the difficult process in allocating spectrum for third generation (3G) mobile phone service:

> While a global common spectrum [plan] ... was generally supported, countries supported different bands in order to protect existing services such as analogue and digital TV, digital audio broadcasting, aeronautical radio navigation service, meteorological radars, fixed wireless access and more. A lack of consensus may not have prevented countries from making mobile spectrum available ... on a national basis, but this would have resulted in higher handset prices for third generation systems because of the need to incorporate more complex circuitry to support international roaming across a large number of frequency bands.
>
> The decision provides for three common bands, available on a global basis for countries wishing to implement the terrestrial component of [3G mobile phone service] ... While the decision of the Conference globally provides for the immediate licensing and manufacturing of [3G service] in the common bands, each country will decide on the timing of availability at the national level according to need. This high degree of flexibility will also enable countries to select those parts of the bands where sharing with existing services is the most suitable, taking account of existing licences.
>
> The agreement effectively gives a green light to mobile industry worldwide in deploying confidently [3G mobile phone] networks and services and provides a stable basis for investors in the industry.[6]

The World Administrative Radio Conference is an important event where worldwide spectrum allocation and radio regulations standards are periodically reviewed, debated and modified to promote and accommodate future wireless technology and services. In conjunction with these conferences, the ITU publishes a set of Radio Regulations and maintains a Master International Frequency Register, which is intended to record all frequency assignments around the world. The current database contains over one million terrestrial frequency assignments.[7]

### 2.4.1  Regional coordination of radio spectrum

To assist in the process of international radio spectrum management, the ITU has divided the world into three regions. North America belongs to ITU Region 2, which also includes Latin America, the Caribbean and South America. Region 1 includes Europe, Russia, the Middle East and Africa. Region 3 encompasses Asia and the South Pacific, including Australia and New Zealand.

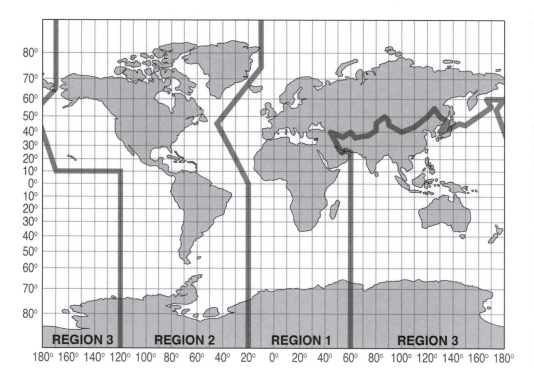

**Figure 2.4**    ITU world regions

The Radiocommunication Committee of **CITEL** (the Inter-American Telecommunication Commission) is the international organization responsible for spectrum management within ITU Region 1 and operates under the auspices of the Organization of American States. While CITEL serves as a regional body for the Americas, it acts in accordance with ITU Regulations and Recommendations. The following are excerpts from the CITEL mandate pertaining to its role in regional spectrum allocation:

To promote among Member States harmonization in the utilization of the radio frequency spectrum and the operation of radiocommunication services ... bearing especially in mind the need to prevent and avoid, to the extent possible, harmful interference between the different services.

To undertake the coordination of regional preparations for ITU World and Regional Radiocommunication Conferences, including the preparation of InterAmerican Proposals (IAPs) and common positions, as well as to undertake interregional consultations in preparation for these conferences.

To undertake the coordination and harmonization of standards related to spectrum use such as over-the-air broadcasting and common air-interfaces for radiocommunication services.[8]

In addition to the work done through CITEL in harmonizing spectrum allocation and representing ITU Region 1 at the WRC, further coordination along national borders within each region often takes the form of bilateral treaties and agreements. In the case of the United States and Canada, for example, the US Federal Communications Commission (FCC) and Canada's Ministry of Industry are directly involved in developing these arrangements.

For the 25 countries that are part of the European Union, radio spectrum management activities are governed by legislative directives pertaining to radiocommunication activities, which are informed by the European Conference on Post and Telecommunications Administrations (**CEPT**). CEPT's role extends beyond the EU to include 46 member states, and its activities are coordinated through the Copenhagen-based European Radiocommunications Office (**ERO**). Among its other activities, ERO is developing proposals for a new European Table of Frequency Allocations, which it expects to implement by 2008.[9]

In the Asia–Pacific (ITU Region 3), coordination among countries in matters related to radio spectrum is carried out through the Asia Pacific Telecommunity (**APT**). In particular, it is the APT Conference Preparatory Group for WRC that is responsible for assisting in developing common proposals for the region that are submitted at ITU World Radio Conferences.[10]

## 2.5 Assigning spectrum at the national level

What are the steps that a country must take to manage the radio spectrum? And how does a national government ensure amidst the challenges and a changing international context that its policy for spectrum management corresponds to the long-term social and economic well being of its citizens? In many countries the generic process is similar. In conjunction with the ITU and WRC, each country develops its own national spectrum management policy. This policy includes a policy framework document that sets out the objectives and public interest mandate for spectrum management in the country. The policy will include provisions for considering and adopting ITU recommendations for spectrum allocation flowing out of the World Radio Conferences. This results in a national table of frequency allocations, or **band plan** for the country. The national band plan will follow many but not necessarily all of the ITU recommendations for frequency allocation because local circumstances or political or economic priorities may require that national government adopt slightly different allocations in some frequency bands.

Having established a national band plan, spectrum managers then develop, consider and adopt specific rules for the operation of different types of radio systems (e.g., maximum power output, radio interference restrictions) and for the licensing of operators within specific bands. Public consultation and expert input are often sought at this point in the policymaking process. Licensing is an activity that takes place within each country and the process plays an important role in balancing requirements for technical and economic efficiency in spectrum use with wider public interest objectives.

### 2.5.1    The case in Canada

The following is a mini-case study of how the government of Canada manages spectrum in that country. The process is similar in other countries although you should bear in mind there will likely be important differences in jurisdiction, as well as in consultation and decision making processes between countries. The policymaking process begins and ends with a government department that is responsible for radiocommunication activities and spectrum management. In Canada, this responsibility belongs to the Ministry of Industry (Industry Canada), which publishes the *Spectrum Policy Framework*. This is a document that sets out the principles and objectives for radio spectrum management in Canada. It is informed by international policy documents as well as by formal statutory requirements such as the Canadian Radiocommunications Act. The *Spectrum Policy Framework* provides a set of policy aims to guide the myriad other activities associated with spectrum management. These activities are listed within a series of guidelines that can be summarized in three broad categories:

*   Allocation and prioritization of radio spectrum for specific services
*   Assignment and licensing of spectrum to specific users
*   Planning and consultation with the public

In recent years the *Spectrum Policy Framework* in Canada has been subject to a major review process in addition to having seen some significant changes due to periodic revisions and modifications over the years. The *Framework* provides basic direction for all spectrum policy and management in Canada, setting out a number of core objectives:

*   To promote and support the orderly development and efficient operation of radio systems in the country
*   To plan and manage spectrum use, and to emphasize efficient use, flexibility, ease of access and responsiveness to technological change
*   To represent and protect domestic interests in the international domain
*   To promote and support research and development in radio communication techniques and systems
*   To consult the general public and interested parties to ensure balanced policies and plans

To meet the first objectives, frequency assignment and licensing is undertaken with the intent of minimizing interference between radio systems while serving the largest user base possible. This is what is meant by the phrase 'orderly development and efficient operation'. A recent development in spectrum management has been to apply economic principles more actively to the process of licensing new services. Canada's *Spectrum Policy Framework*, for instance, refers to an increasing reliance on market forces in the assignment and licensing of spectrum. This translates into a number of initiatives intended to meet the objective of emphasizing flexibility, ease of access and responsiveness to technological change.

Accompanying the spectrum policy framework document, the government also publishes a national band plan, called *The Canadian Table of Frequency Allocations*. This document establishes specific spectrum allocations within the country and is based on ITU and CITEL recommendations. The allocation of spectrum in certain frequency bands does not always conform exactly to international recommendations because of conditions unique to Canada's regional and domestic matters, but these exceptions are cited as footnotes in the document.

An important activity related to the band plan is the need to provide industry and the public with a reliable forecast about the release and licensing of future portions of radio spectrum as a means of encouraging investment in new equipment and services. This is in part what is meant by 'responsiveness to technological change'. In Canada, the government issues a document entitled the *Spectrum Release Plan* that sets out the details of future licensing activities and provides valuable strategic information for research and development, as well as for investment in the wireless sector.

In conjunction with the *Release Plan*, numerous other policy documents such as a series of very technical plans are published that establish quite detailed technical parameters and regulation pertaining to the operation of radio equipment and devices in specific bands. For instance, a document with the complicated title *SRSP-510 – Technical Requirements for Personal Communications Services in the Bands 1850–1910 MHz and 1930–1990 MHz* sets out the specific technical requirements that Canadian carriers must follow when deploying digital mobile phone service. The point here is that spectrum management is an activity that extends from the lofty aims of the *Spectrum Policy Framework* to the finicky engineering details of radio systems specifications.

## 2.5.2 Bands, blocks and bandwidth

As you are now aware, the radio spectrum is classified into specific groups of frequencies known as *bands*. Within each band, specific services are allotted to smaller groupings of frequencies. For mobile phone service, the Canadian government allots **blocks** of frequencies that comprise the *bandwidth* required for the technology. In this case, bandwidth describes the range of frequencies needed to operate a specific service. For example, prior to assigning digital mobile phone service in Canada, spectrum managers divided the 2GHz band into 30MHz blocks of frequencies, which is a bandwidth that accorded with the technical requirements of the service. During this initial licensing period, spectrum managers also kept some blocks of spectrum in reserve, correctly anticipating future growth in the digital mobile phone market.

## 2.5.3 Spectrum release and licensing

An important aspect of Industry Canada's role in spectrum management is spectrum release and licensing. Before any band or block of frequencies can be licensed, they must be released for licensing. In some cases, this will require the displacement of incumbent users already established in a particular band – sometimes referred to as '**band-clearing**'. While the Canadian government retains the right to modify its Table of Frequency Allocations when it deems necessary, it also attempts to do so through public consultation. The time frame for spectrum release and licensing must therefore take into account the cost and timing of relocating incumbents who are currently using spectrum in the reallocated portions.

Perhaps the most significant step in the spectrum management process, following the allocation of frequencies, is to assign spectrum to specific users through a licensing process. The Canadian government does this by issuing '**radio authorizations**' to specific individuals or to companies. A radio authorization provides an exclusive right to operate on a specific frequency in a geographic area and under specified technical conditions. In Canada, a radio authorization takes one of two forms: a radio apparatus licence or a **spectrum licence**.

Strictly speaking, a radio licence permits operation of specific type of radio equipment conforming to a set of standards – like those set out in the *SRSP-510* document noted above – and to operate within a specific geographic area. A spectrum licence, on the other hand, permits operation within a designated portion of the radio spectrum for a specific geographic area, with far less emphasis on the specific type of radio apparatus being used – although there will be some minimal technical conditions imposed on the licence that are intended to prevent unwanted interference with nearby frequency bands.

The assignment of radio authorizations can be done in one of two ways: either a **first come first served** (**FCFS**) or a competitive process involving either a **comparative review** (sometimes called a 'beauty contest') or with a market-based process called a **spectrum auction**. Where the supply of spectrum exceeds the demand from potential users, the FCFS process is often used. When demand for spectrum is greater than the available spectrum, the comparative review has been the traditional means for assigning it. Today spectrum auctions are increasingly being used in cases where there is high market demand for spectrum, as in the case of mobile phone service. Another method that was attempted in the United States for the licensing of first generation mobile phones in the 1980s was a **lottery** system that proved to be a major headache for the government and resulted in a questionable outcome for the public interest.

Spectrum auctions are a relatively new development in the licensing process, first used in New Zealand in 1990, they are now a popular means of issuing licences for both second and third generation mobile phone services. Where there is strong commercial interest in providing a radio service, such as mobile phones, this method is regarded as superior to the traditional comparative review process for a number of reasons:

- Auctions promote both technical and economic efficiency by establishing a market-based price of the licence rather than one set arbitrarily by a government
- Auctions are quicker and more efficient than other review processes
- Auctions are transparent, unlike a comparative review where the government's specific criteria for evaluation are not always evident to the public[11]

An important policy concern to be addressed during the issuing of spectrum licences is that one user may try to hoard or 'warehouse' blocks of spectrum in order to gain a future advantage in the market. For this reason, the governments introduce a spectrum aggregation limit, or **spectrum cap** as it is known in Canada. The spectrum cap restricts the amount of bandwidth that any single operator is permitted to acquire or hold at any time. Over time a spectrum cap might be modified to allow operators to expand their wireless networks but within a 'level playing field' intended to keep the marketplace competitive.

### 2.5.4   Licence exempt bands

An alternative strategy to licensing bands to specific groups is that of giving some bands **licence exempt status**. Licence exempt status simply means that members of the public can purchase and operate radio equipment that operates in these bands without applying to the government regulator for an individual radio authorization. The idea behind providing licence exempt bands is that it creates a mass market for manufacturing and selling radio devices to the general public. Common examples of licence exempt technologies include 900MHz cordless telephones, 460MHz Family Radio Service (FRS) and 2.4GHz wireless LAN systems (also known as Wi–Fi systems).

Mobile phones are something of an anomaly in this case. While consumers can purchase a mobile handset without obtaining an operator's licence, the mobile operator is obliged to obtain a radio authorization from the government in order to operate a mobile telephone network. Strictly speaking then, mobile phones are *not* part of a licence exempt band, whereas a cordless home telephone phone or a Wi–Fi enabled computer are radio devices that fall under the licence exempt designation.

## 2.6   Contemporary policy issues

Over the course of the 20th century, radio spectrum has become an increasingly important resource and presents a host of new challenges for public policy. It is possible to identify at least three major trends that spectrum managers are now facing: first, the convergence of telecommunications and broadcasting industries; second, the globalization of economy/trade; and, third, rapid developments in telecommunications technology.

### 2.6.1   Convergence of communications industries

With the advent of the Internet in the mid–1990s a number of countries began to review their regulatory frameworks for broadcasting and telecommunications. In many cases, these two areas of activity were regulated as distinct sectors often with strict prohibitions on cross–media entry. The outcome of many of these reviews, such as 1996 Convergence Policy Decision issued by the CRTC in Canada, established a set of conditions that would allow cross–media entry for tele-communications and broadcasting service providers. In those countries where a similar convergence policy has been established, these formerly closed markets have now been opened to new forces of competition between telecommunica-tions carriers and cable TV distributors. Cable TV providers, for instance, are now permitted to offer telephone services to their customers and local telephone companies are now allowed to offer TV services over their broadband service. In the past, these services tended to be strictly segregated.

In terms of spectrum management, convergence policy directives mean that additional radio spectrum is needed to support the growth of new competitive service providers in both the telecommunications and the broadcasting sectors. Previously the spectrum policy framework in many countries tended to *discourage* the use of radio systems that would create duplicate services already provided by wireline–based technology. This policy was intended to reserve spectrum for those services that were absolutely dependent on radio systems.

The need to make room for new competition in the media and communica-tions sector means that the spectrum policy framework in many countries has been revised to *expand* the role of radio as a substitute for delivering communications services. This shift in the outlook for spectrum management is related to what is sometimes called the 'Negroponte Switch'. The term refers to comments by the director of MIT's Media Lab, Nicholas Negroponte, that suggested as we move into the future that wired and wireless information would trade places. In other words, the old regime of telephone service provided over wires would be better served by wireless technology, and that the old broadcasting regime of TV/radio was more suited to wireline (i.e., cable) delivery:

What is in the air will go under the ground. And what is underground will go into the air. ... more and more television will go through cables than over airwaves and more and more telephone will use airwaves instead of copper wires buried along roads. That's the Negroponte switch.[12]

In making this observation, Negroponte was raising a question about the need for new spectrum allocation for high definition television.[13] His point was that many high bandwidth services such as television are better served by a wireline infrastructure and that low bandwidth services such as voice telephony should be wireless. For policymakers the Negroponte Switch suggests that prioritization of spectrum allocation and assignment of licences must now be assessed differently, using a new set of objectives and may require band-clearing activities to make room for firms wanting to use new types of radio systems to enter the marketplace.

A case in point is a radio system called **WiMAX**, which is a fixed (not mobile) wireless access technology that offers a new way to access broadband services. In order to permit this technology to be deployed and to become a viable alternative to traditional wireline broadband offered over cable TV or telephone networks, it was necessary to allocate new radio spectrum in the 10–66GHz band. This is a case where the impact of convergence policy on spectrum management has been to increase in the supply of radio frequencies, particularly in the UHF and SHF bands, in order to promote the deployment of competitive wireless services, such as WiMAX.

### 2.6.2   Globalization of trade

In 1997, the World Trade Organization (WTO) multilateral agreement on basic telecommunications opened domestic telecom markets to foreign entry. As a result, spectrum policy frameworks today must adopt a more global perspective than ever before. In effect, this opening up of markets could mean that many countries will have to harmonize their radio regulations and equipment approval processes with other trading partners in order to support the flow of goods and services across international borders. Without such harmonization, there could be cross-border interoperability problems for competing radio systems. These problems could be construed as an unfair barrier to trade. As a result, spectrum management and other radio regulations will likely continue to be affected by the globalization of trade in radio equipment.

### 2.6.3   Technological change

Over the past decade, a number of important technological developments have impacted on spectrum management. On the one hand, the replacement of legacy radio systems by fibre-optic networks (part of the Negroponte Switch) has opened up spectrum for new users, resulting in re-allocation activities and new opportunities for innovation in the wireless sector. On the other hand, the dramatic growth of mobile phones and satellite systems, as well as other wireless technologies has created new demands for radio spectrum and in some bands is leading to demand that far exceeds current capacity.

The advent of the Internet has also had a dramatic effect on spectrum management, as there is today a seemingly insatiable demand to build new wireless networks to deliver voice and data services. New demands on radio spectrum management will continue as research and development extends the range of products and services based on wireless technology, leading to radical new proposals for spectrum management that will be described in Chapter 8.

## 2.7 Marconi's legacy

While much of spectrum management is a technical matter for radio engineers, it is also very much a social and political concern when it comes time to make decisions about how to organize this resource to meet fiercely competing interests. Historically these interests have changed over time, requiring different policies and priorities for spectrum management. As one expert writes about the policy approach of the last century:

> The basic design of spectrum regulation and management that emerged was rooted in the radio technology that Marconi developed, which required high signal to noise ratios.[14]

High signal–noise ratios refers to the problem of interference in these radio systems, particularly those that produce high power outputs. Spectrum management was conceived on a primary objective of organizing the use of frequencies so that there is sufficient space between users on the bands to prevent unwanted interference across those bands. Today, some digital radio systems have the capacity to share frequencies with other technologies while minimizing many of the older problems of interference.

Looking ahead at these emerging technologies, the spectrum release plan in any country can have a significant influence on investment in technology research and development, which means that policy decisions on spectrum management are also very influential in making new technologies and services feasible from a commercial perspective. As a result, radio equipment suppliers and wireless service providers are motivated to influence policy decisions to their advantage and are active participants in the ITU-WRC and at regional and national meetings where important decisions are made. Indeed, spectrum is 'technology, industry, money, culture and power'. The next chapter looks at how these forces came together in the 20th century to make possible the earliest forms of mobile telephony.

## 2.8 Further reading

In 2004, the ITU held a workshop entitled 'Radio-spectrum Management for a Converging World' which featured a number of non-technical background papers and specific national casestudies on spectrum management. These documents are available online at the ITU website: http://www.itu.int/osg/spu/ni/spectrum/index.html

The United States Federal Communications Commission website on spectrum management can be found at http://www.fcc.gov/oet/spectrum/

The How Stuff Works website provides additional information about the physical properties of radio spectrum with some helpful illustrations: http://electronics.howstuff works.com/radio-spectrum1.htm

A more in-depth source of information on the properties of radio spectrum and its use, as well as more details about the international governance of spectrum management can be found in Amit K. Maitra's (2004) book *Wireless Spectrum Management* (McGraw-Hill Professional).

For those interested in the social history of wireless technology, there are two books on the subject of early developments in the field: S. Hong (2001) *Wireless: From Marconi's Black-Box to the Audion* (MIT Press) and G. Weightman (2003) *Signor Marconi's Magic Box: The Most Remarkable Invention of the 19th Century and the Amateur Inventor Whose Genius Sparked a Revolution* (Da Capo Press).

# 3 Going mobile

... in 1981, 'mobile phone' meant pretty much one thing: a big suitcase full of electronic equipment, wired and bolted into a millionaire's Cadillac limousine, with a three-foot steel antenna drilled through the trunk lid.

(Murray Jr. 2001)

## 3.1 Introduction

For much of the last century, the term 'radiotelephony' was used to describe what we now refer to as mobile phones or cell phones. As far back as the 1940s, early radiotelephony services were available for a limited number of people. Spectrum scarcity, however, has long been part of the problem in extending mobile phone service to a wider market. Another part of the problem was the power consumption requirements and size of early radio equipment. Each of these factors had to be overcome in order to enable the mass consumption of mobile phone services that we have today.

The aim of this chapter is to provide a social history and technical overview of the events and innovations that preceded the mobile phone system we have today. The chapter looks at the origins of early radiotelephone service, highlighting the problem of spectrum scarcity, as well as the high cost and long waiting times of early service providers. The chapter then discusses some of the key innovations that enabled miniaturization of electronic components that made possible the development of the first 'mobile' phone in 1973. Some basic terms and concepts of radio networks are introduced in the chapter to provide the background necessary for understanding the significance of the cellular network concept that was first conceived in the 1940s. The chapter ends with a discussion of how the combination of smaller, lighter handsets and cellular networks formed the first generation of mobile phone service and sowed the seeds of a revolution in personal communications.

## 3.2 Origins of the mobile phone

The very first mobile phones were referred to as 'radiotelephones' and were first used in the early part of the last century for ship to shore or ship to ship communications. The inventor and entrepreneur, Guglielmo Marconi, is credited with developing the first successful wireless telegraph, but this system could only transmit the dots and dashes of Morse Code. We might say, without stretching the analogy too far, that Marconi pioneered the first *wireless data system*. In 1901,

Marconi placed a radio aboard a steam-powered truck, in effect creating the first land based wireless mobile data network.[1]

The first successful wireless transmission of human speech, however, had to wait until Christmas Eve in 1906, when Reginald Fessenden used a radio to transmit music and spoken word to ships at sea in the Atlantic Ocean. The origins of mobile radiotelephony stretch back to these key moments in history, when voice and data transmission by radio captured the imagination of the public, not to mention catching the eye of entrepreneurs and investors alike.

By the 1920s, mobile radio systems in the United States were operating at 2MHz (just below the present AM broadcast band) and were used mostly by law enforcement agencies for dispatch. These first systems were one-way only and used Morse Code to send alerts to police officers in their patrol cars. In many respects, this system was something like an early form of radio paging because when the officer in a patrol vehicle received a radio alert, he would then have to drive to the nearest telephone calling station (often located at street corners) to obtain the details from the dispatcher.

While police and emergency services were instrumental in pioneering mobile radio systems well into the 1940s, very few of these systems were actually inter-connected with the **public switched telephone network** (**PSTN**). This meant that the system was not a 'telephone' as we know it today because transmissions were limited to a very small network connecting the dispatcher to the patrol vehicles equipped with radios.

## 3.2.1   Early radiotelephone systems

Some of the first true mobile radiotelephone systems appeared in the United States just after World War Two in 1946. Known as **Mobile Telephone Systems** (**MTS**), these services did provide interconnection with the public switched tel-ephone network, thereby enabling telephone calls to be made from a mobile radio permanently mounted in an automobile (in most cases). These systems were based on simple network design with a large powerful antenna to provide blanket coverage across a wide area, usually an entire city.

The early MTS networks were plagued with inherent problems due to the limits of available radio spectrum and the radio technology available at the time. A major drawback with the early systems was that they required considerable bandwidth to transmit and receive signals, which meant that they required lots of spectrum to provide a small number of communication channels. MTS systems in some cities were heavily congested, particularly at peak calling hours when fru-strated customers – who were paying a great deal of money for the service – would have to wait patiently for one of the few **radio channels** to become available before they could place a telephone call. The availability of radio channels was a function of the amount of radio spectrum allotted to the MTS service providers:

> In mobile telephony a channel is a pair of frequencies. One frequency to transmit on and one to receive. It makes up a circuit or a complete com-munication path [and] sounds simple enough to accommodate. Yet the radio spectrum is extremely crowded. In the late 1940s little space existed at the lower frequencies most equipment used. Inefficient radios contributed to the crowding, using a 60kHz wide bandwidth to send a signal that can now be done with 10kHz or less. But what could you do with just six channels, no matter what the technology? With conventional mobile telephone service you had users by the scores vying for an open frequency. You had, in effect, a

wireless party line, with perhaps forty subscribers fighting to place calls on each channel.[2]

In addition to spectrum scarcity, there was another factor that compounded the problems for early MTS customers: the very early systems required the intervention of a human operator when placing all outgoing telephone calls. Each customer would have to contact the operator, tell him or her the number to be dialed, and the operator would then dial that number to make the connection. In effect, the operator provided a bridge between the mobile radiotelephone network and the public switched telephone network. As you can imagine, this could be a slow process compared with the speed dialing and instant reply functions we have available on our mobile phones today. To make matters worse, sometimes the customer's patience and persistence would be greeted with a busy signal or no answer at the other end – these were, after all, the days before answering machines and voice mail. Making a call on an MTS service was by no means a casual or convenient affair.

Early MTS systems also operated in **half duplex mode**, meaning that conversations had to take place using a push to talk procedure. This meant that the mobile customer would have to push a button on their handset before speaking and then release this button in order to listen to the response. Simultaneous two-way conversations, known as **full duplex mode**, were not possible at the time. Eventually, an improved MTS systems, known as **Improved Mobile Telephone Service** (**IMTS**) would come to offer full duplex mode communication in the 1960s. Further innovations also allowed customers to bypass the human operator altogether and to direct dial their calls.

Those customers who wanted to *receive* incoming calls on their mobile radiotelephone were quite limited in their ability to 'roam' from place to place. The early systems did not have any way of tracking the customer as they moved from one coverage area to another, and roaming between cities in most countries – let alone between countries – was limited by a lack of business agreements between the service providers and also in some cases by technical incompatibility. Part of the problem was that spectrum allocation and radio licences were not contiguous from one city to another, and many mobile handsets at that time were not equipped to transmit or receive on all the possible channels that were needed for wide area roaming.

The user friendliness of early mobile radiotelephones was another factor that limited their appeal to the wider public. These devices were large and bulky, and for that reason were often mounted under the dashboard of an automobile. Some devices were mounted in briefcase style carriers. One reason for their bulkiness is that the early radio systems required a great deal of electrical power to operate and an automobile battery was the only source that provided enough current. While it may not be apparent today, major innovations in power supply were essential for the development of the modern mobile phone:

> Early practical mobile phones were carried by cars, since there was room in the trunk for the bulky equipment, as well as a car battery. One of the most important factors allowing phones to be carried in pockets and bags has been remarkable advances in battery technology. As batteries have become more powerful, so they have also become smaller. Partly because improvements in battery design have been incremental, their role in technological change is often underestimated. [3]

Early MTS systems also required a certain degree of technical expertise in order to switch between channels, set transmission modes and so forth. Another

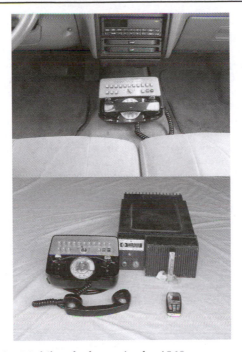

**Figure 3.1**   Mobile telephones in the 1960s

*Source*: Farley, T. (2004) Mobile telephone history, *Privateline.com*. Available at http://www.privateline.com/PCS/mobilephonepictures.htm (reproduced with permission).

significant deterrent to the popularity of early mobile radiotelephony was simply the cost of service. Both the handsets and the service plans were very expensive, especially by today's standards for mobile phone service. The value for money was not great either, as the quality of voice transmissions on these early MTS/IMTS systems was unreliable and privacy was practically non-existent because other customers and anyone with a radio scanner could listen in on the telephone conversations.

Despite the drawbacks of the early MTS/IMTS systems, a small number of business customers and others *did* use them because they saw value in having mobile access to the telephone network. But even at this very modest level of popularity, the limitations caused by channel scarcity and the lack of available radio equipment meant that potential subscribers often waited several months to obtain service. For the MTS service providers, the limited spectrum meant frequent congestion of their radio network and created an obstacle to the expansion of these systems to accommodate more customers.

In fact, many MTS/IMTS systems could not accommodate more than 250 subscribers in any given market. Yet, for all these limitations it seems that waiting lists did develop in every city where mobile telephone service was introduced. For example, telecommunications historian Tom Farley writes that,

> [w]aiting lists developed in every [American] city where mobile telephone service was introduced. By 1976 only 545 customers in New York City had Bell System mobiles, with 3,700 customers on the waiting list. Around the country 44,000 Bell subscribers had AT&T mobiles but 20,000 people sat on five to ten year waiting lists. [4]

Despite the costs and problems associated with MTS service, demand still exceeded supply. This situation clearly called for some kind of solution to the problem of spectrum scarcity, which was partly responsible for the supply problem facing the early service providers. Luckily, a solution had been in the works at Bell Labs in the United States from about 1947, where the idea for a *cellular network* design was being studied. Farley points out, however, that despite the apparent demand for early mobile radiotelephone service, it took almost four decades for the technology to move beyond the technical limits of the MTS systems. The delay was not necessarily due to technological barriers either, but rather it is attributed in part to the United States' government and in part to the American private monopoly telephone operator at the time, AT&T. The government was blamed for being slow to allocate spectrum for a cellular service, and AT&T for its part did not foresee any business reason for expanding its mobile phone service for the general public.

Despite the reluctance of government and industry, additional spectrum for a cellular phone system was released in the 1960s and resulted in the development of the first generation of cellular mobile phone service. Known as the analogue mobile phone system or AMPS, the new concept was first tested in Chicago in 1978. Prior to these tests, however, there were a number of specialized cellular networks operating in North America. Among these included the first commercial cellular radio system to employ frequency re-use along the New York City–Washington DC corridor, starting in 1969. This system used special payphones installed on Amtrack Metroliner trains, giving commuters the opportunity to make telephone calls while moving along at one hundred miles an hour. The system was designed to use six radio channels in the 450MHz band along nine zones of the 225-mile route.[5]

### 3.2.2    The birth of the 'mobile' phone

While the cellular network concept was implemented on a very small scale in the late 1960s, the widespread adoption of cellular mobile phones would have to wait for a number of other important technical innovations. Among these innovations was the **transistor**, another Bell Lab invention that appeared in 1948. The transistor is an electronic component that would come to replace the bulky and power hungry vacuum tubes that were once needed for radio systems. In effect, the transistor started a revolution in miniaturization that was accelerated further with the invention of the **integrated circuit** by Texas Instruments in 1958. Radio devices, including radiotelephones could now be made smaller, consume less power and could be more accurately described as 'mobile' phones.

In the 1970s, miniaturization made another quantum leap when Intel began to market its first microprocessors for the production of electronic calculators. At the time, these early microprocessors contained hundreds of tiny transistors located on silicon wafers, performing thousands of calculations per minute. Compared with today's microprocessors that do millions of calculations per second, they may seem primitive, but they were the key to a process of microminiaturization that make today's tiny mobile phones possible.

To provide some sense of how quickly innovations in miniaturization have impacted the electronics industry we need only consider Moore's Law of computing power. More than a quarter century ago, during the time when Intel was filing its first patents, one of its founders Gordon Moore forecasted that the number of transistors on a microprocessor would double approximately every 18 months. This effectively meant at least a quadrupling of computing power every three years. Today it appears that Moore's law has been proven accurate, which means that computing devices have become smaller and more compact but with more capabilities. The mobile phones on the market today are a testament to the prescience of Moore's insight and the relatively short but rapid history of innovation in the electronics industry.

## 3.3   Wireless networking

In addition to the amazing advances in miniaturization, today's mobile phone services are possible because of innovations in the design of radio networks. Many of these innovations were prompted by the need to address the problem of spectrum scarcity and to find ways of using fewer frequencies more efficiently. A major milestone in radio system design mentioned briefly already, is known as the 'cellular' network. To understand the significance of the cellular idea it is helpful to first know some of the basic terms used to describe radio networks.

### 3.3.1   Communication modes

One way to describe a radio network is to consider the way in which signals are transmitted and received between radio devices. This is also known as the *communication mode*. There are three basic communication modes: simplex, half duplex and full duplex modes.

When in **simplex mode,** a radio network transmits in one direction only, or *uni-directionally*. Typically this means a single transmitter can communicate to one or more receivers. An example of a simplex mode network is broadcast radio or TV, where the network is designed with a powerful transmitter providing wide area coverage for many receiving devices.

When a radio network is **half duplex mode**, however, it is capable of two-way, or *bi-directional*, communications. This means that the network will consist of two or more transceivers capable of both transmitting and receiving radio signals. However, it is important to note that a half duplex communication mode also means that radio signals can flow only in *one direction at a time*. A contemporary example of a half duplex mode network is the 'push to talk' walkie-talkies that can be purchased at local electronic retailers. As described above, early MTS systems operated in half duplex mode.

In **full duplex** mode a radio network is capable of *simultaneous bi-directional* communications. This means that the network will be designed around two or more transceivers capable of sending and receiving radio signals at the same time. Mobile phone service today operates in full duplex mode, which as you can imagine creates additional demand for spectrum and therefore encourages the search for means of increasing the spectral efficiency of the radio network. Whereas simplex mode can operate using a single radio channel, both the half duplex and full duplex modes require two 'paired' channels per transceiver, which effectively doubles the number of frequencies needed to operate a network using either of these modes of communication.

### 3.3.2   Basic network designs

In addition to communication mode, it is important to consider the basic architecture of a radio network. There are three basic design types in common use today for half and full duplex systems: direct, single site and cellular. Each type is associated with a range of specific communication services and infrastructure requirements.

**Direct radio networks** are those in which two or more radio transceivers are linked without the need for any intervening infrastructure. The Family Radio Service (FRS) two-way radio or Citizen Band (CB) system, are a popular example of this type of network design. The range of direct radio networks is often very small because it is limited by the output power of the radio transceivers. In some direct link radio networks a device called a 'repeater' may be used to extend its range across a wider geographical area.

**Single site radio networks** are those in which two or more radio devices communicate with one fixed location transceiver. The fixed location transceiver, which often has a large antenna mast associated with it, might also serve as a gateway between the radio network and another, such as the public switched telephone network. Radio paging systems and dispatch services often use a single site radio network design, and the MTS radiotelephone systems were based on a single site network design.

There are two fundamental shortcomings when dealing with direct and single site radio networks. On the one hand, the range of the network is limited by the power of the radio devices deployed in the network. To achieve better range, it is necessary to use higher powered radio transceivers that tend to be large, bulky and consume a lot of electricity, which of course makes them less than ideal for mobile applications. On the other hand, these designs are usually confined to a relatively small amount of bandwidth, thereby placing constraints on the number of potential users in any area at any given moment in time – one of the major limitations of the early MTS services.

In order to address these two shortcomings, the **cellular network design** was studied in Bell Labs in the late 1940s. Cellular networks are based on two principles: small radio coverage zones known as 'cells' and something called 'frequency re-use'. Instead of installing a single high powered transceiver at the city centre to provide service for everyone, the cellular network design is based on many low powered transceivers located throughout the city and that serve geographically small areas, sometimes only a few kilometres in diameter. Because each cell provides coverage for a very small area, the same frequencies used for radio channels in one cell can be re-used in other more distant cells where interference will not be a problem. In effect, this design permits network operators to recycle a relatively small number of frequencies but provide service to more customers.

In a large city there may be hundreds of cells that make up the network, but these networks are designed in groups that can vary in size from three to 21 cells per cluster depending on number of *channels* desired in each cell as well as other geographical factors. For example, in a dense downtown urban setting with many potential users and plenty of physical obstructions (i.e., buildings), there are usually many small cells with fewer channels. In a rural area with fewer customers and fewer physical obstructions, however, there can be fewer cells with much larger coverage areas and more available channels per cell. Ideally, the network operator would like to optimize the number of channels per cell because this means using less of the expensive infrastructure needed for each cell site. Such infrastructure includes antennas, support structure (often using someone else's property, such as a rooftop), network gateway connections and access to commercial power.

While the cellular network design achieves a major breakthough with frequency re-use it now has to overcome an associated problem of managing connections as customers travel around the city. What happens when a customer moves from one cell into another while making a telephone call? How does the network prevent the call from being disrupted as the customer crosses this

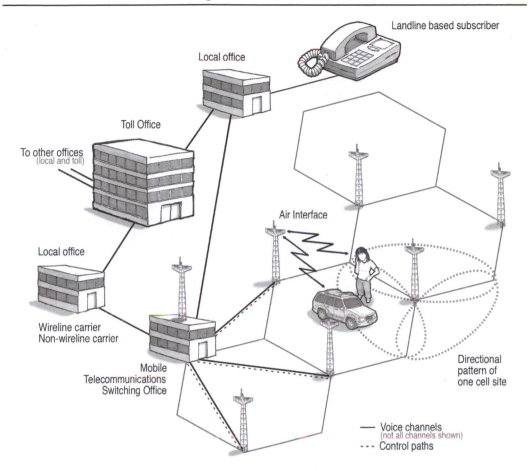

**Figure 3.2**  Radio cells in a typical configuration for Bell AMPS system

*Source*: AT&T (c. 1984) *A History of Engineering and Science in the Bell System: Communications Sciences (1925–80)*. New York: AT&T.

threshold? This problem leads to the most distinguishing feature of a cellular network design: the **hand-off**. The hand-off is the process that permits a mobile customer to move between radio cells without losing their connection. In practice this is a very sophisticated process that requires a complex system of radio control signals and computers to relocate a radio transmission from one cell to another without disruption. However, it is this combination of frequency re-use and the ability to hand-off customers from one cell to another that makes today's mobile phone service a commercial success.

There are two basic kinds of hand-off techniques. The first is called the *hard hand-off*; the second is the *soft hand-off*. The *hard hand-off* technique requires that the radio transmission be temporarily broken before a new transmission in the next cell is established. The break might take place very quickly but there will be a moment of disruption to the call. A hard hand-off can result in a lost connection if the new cell does not have an available channel at the moment this takes place. However, this technique also requires less computer intelligence to coordinate the process and therefore reduces the technical complexity of the network.

By contrast, a soft hand-off (sometimes called 'make before break') works by establishing a transmission in the new radio cell before the active one is terminated or 'torn down'. This requires the handset to be capable of tuning into multiple channels at the same time and also requires more computer processing in the network during the hand-off process. However, the soft hand-off also provides for a smoother transition and higher reliability during mobile transmissions, and most mobile phone networks today use the soft hand-off technique.

### 3.3.3   Cellular infrastructure

Having now introduced the basic concept, we turn to the physical infrastructure required for a cellular telephone network. A cellular network can be described in three segments, and the first is called the *air-link,* which refers to the portion that connects the mobile phone to the *base station* with a radio transmission. Each base-station provides a transceiver and antenna at the edge of every cell. The antenna mast is often mounted on a tower or the side of a building and is a common sight in many cities today. Taken together, the various pieces of equipment at the base station are sometimes referred to as a 'cell-site'.

Cell-sites can be found at the side of the highway on large monopole structures, on the tops of large buildings, and small antenna systems are sometimes located inside shopping malls and other buildings to provide extra coverage. If you know what to look for, the antenna structures will become a familiar sight. In a typical network arrangement, the many cell-sites that are spread across a city are then linked to a centralized **base-station controller** (**BSC**).

The second segment of a cellular phone network is known as the **backhaul**, which describes the link connecting the base-station controller to the **mobile switching centre (MSC)**. The MSC is the brain of a cellular network because it keeps track of users, coordinates incoming and outgoing calls and controls the hand-off between mobile phones and the cell-sites. These functions are in part controlled by two databases. The first is called the **Home Location Registry (HLR)** and other is the **Visitors Location Registry (VLR)**. The HLR is a database that contains a record for every mobile phone registered to a specific mobile switching centre. In other words, this MSC acts as the 'home base' for those mobile phones. When a new mobile phone is issued to a customer, its phone number and other information is registered with a local MSC. For example, a phone with a North American '415' area code will likely be registered in an HLR database associated with an MSC in San Francisco (which is within the 415 area code). Each mobile phone number is permanently registered in a specific HLR somewhere in the world.

When a mobile phone is roaming beyond the boundaries of cell-sites under the control of the MSC, its telephone number is entered automatically into the Visitors Location Registry of another MSC. So, for example, if a customer from San Francisco arrived in Hawaii (area code 808) on vacation and then activated his or her mobile phone, the computers managing the network would check and realize that a phone with a '415' area code does not belong to any MSC in that local area, and would then place his or her number in the local VLR database. The computer at the local MSC would then communicate back to the computer in the MSC in San Francisco and notify it of the customer's location, telling it also where to route any calls that might be made to him or her. The mobile phone is *temporarily registered* in the Hawaii VLR only for as long as he or she is visiting there.

This automated registration process enables national and international roaming for mobile phone customers. Behind the relatively mundane customer experience

**Figure 3.3**  A typical antenna mast at a cell-site base station

*Source*: http://bosquet.cprost.sfu.ca/~smith/wibo/3-3.jpg
*Note*: Photograph courtesy of Tod Klassy.

of roaming is a complex exchange of data required to manage this process. For example, if a customer in San Francisco decides to call a friend who is on vacation in Hawaii, that customer simply dials the phone number as usual. A computer at a San Francisco MSC checks its HLR database then discovers that the number was last registered with a VLR database in Hawaii. The computer in San Francisco then redirects the call to the appropriate MSC in Hawaii. The local MSC in Hawaii then sends a signal to 'page' that mobile phone number among the various base-station controllers and cell-sites in its network, in most cases finding the phone and connecting the call.

The third segment of a cellular network is known as the **point of inter-connection**, which links the gateway mobile switching centre (**GMSC**) to the public Switched Telephone Network (PSTN). This third segment is necessary to

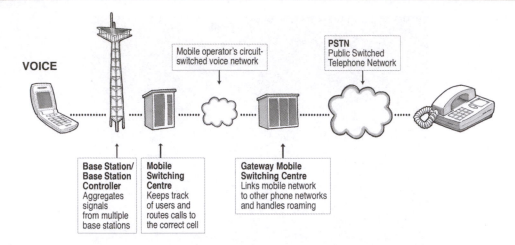

**Figure 3.4**   Three segments of a mobile phone network

enable a mobile phone customer to connect with other customers operating using other wireless and wireline service providers. Without this **gateway** element, a mobile phone customer could only connect with other mobile phone customers using the same network, which of course would not be very helpful in most cases. As contrasted with the older MTS systems, the point of interconnection in cellular networks is managed without the need for human operator, enabling direct dialing to and from the mobile phone customers and the wider public switched telephone network.

## 3.4   The first generation mobile phone

With the deployment of the first functional cellular networks as early as the late 1960s, one remaining obstacle to the mobility of customers using these networks was the telephone handset itself. It was a combination of crucial innovations – increased processing power, miniaturization of components and lower power consumption – that finally created the right technological conditions for the first truly 'mobile' phone to be introduced to the public.

In 1973 Martin Cooper, an engineer employed with Motorola, filed the very first patent on a *handheld* cell phone and is also widely credited with being the first person to place a call with it. As the story goes, that first call was from a sidewalk in New York City to a rival colleague, Joe Engel, who was then head of research at Bell Labs. He and Engel had been involved in a fiercely competitive race to be the first to develop a handheld device and Cooper was calling to inform Engel that he had won. Cooper's successful invention was later improved upon and marketed by Motorola as the DynaTAC 8000X. It weighed over two pounds (about one kilogram), it had 35 minutes of talk time with eight hours' standby, and a ten hour recharge cycle. The DynaTAC 8000x is known as the original 'brick' phone. As for its features, it offered a simple one colour LED display, enough memory to store about 30 telephone numbers and retailed at the time for about $3995.[6] Compared with an average mobile phone today, the brick was hardly a bargain either in terms of cost or features.

**Figure 3.5** A mobile phone from the 1980s

*Source*: Farley, T. (2004) Mobile telephone history, *Privateline.com*. Retrieved May. Available at http://www.privateline.com/PCS/history9.htm#anchor814580

The Bahrain Telephone Company is alleged to have established the first city-wide commercial analogue cellular service in May 1978. This system was rather small, with only two 'cells' in operation and limited to 20 channels, supporting 250 subscribers and operating in the 400MHz band. Japan is reported to have followed shortly thereafter, with the operator Nippon Telephone and Telegraph (NTT) introducing the first generation cellular service into Tokyo in 1979.[7]

In northern Europe, cellular service first became available in 1981 when the Nordic Mobile Telephone Service (NMT) went into operation across Sweden, Norway, Denmark and Finland in the 450MHz band. Western Europe was introduced to cellular service in 1985, when the TACS (Total Access Communication System) entered into service in the UK, Italy, Spain, Austria and Ireland. In the same year, France and Germany introduced their own standards to provide analogue cell phone service to their citizens.

First generation cellular service was not introduced in North America until 1983, when a regional Bell operating company called Ameritech began serving the city of Chicago. The first orders for mobile handsets in North America went to American-owned Motorola and a Japanese company called Oki Electric. Soon, however, the service expanded across the country following a US government lottery to give away licences in the 800MHz band to prospective mobile phone operators. In Canada, Alberta Government Telephones introduced the AURORA-400 system, thereby inaugurating that country's first generation of cellular mobile phone service. A few years later, two cellular services were licensed to provide service in Canada's major cities on the 800MHz band using the AMPS standard.[8]

### 3.4.1   A phone you could carry anywhere

We may not realize today how significant the invention of a handheld mobile phone was for many people at the time. Take, for instance, this lively description from James Murray's book *Wireless Nation* about his first encounter with a handheld cell phone:

> Looking down at the bulky, molded-plastic box in my hand, I was momentarily confused. It looked like a big portable calculator, but why did it have that rubber stick pointing out of one end? My brother-in-law Graham Randolph, who had just handed me the odd-looking instrument, grinned knowingly and said, 'Why don't you call home?' When I glanced again at the box in my hand, I recognized the stick as an antenna and the numbered buttons as a telephone keypad.
>
> It was March 5, 1981, and Graham and I were standing on a Baltimore sidewalk outside his office in the bright, late-winter sun. I punched in my home phone number as Graham sauntered off in the direction of our luncheon engagement, and after a ring or two I was doing something I'd never done before: talking on a phone as I walked down a city street.
>
> Like many other businesspeople, I'd seen mobile phones before, but in 1981, 'mobile phone' meant pretty much one thing: a big suitcase full of electronic equipment, wired and bolted into a millionaire's Cadillac limousine, with a three-foot steel antenna drilled through the trunk lid. Mobile phones were car phones, and not very good ones at that − but this was something different: a phone you could carry anywhere.[9]

The novelty of these first generation mobile phones was partly due to their relative scarcity on the street. While the revolution in microelectronics had reduced the handset to the size of a small brick, the cost of purchasing them and making calls still made it prohibitively expensive except for business executives. This also led to the fashionable use of mobile phones on television and in the movies, which lent this technology a symbolic power that would come to play an important role in creating pent up demand for the next generation of mobile phones in the 1990s.

### 3.4.2   Not for everyone (yet)

To get some sense of what the first generation of mobile phone service might have cost, the following excerpt presents some typical North American prices from 1986. Mind you this was the dawn of first generation service and it is important to note that the authors in this passage are discussing the 'drastic reduction' of prices that cellular service has introduced compared with the older MTS systems:

> The [cell phone] equipment needed in a single vehicle runs anywhere from $1200 to $3000 and it is estimated that the average monthly telephone bill will be around $150. If the cost of service remains as high as it has historically been, as much as 500% higher than landline telephone rates, cellular telephones will probably remain a technology used exclusively by those few business people and professional people that can justify the expense.[10]

In fact it was the exorbitant cost of mobile phone service in the 1980s that provided the context for a number of high profile industry speculations about the future market for mobile phone service − speculations that proved to be wildly inaccurate with the introduction of second generation mobile phone service in the 1990s.

The eventual reduction in cost and other improvements that have led to the emergence of a popular culture in mobile phones were important, but it was also a series of regulatory reforms stretching back to the late 1960s that paved the way for a mass market in mobile phone service. More specifically, these reforms can be traced to two key events that coincided in 1968. The first was the launch of regulatory hearings by the FCC in the United States that eventually led to the allocation of spectrum for cellular phone service. The second has come to be known as the Carterfone Decision.

## 3.5   Regulatory reform

Almost from its origins, cellular was viewed as a service that should be offered on a competitive basis. This was at a time when telephone service in most countries operated under a monopoly, either private (as in the US and Canada) or state owned (as in most of Europe and the rest of the world). One important exception to the monopoly provision in the United States was in the provision of MTS radiotelephony. In 1949, the Federal Communications Commission licensed the Radio Common Carriers (RCCs) in the 450MHz band to provide this service to the public. It is significant that even under the AT&T monopoly regime, the FCC in the United States still viewed mobile phone service as something that could and should be open to competition. The RCCs played an important role because they were granted limited access to spectrum and provided what amounted to some of the first FCC permitted competition for AT&T.

### 3.5.1   Thomas Carter versus Ma Bell

During most of the last century, monopoly service providers controlled the telephone systems of the world, from the very core of the network all the way to its very edges including customer premises equipment (CPE) such as telephones, modems, facsimile machines and modems. In the United States, for example, AT&T (American Telephone and Telegraph) had so much influence that it could veto *anything* that a customer might want to use to connect to the network. As a result, customers could use only AT&T telephone authorized equipment. The reason for this was often cited as technical concerns and a claim that non-approved equipment might cause problems to AT&T's national network in the US. This is sometimes known as an 'interoperability' argument, and AT&T as well as monopoly operators in other countries used it for many years to claim that equipment from competing firms had the potential for emitting excessive signal power, hazardous voltages or to create other technical incompatibilities that could compromise the integrity and safety of its network. The effect of the interoperability argument was to seriously limit the growth of competition in the manufacture and sale of telephone equipment.

The Carterfone Decision in 1968 challenged AT&T's position on this matter and paved the way for a competitive telephone equipment market, first in the United States and eventually in other parts of the world. Thomas Carter was a Texas businessman who was selling and installing two-way radios for the petroleum industry in the 1950s. Carter recognized that many of his customers worked in remote oilfields and used two-way radios to relay messages through a mobile radio operator to executives located at corporate head office. This was a cumbersome process, even more so than the early MTS systems because the operator

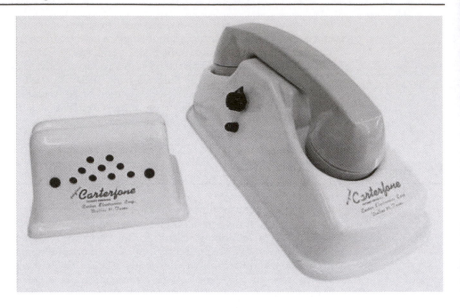

**Figure 3.6**   The Carterfone (circa 1965)

*Source*: Photograph courtesy of http://www.sandman.com/tellhist.htlm

had to act as a intermediary, literally conveying messages word for word from the field radio to the executive on the telephone back at the head office.

Carter saw in this situation a business opportunity and developed an 'acoustic coupler' that would permit his customer base of radio users to speak directly with their head office counterparts without the need for an operator mediating the conversation. His invention became known as the Carterfone and it was unique because it did not make a direct electrical connection to AT&Ts network but instead used a simple cradle into which the telephone handset was placed. This ingenious solution seemed to get around the interoperability argument used by AT&T to discourage competitive equipment providers, and the Carterfone was on the market for many years. In the mid-1960s AT&T (aka 'Ma Bell') decided to take action against Thomas Carter for violating the prohibition on interconnecting unauthorized equipment to its network. Carter then retaliated by filing an antitrust suit against AT&T.[11]

In 1968, the US Federal Communications Commission (FCC), which had been hearing arguments in the Carterfone case, decided against AT&T. This decision was important for a number of reasons including the precedent it set regarding the attachment of private equipment to the network, thereby spawning what would eventually become a competitive telephone equipment industry in North America. Competitive offerings in telephone equipment would later prove to be a significant factor in the widespread growth of mobile telephone service.

The Carterfone Decision was also the first in a series of court challenges to Ma Bell's monopoly over telephone service. Another case involved Microwave Communications Inc. (MCI), which led to a decision that opened up the long distance market to competition. A third case was the so-called computer decisions of the 1970s and 1980s, which created new markets for data services and paved the way for early experiments in **packet–switching** that eventually led to the Internet.

Altogether these events were part of a long battle between AT&T – which at that time was the largest corporation on earth – and the US Department of Justice and various other private interests. This difficult confrontation was finally resolved in 1982 when AT&T was ordered by a US court to split itself into six Regional Bell Operating Companies (RBOCs, or 'Baby Bells'). AT&T was allowed to remain in the long distance business in the US but would now operate in a competitive market with other long distance carriers. Bell Labs, which had produced so many technical innovations (including the transistor) under the authority of AT&T, was also separated from Ma Bell, leading eventually to a competitive market in telecommunications equipment.

AT&T's break up set the stage for a wave of regulatory reform in telecommunications around the world, and one that progressed quite rapidly from the mid-1980s into the 1990s, with the UK, Canada and countries of the European Union soon dismantling the old monopoly regime in favour of a new kind of telecoms industry.[12]

## 3.6   The seeds of revolution

In the late 1970s, when the Federal Communications Commission in the US finally decided to assign radio spectrum nationwide for commercial cellular services, it decided on a policy of competitive service provision and granted two licences in each regional market. This was similar in some ways to the Radio Common Carrier model that had prevailed with early mobile radiotelephone service. When cellular services finally began in the US, one licence went to the incumbent carrier (one of the RBOCS) and the other licence was granted to a new entrant (often with an affiliation to the old MTS system).

The role of the AT&T divestiture in shaping the development of mobile telephony is not to be underestimated. For example, the fact that we can choose from a wide variety of mobile phones and from competing service providers is a direct result of the creation of a competitive equipment market spawned in part by the Carterfone Decision of 1968. Access to cheap long distance service as well as the ability to use a mobile phone handset for data services is also a spin-off of a series of decisions in the US that subsequently influenced telecom policy in other countries around the world. The introduction of a competitive market for mobile phone service has created lower prices for customers and extended market reach far beyond the business executives to now include the general public. Nowhere is this more evident than in Europe, where EU-wide regulatory reform and technological innovation came together to sow the seeds of a second generation (2G) digital revolution heralded by the arrival of GSM in the mid-1990s and the astonishing popularity of the mobile phone across Europe.

## 3.7   Further reading

There are a number of books that chronicle the early days of cellular phone service in the United States, such as James B. Murray Jr.'s (2002) *Wireless Nation* and O. Casey Corr's (2000) book *Money from Thin Air*. Dan Steinbock's (2002) *Wireless Horizon* offers an international perspective on the early history of the mobile phone sector.

For his (2003) book, *Constant Touch: A Global History of the Mobile Phone* (Icon Books), John Agar decided to smash his mobile phone to bits and examine the results. The first part of the book reports on the history of what he finds, including the origins of the battery, the LCD screen and the controversial element used in modern mobile phones, coltan.

Tom Farley's website, Privateline.com, provides a very good history and pre-history of wireless telephony leading up to the modern mobile phone. It is oriented towards North America but does include international material. The website also includes some fascinating images of the early technology: http://www.privateline.com/PCS/history.htm

Tom Farley with Mark van der Hoek also has an excellent background paper on cellular telephone basics that provides additional technical details. It is a very useful source of information for those interested in this topic: http://www.privateline.com/Cellbasics/Cellbasics.html

Geoff Fors' website offers an interesting glimpse of some of the mobile radio equipment produced by Motorola during the 1940s. The website includes images that give a good sense of the bulkiness and rather limited mobility of the early technology as compared to what is commonplace today: http://www.mbay.net/~wb6nvh/Motadata.htm

Martin Fransman's (2002) book, *Telecoms in the Internet Age: From Boom to Bust to ... ?* (Oxford University Press), provides a historical account of changes in the telecom sector from the old telecoms industry through to what he calls the 'infocommunications industry' of today. Fransman examines the changing relationship between equipment providers and monopoly operators, and the unanticipated role of the Internet and of mobile phones in the evolution of the telecom sector.

# 4 | Getting personal

My only goal is to create something people need to have.
(Nokia designer, Frank Nuovo in Specter 2001)

## 4.1 Introduction

In the 1990s, cellular networks around the world went digital and mobile telephony was suddenly transformed into 'Personal Communication Services'. PCS, as it is known in North America, represents the second generation of mobile phones. It was at this time in particular that the mobile phone evolved into a mass consumer item and joined the Internet as the one of the most influential technologies of the late 20th century. Through innovative industrial design, exemplified by the work of Nokia's Frank Nuovo, and with the use of creative marketing strategies and business plans by new entrants in the telecom sector, what was once known to the world of technical experts as 'radiotelephony', became known to everyone as *my* mobile phone (in Europe) or *my* cell phone (in North America). No longer a utility object for communicating, the mobile phone is now more like a *Tamagotchi* – a fashionable plaything, somewhat enigmatic yet congenial, and something to which owners would often become deeply attached.

The aim of this chapter is to provide a historical and technical overview of this personal communications revolution that began with the launch of digital cellular networks and services in the mid-1990s. Important technical terms and concepts of digital cellular systems are introduced to provide background to the changes, as are some of the major influences in the areas of business strategy and public policy that helped to create today's techno-culture of mobility.

## 4.2 Analogue days

Estimates made in the analogue days of the 1980s about the future market for mobile phones have proven to be far from the mark. When digital mobile phones appeared on the scene in the latter half of the 1990s they shattered all expectations of growth. In fact, the early estimates were so wildly inaccurate because they were based on mistaken assumptions, namely, that mobile phone service would be too expensive for most people and that only a relatively small set of business customers would really see any value in talking on the telephone while mobile.

Yet, as we will see in this chapter, the experts did not take into account the fact that a number of influences from Europe, including a relatively obscure company from Finland, would alter our thinking about the mobile phone and transform it into mass-market consumer good. Around the same time that the dotcom boom was bringing the Internet into everyday life, the mobile phone was also starting to garner considerable media attention. It was at this time too that the *Economist* published a feature length editorial on the subject, in which it offered readers 'a cautionary tale' about taking advice from consultants on the subject of mobile phones:

> In the early 1980s AT&T asked [its management consultancy] to estimate how many cellular phones would be in use in the world at the turn of the century. The consultancy noted all the problems with the new devices – the handsets were absurdly heavy, the batteries kept running out, the coverage was patchy and the cost per minute was exorbitant – and concluded that the total number would be about 900,000. At the time this persuaded AT&T to pull out of the market, although it changed its mind later. These days 900,000 new subscribers join the world's mobile-phone services every three days. In eight countries more than a third of the population owns mobile phones ... Almost everywhere ownership is growing relentlessly, and some times exponentially. In both France and the Netherlands, for example, the number of mobile phones doubled during 1998. The tipping point seems to be somewhere between 15% and 20% of the population. Below that, people regard mobiles as expensive toys for business people, so it takes a long time to reach that point; but from there on, growth takes off.[1]

The *Economist* was reporting on a phenomenon that many others were taking notice of – that mobile phones were becoming wildly popular. Something important had taken place between the first generation of the analogue cellular phone and the digital second generation. This 'something' seemed to be about more than technical innovations, although it was true that handsets were lighter, batteries lasted longer and costs had dropped. The fact of the matter was that mobile phones had become personal and the term PCS (for 'personal communication services') was a term used in North America to describe the second generation networks. According to some in the industry, the mobile phone was evolving into a 'personal trusted device'. Before America really entered the scene, however, it was the European Union – a region that had faced tremendous barriers in deploying first generation cellular service – that spearheaded what one writer has referred to as 'the great mobilization of the year 2000'.[2] Behind the EU effort was a desperate need to resolve an interoperability problem at the last mile of the analogue networks that had sprung up throughout Europe in the 1980s.

## 4.3    The last mile

As you may recall from the previous chapter, the 'air-link' is a technical term that refers to that segment of a mobile phone network between the handset and the base station – the only portion of the system that is actually wireless. If you were to look carefully at a diagram of a wireless network it may come as a surprise to realize that only a small portion of the signal path actually happens by radio. This relatively tiny but crucial segment is sometimes called the 'last mile' of the network.

In addition to the air-link, some mobile operators will use a separate radio link to connect the cell-site back to the Mobile Switching Centre. This link does not directly involve the mobile phone users but is known in the telecom industry as

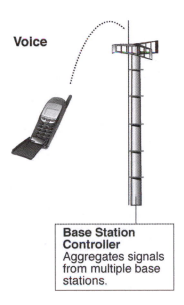

Voice

**Base Station
Controller**
Aggregates signals
from multiple base
stations.

**Figure 4.1**    The last mile of a mobile phone network

'trunking' or *backhaul* service. Some cell-sites will have a small dish-type antenna in conjunction with the regular cellular antenna mast. This dish is a microwave antenna that provides wireless backhaul from the local cell-site to the switching centre and can save a mobile operator the expense of installing and maintaining fibre–optic or buried wireline trunks. Note, however, that in these instances the wireless carrier might actually require two separate radio authorizations from the government regulator: one authorization is needed to operate a public mobile phone network and the other is needed to operate a private wireless backhaul network.

For many customers in North America, the analogue air-link offered relatively good coverage and was certainly a step up from the older single point radio network design of the MTS systems. In Europe, the problem was a situation involving multiple standards and frequency assignments for the last mile air-link, making it difficult for customers to roam between countries. Part of the EU drive for digital standards was to resolve this interoperability dilemma but analogue operators in Europe and America also faced a common problem of congestion.

Analogue cellular systems *did* increase the number of customers compared with the old MTS systems, but capacity was still limited by the relatively poor spectral efficiency of the analogue design. This is because analogue systems require a pair of channels (i.e., frequencies) for each mobile caller, plus a set of 'guard bands' to ensure enough separation between channels to avoid interference between calls. Even with frequency re-use in a cellular network, the paired channels and guard bands consumed a lot of spectrum and seriously limited the number of mobile phone customers that could be accommodated on the network. If a growing demand for mobile phone service were going to be satisfied then operators in Europe and America would eventually need access to more spectrum, but in the shorter term they would also need to squeeze more value out of the spectrum that they already were authorized to use.

### 4.3.1   Squeezing spectrum (some more)

**Spectral efficiency** is a term that simply means how much value a wireless system can draw from a specific amount of bandwidth. The challenge for mobile operators of course is to find a way to achieve greater efficiency with the spectrum they already have allotted to them. One way, as we have already seen, is to adopt a cellular network design based on frequency re-use. This enables a small number of radio channels to be recycled within a designated geographic area, thereby permitting more customers to access the network at any given moment. However, a cellular network infrastructure is very expensive to build and it has practical limits to growth in terms of constructing additional cell-sites.

Another means of achieving spectral efficiency is called **multiplexing**. This term is related in part to the communication modes – simplex, half and full duplex – introduced in the previous chapter. These modes refer to the capability for simultaneous two-way voice or data communications on a wireless radio network. Analogue first generation mobile phones are 'full duplex' and use two radio channels per call – one for transmitting and another for receiving ('paired spectrum'). This is also known as **Frequency Division Duplexing (FDD)** because the duplex mode is achieved by assigning the spectrum into one set of channels for the uplink and another set for the downlink between the phone and the cell-site.

By way of comparison, **Time Division Duplexing (TDD)** refers to a method whereby a single channel is used for both uplink and downlink in an alternating fashion, divided by small increments of time. With the help of computers and microchips this type of simplex mode of communication can be automated, making the back and forth alternations extremely rapid and effectively invisible to the user. TDD is used in some wireless LAN systems but second generation digital cellular systems have been developed using FDD-based designs.

FDD for cellular systems is based on symmetric paired spectrum, which means that the bandwidth allocated for uplink and downlink is the same. **Uplink** refers to the transmission from the mobile phone to the cell-site, whereas **downlink** refers to the transmission from the cell-site to the mobile phone. In an FDD design, the uplink and downlink transmit on separate frequencies:

> Spectrum pairs always use the higher frequency for the downlink and the lower one for the uplink. This is because high frequencies have a slightly shorter range, thanks to atmospheric interference, and the base station can increase its transmission power to compensate. Mobile terminals can transmit using slightly lower power, which lengthens battery life and reduces the risk of radiation harming the user.[3]

One limitation of duplexing of course is the need for paired channels for each mobile phone call and therefore extra spectrum to provide these channels. This limitation has been overcome with a fairly recent innovation known as **multiplexing**. In the world of digital cellular the term refers to the method by which multiple full duplex transmissions can be simultaneously threaded together using a single pair of channels. As you can imagine, this technique of combining several transmissions on a single pair of frequencies can dramatically improve spectral efficiency.

How do you thread multiple phone conversations together on a single pair of channels? Modern multiplexing techniques depend very much on the sophisticated capabilities of computers and digital transmission systems. Computers can enable a single pair of channels to be divided in very small increments by assigning them a time slot or a specific code. These methods are known as *time-division* multiplexing or *code-division* multiplexing.

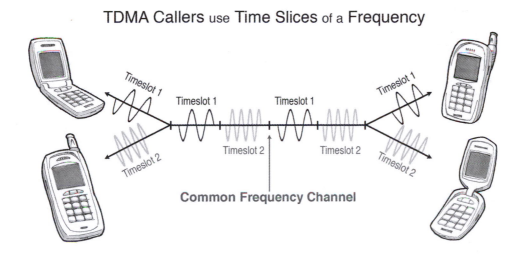

**Figure 4.2** Illustration of the TDMA concept

### 4.3.2 Time-division multiplexing

In **time–division multiplexing**, a single pair of channels can be sliced up into tiny individual timeslots. The speech captured by the microphone in a mobile phone is digitally sampled and then sliced up into tiny fragments that are assigned to one or more of these timeslots. Other mobile phones within the cell might share the channel but are assigned their own timeslots in the multiplexed signal. This is done extremely rapidly with a microprocessing computer, and some multiplex systems are based on eight or more timeslots, which means that up to eight separate telephone calls can be simultaneously supported on each paired channel. With older analogue systems that same pair of radio channels could only support one phone call. This amounts to a potential eight-fold increase in capacity using the same amount of radio spectrum!

### 4.3.3 Code-division multiplexing

Code-division multiplexing is a bit more complex but adheres to the same goal of increasing spectral efficiency. Because it is a complicated technique to understand, an analogy is often used to explain code-division multiplexing, which begins with, 'Imagine you are at a cocktail party with an international guest list . . . ' The room is crowded with people from all over the world having conversations in different languages. In order to have a conversation with another English speaker, you must either go to another room or be able to tune-out all the other conversations. Luckily for us this is relatively easy to do since the other conversations are in languages you don't speak and can't understand. Many simultaneous conversations are happening in the room and yet, if it doesn't get too noisy, it is still possible to concentrate on what your partner is saying to you.

Your conversation at the cocktail party is like a single channel of paired fre-quencies (i.e., sender/receiver), and each language being spoken around you represents a coded set of transmissions between other senders and receivers. The

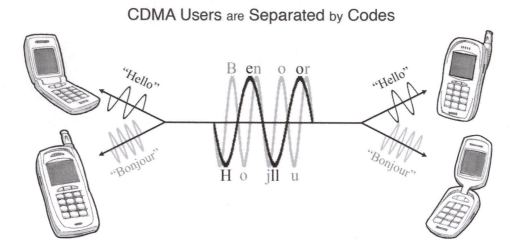

**Figure 4.3**   Illustration of the CDMA concept

speakers of each language understand their own codes and ignore the others, making it possible to conduct a single conversation in the midst of many others. At this party there are many simultaneous conversations but because each conversation is uniquely 'coded' in its own language, it doesn't interfere with others taking place in other languages. In fact, from your point of view (unless of course you are eavesdropping) the other conversations are simply background noise to be ignored.

In code-division multiplexing a single pair of channels can support many simultaneous transmissions because each separate telephone call has been assigned its own special code. Computers do the work of coding and decoding the signals in the mobile phone and at the cell-site, thereby multiplying the spectral efficiency somewhere between eight and 20 times that of analogue systems.

Code-division multiplexing is also called *spread spectrum*, referring to the fact that it uses a wide band of frequencies simultaneously. Rather than using a single pair of frequencies per transmission, CMDA transmissions are 'spread' across a range of many frequencies and either hop from one to the other in a coded pattern or are spread out all at once across the whole bandwidth in a coded sequence. The former is known as **Frequency hopping (FH-CDMA)** the latter as **Direct Sequence Spread Spectrum (DSSS, or DS-CDMA)**. Short-range wireless technologies such as Bluetooth are based on frequency hopping. DSSS is the basis for third generation mobile phone networks as well as the IEEE 802.11 family of wireless LAN systems, also known as Wi-Fi.

The spread spectrum concept has a fascinating history that dates back to the 1940s when it was first patented by the Austrian actress Hedy Lamarr and American composer, George Antheil. Here is part of that intriguing story:

Lamarr had fled the Nazi regime in Germany, where she'd been married to an arms dealer and noticed that most of the torpedoes he sold missed their targets. Spread spectrum was intended as an unjammable radio system that would enable torpedoes to be guided by remote control. The Navy initially dismissed it as too complicated, but the complexity later became manageable, with the arrival of transistors and silicon chips. Spread spectrum is now the basis of most mobile data systems, including Bluetooth, 3G cellular, and wireless Ethernet.[4]

Whereas the first generation of analogue mobile phones used a relatively simple system of frequency division duplexing, modern digital mobile phone networks have employed more sophisticated multiplexing techniques to achieve better spectral efficiency and greater performance. With the deployment of digital second generation or '2G' systems in the 1990s, the world gradually became divided into regions dominated by a TDMA-based system or one based on CDMA. The European Union sought to resolve its last-mile dilemma by developing a universal TDMA-based system that would come to be known simply as 'GSM'.

## 4.4   Europe leaps ahead

By the mid-1980s, the AMPS (Analogue Mobile Phone System) standard was in widespread use with roaming capabilities across significant regions of North America. As a result, there was no urgent case for developing a unified digital standard even though there were growing concerns around congested spectrum in major urban centres. The AMPS system also faced other problems related to its analogue technology. Among these was an ongoing concern about privacy because anyone with a radio scanner could intercept telephone calls made from a mobile phone. There was also the persistent problem of phone fraud since certain technical limits of analogue systems made it relatively easy to use stolen network access codes to obtain phone service without paying for it. Nevertheless, North America by the late 1980s had a reasonably well developed analogue network with wide area roaming available in most major cities.

By contrast, the countries in Europe had developed and deployed nine incompatible analogue systems. For those business clients who were constantly crossing international borders within the European Union, this situation often made mobile phones impractical. A notable exception was in the countries of Scandinavia, which had developed the Nordic Mobile Telephone (NMT) system. NMT was a first generation analogue service that allowed users to roam throughout the Nordic countries. Mostly, however, roaming was very difficult for first generation mobile phone service in the European countries, and it was this situation that eventually spurred interest in developing a single international standard for the EU.

Europe's patchwork of standards and frequency assignments for mobile phone systems was partly a legacy effect stemming from the telecommunications policies of the monopoly era. As noted in the previous chapter, telephone service in most countries prior to late 1980s was provided by private or state owned monopolies. In Europe and elsewhere these were called PTTs (Post, Telegraph, Telephone). Over time, the PTTs came to be regarded by influential policymakers as barriers to innovation that were often used to support the national economic interests of countries in Europe.

If you have ever had the pleasure of travelling throughout Europe, you may have noticed that each country has a different adapter plug for its telephone sockets. The most obvious effect of this arrangement is to make it difficult to import telephone equipment from one country into another (at least without making modifications to it). This is one example of how European countries attempted to control the interconnection of unauthorized telephone equipment to their networks – not unlike the situation in the Carterfone case.

In the European countries the incentive to prevent unauthorized inter-connection was partly economically driven, insofar as many countries enforced a policy that protected a close relationship between the domestic equipment manufacturer and the national PTT. The domestic manufacturer of switches and telephone handsets was given exclusive rights to provide these for the national network, while also being allowed to try and sell its wares in other countries. In this way, telecom policy was used to support domestic equipment manufacturing, as well as the research and development that went along with it. This was the longstanding arrangement between equipment vendor Alcatel and the French PTT. It was the same for Siemens and the German PTT, Deutsche Telecom. In fact, most of the major telecom equipment manufacturers in the world today were once in similar relationships to an incumbent operator. These included Nortel (former supplier to Bell Canada), Lucent (formerly Bell Labs working for AT&T) and Cable & Wireless (supplying British Telecom).[5]

The patchwork of technical standards and frequency assignments that plagued the mobile phone sector was partly a result of these protectionist policies and resulted in fragmented and relatively small markets for analogue cellular service in Europe. Nine different analogue standards were adopted, using incompatible frequency assignments. The mobile operator in the UK, for instance, began in 1985 to deploy the TAC (Total Access Communications) system in the 900MHz band whereas France, Germany and Italy were each deploying their own pro-prietary analogue systems.

Another example of the many standards in Europe was the 'Netz' series developed in Germany and later deployed in other countries including Austria, the Netherlands and Luxembourg. The Netz series began in 1958 with the A-Netz standard operating in the 160MHz band and provided basic radiotelephony service much like the MTS systems in North America. B-Netz was introduced in 1972, offering some enhancements but still providing basically an MTS-type service. C-Netz was similar to AMPS and appeared in the 1980s. It was one of a number of proprietary European cellular systems; it operated in the 450MHz band, and provided voice service with some limited data capabilities. With the succession of digital mobile phone service in the late 1990s, the C-Netz analogue network was shut off in 2000.[6] Today, there are two digital 900MHz systems operating in Germany (T-Mobile and Vodafone) that are referred to as 'D-Netz' while the digital service on the 1800MHz band is called 'E-Netz'. These digital networks belong to a pan-European standard known as GSM.

### 4.4.1  GSM

With the continued pressure toward regional integration, global trade agreements and a growing telecom reform movement spreading across the continent, Eur-opean governments perceived advantages and opportunities in developing not only a unified standard for mobile phone service but in developing a single digital standard that could provide advanced features to meet anticipated future demand for data services.

GSM stands for *Global System for Mobile Communications*, although the original name of the initiative that developed the standard started out as *Groupe Spéciale Mobile*. This is a non-proprietary European designed digital air-link standard, which means that its specifications are available without licence to anyone wishing to manufacture equipment based on the GSM standard. Development of the standard began in the 1980s when the continent began to experience growing demand for access to analogue mobile telephone service. GSM was developed with four ideas in mind: to adopt a pan-European frequency assignment at

900MHz; to permit roaming across borders; to design a completely digital system; and to offer both voice and data features.

The Nordic Mobile Telephone System (NMT), a first generation mobile phone system developed in Scandinavia, came to play an important role in the development of the European initiative. The NMT standard provided a model for the development of GSM and helped to provide both Sweden and Finland with a first mover advantage in the global mobile communications market, something that equipment manufacturers like Ericsson and Nokia would use to their advantage. Jon Agar, in his book *Constant Touch: A Global History of the Mobile Phone*, describes how other preceding systems that had created so much difficulty in Europe actually helped the GSM development programme, which in turn launched the mobile phone boom in Europe:

> The European digital standard benefited, bizarrely, from the chaos of what went before. Many different national systems at least produced a variety of technical possibilities from which to pick and choose. NMT provided a basic template onto which extra features – such as SIMS cards, from Germany's Netz-C – could be grafted. Furthermore, the relative failure of the fist cellular phones in countries such as France, and especially Germany, created a pent-up demand that GSM could meet. In the USA, where customers were satisfied with the analogue standard, there was little demand for digital until spectrum space began to run out. Paradoxically, the USA lost the lead because its first generation of cellular phones was too successful.[7]

Standardization work on GSM began with CEPT (Conférence Européenne des Postes et Télécommunications), an organization that was once the forum in which European PTTs cooperated on technical standards and operating procedures. In the late 1980s, the European Telecommunications Standards Institute (ETSI) was created and then took over the work on GSM. In 1991, GSM was finally standardized in a 5000-page document that described a range of specifications, including those for international roaming, fax and data services. The GSM standard also included the provision for a short messaging service (SMS) that would have a profound impact on the popular use of mobile phones. With respect to improved spectral efficiency, GSM achieved this with time division multiplexing based on eight timeslots, which means that it is capable (in theory) of threading together eight separate telephone calls over a single paired channel.

Since first being deployed in the early 1990s, GSM quickly achieved the pan-European coverage that it was hoped it would. Then, however, it continued to be adopted by other countries and soon became the most widespread standard for mobile communications in the world. The GSM World website reports that in 2003 there were 541 GSM networks operating in 185 countries, which is about 70 percent of the world market for mobile communications. In Europe, GSM is deployed in the 900 and 1800MHz bands but GSM networks are sometimes available in other countries on the 450MHz band. In North America, GSM is deployed on the digital PCS band at 1900MHz, which is sometimes referred to as GSM-1900.[8]

## 4.5    North America

As noted, AMPS was the first generation analogue air-link standard developed in North America and deployed for the first time in the early 1980s. The AMPS air-link was designed primarily for voice service but it did have simple data services including limited short messaging capabilities that were not widely used. In the US and Canada, AMPS-based systems operated in the 800MHz band, and achieved good coverage in most of the populated regions of those countries. Today, with the advent of digital networks, mobile phones that use the AMPS air-link exclusively are now disappearing. In their place have come the 'dual-mode' or 'tri-mode' models that are backward compatible with AMPS. Although most urban centres will now have digital coverage exclusively, having an AMPS mobile phone may still be necessary when roaming in remote areas that lie beyond the boundaries of digital coverage.

### 4.5.1    D-AMPS

In 1984 the Cellular Telecommunications Industry Association was founded in the United States to provide representation for the growing mobile phone sector and gave its approval for a new *digital* 'dual mode' standard called D-AMPS ('D' for digital). D-AMPS was the first North American digital cellular standard, which is also known by the official names IS-54 or ANSI-136.

An important consideration in creating the first North American digital cellular standard was not only to improve spectral efficiency but also to do so without the need for assigning new spectrum. Spectrum scarcity meant that the digital systems would have to work with the existing allotments for AMPS service. The D-AMPS standard was therefore developed to work with the 30kHz channels established for the analogue system, thus obviating the need for new spectrum allocation and permitting incumbent operators to easily upgrade their 800MHz-based systems from analogue to digital.

Like the GSM standard, D-AMPS also uses a time division method for multiplexing and thus earned the name **TDMA (Time Division Multiple Access)**. Whereas each 30KHz of bandwidth in the old AMPS system could support one user only, the D-AMPS version of TDMA could provide service to three callers over the same 30kHz of spectrum because each channel was divided into three unique timeslots.

TDMA was developed initially for North America and was adopted by mobile operators in both the US and Canada. It soon faced stiff competition from a second air-link standard called CDMA, which eventually resulted in the rise of two competing standards in those countries. This fragmentation effectively split North America into two incompatible mobile phone systems, affecting roaming to some degree and, according to some observers, has been partly responsible for the slow adoption of text messaging in North America.

Today, former TDMA-based operators, like Cingular in the United States, are changing over to GSM because of its global roaming and widespread appeal. GSM also offers improved spectral efficiency over TDMA and a well defined upgrade path to third generation mobile phone service. The transition between these two air-link standards is being made possible with something called GAIT. GAIT is yet another acronym and stands for 'GSM ANSI-136 Interoperability Team', which is a group of experts that has been working on technical specifications that enable a GSM overlay for TDMA networks. GAIT is also supporting the development of mobile phones capable of roaming on either GSM or TDMA networks.[9]

Despite the gradual decline of TDMA in North America, it remains an important second generation standard, particularly in other parts of ITU Region 2, where more than 90 operators continue using it as their primary air-link standard. In fact, it is reported to be the only standard with nationwide coverage in countries such as Brazil, Colombia, Ecuador, Mexico, Nicaragua and Panama.[10]

### 4.5.2 Qualcomm's cdmaOne

In 1995, the American company Qualcomm introduced a CDMA-based standard based on the spread spectrum technique first patented by Lamar and Antheil in the 1940s. Many large carriers in both the United States and Canada soon adopted CDMA and, unlike the open source standard of GSM, Qualcomm has maintained tight control over licensing of its CDMA technology, sometimes referred to as 'cdmaOne'. Qualcomm now focuses on developing and licensing wireless technologies based on its CDMA patents, having sold its base-station business to Ericsson and its mobile phone manufacturing to Kyocera.

Today, CDMA is perceived as *the* North American digital standard but it is also seeing widespread deployment in South America and the Asia Pacific region. While it does not have the reach of GSM in Western Europe, a number of countries such as Russia, Ukraine and Poland now have CDMA networks. A small number of countries in Africa and the Middle East including Israel also have wireless operators with CDMA networks.

In North America, CDMA-based systems operate in the 800MHz and 1900MHz bands. Digital PCS phones that are capable of working in both bands may be called 'dual-mode' but sometimes they include AMPS 800MHz capability and are then called 'tri-mode'. As the name implies, CDMA uses code division multiplexing that does away with the need for physical paired channels with a spread spectrum technique. Known by the official term IS-95, CDMA standard shares a 1.25MHz channel in contrast to the individual 30kHz channels of AMPS and TDMA. This means that when it was first being deployed, governments had to allocate and assign blocks of spectrum to support the technology, which required mobile operators to bid for PCS spectrum in North America and elsewhere in the mid-1990s in order to deploy CDMA technology.

## 4.6  Japan and PDC

In contrast to the rest of the world, Japan went its own way and developed a TDMA-based system called Personal Digital Cellular (PDC). Facing a situation somewhat similar to that in North America, the Japanese sought to develop a standard that would be backward compatible with the J-TACS analogue system that had been in service since the 1980s. The Association of Radio Industries and Businesses (ARIB), the Japanese standards organization, based PDC on the North American D-AMPS standard but the Japanese added a packet switching capability for data that would later have significant implications for the use of wireless Internet in that country.

PDC is designed with 25kHz channels, each with capacity for three timeslots (much like TDMA) and mobile operators have implemented PDC in Japan at 800MHz and 1.5GHz. NTT DoCoMo first deployed it for the Digital MOVA service in 1993. In late 2003 there were a reported 62 million users of the standard in Japan but PDC is gradually being phased out by third generation standards based on CDMA.

## 4.7   The world in 2G

Table 4.1 is a summary of the world's major mobile phone operators, listing regional coverage, the 2G air-link standards they use, as well as their subscriber base.[11] It is evident from this table that GSM is dominant.

**Table 4.1**   Mobile phone operators

| Country/region | Operator | System | Subscribers (millions) |
| --- | --- | --- | --- |
| China | China Mobile | GSM | 204 |
| EU | Vodafone | GSM | 152 |
| EU | T–Mobile | GSM | 69 |
| South America | Movistar | GSM | 51 |
| United States | Cingular | TDMA/GSM | 50 |
| Japan | NTT DoCoMo | PDC | 46 |
| United States | Verizon | cdmaOne | 45 |

Some countries have assigned different bands for analogue and digital mobile phone systems. For instance, in Europe and Hong Kong digital services operate using GSM in the 900 and 1800MHz bands. If you are travelling to these parts of the world from North America, an older model CDMA or GSM mobile phone might not be able to connect with a network. This is why travellers need to obtain a special GSM 'world phone' that is capable of operating in 900, 1800, 1900 bands.

Table 4.2 compares second generation mobile phone standards, looking at spectral efficiency and market share as of December 2004.[12] As you will recall, the term 'bandwidth' describes the range of frequencies needed for each assigned channel while multiplexing enables more than one telephone call per channel. The efficiency of each air-link standard is a combination of factors, including bandwidth and the theoretical number of calls that each multiplexing design can support (other factors related to the design of the cellular network are also important but are not discussed here).

**Table 4.2**   2G standards, bandwidths and market size

| Air link standard | Channel bandwidth | Calls per channel | Subscribers (global) |
| --- | --- | --- | --- |
| GSM | 200kHz | 8 | 1.3 billion |
| cdmaOne | 1250kHz | ≈ 15 | 238 million |
| D-AMPS | 30kHz | 3 | 94 million |
| PDC | 25kHz | 3 | 58 million |

Readers should note that when purchasing and using a mobile phone there is an important difference between multi-*mode* and multi-*band* phones. Multi-mode phones usually provide two or more air-link standards. For example, certain models of mobile phones on the market in North America are designed to operate on CDMA and AMPS networks, enabling customers to roam in areas where digital is not yet deployed. Mobile phones are now available that will also provide for tri-mode service, enabling customers to roam across TDMA, GSM and AMPS networks.

In other cases, the mode of the phone may remain the same but the *bands* may be different depending on the specific country in which the phone is roaming. For instance, as noted above a GSM world phone is multi-band capable of operating in the 1900MHz band for North America as well as the 900/1800MHz bands for Europe and other countries. A multi-band phone, in other words, is capable of switching between radio frequencies when necessary. Recent advances in the design of mobile phones are making these subtle distinctions increasingly less important, as new models are introduced with both multi-mode and multi-band capabilities, including ones that operate on both CDMA and GSM networks.[13]

## 4.8   The personal trusted device

With the advent of 2G digital mobile phones, many of the technical barriers of the analogue service were solved. Digital networks are more secure, they are more efficient, consume less power, allow for smaller handsets, and they provide high quality voice service plus new data services at better prices than their analogue counterparts. But looking back at the period between about 1995 and 2000, it is possible to see that the success of the second generation mobile phone is much more than a technical achievement.

During this period in history the mobile phone was also embraced as something of a cultural icon, a fashion item and a personal trusted device. No longer the black brick with an antenna stuck in the top, the mobile phone was now an object of mass consumption that would set into motion an upheaval in the telecom sector – one that very few experts saw coming and yet would have a global influence almost on par with the Internet. Certainly there was the matter of new competition in telecom markets and the lower prices that came with the second generation, but there was also more to this movement that just economics. Looking a bit further into the story, it is possible to discern two other major forces at work during this time. The first involved a radical shift in the industrial design of the mobile phone pioneered by companies like Nokia. The second was a decision to include a simple data service in the GSM standard that would enable mobile phones to send and receive short text messages of up to 160 characters.

### 4.8.1   Nokia and Nuovo

Recent history in this field has been deeply influenced by the Nordic countries, not only because of NMT's formative influence on the GSM standard but by the Finnish company, Nokia, for first recognizing the unique personal appeal of the mobile phone. Nokia first entered the mobile phone marketplace in the 1980s, but it has a long history in a diverse range of activities including timber and rubber industries. By the late 1990s, it had become the world's largest manufacturer of mobile phones, surpassing industry giant, Motorola, in 1998. By 2002, Nokia controlled one-third of the global handset market, with sales of over 100 million units per year. Nokia's influence should not be underestimated: through its prominence in the consumer marketplace it has deeply influenced the visions, the technologies and the services that will continue to drive developments in the wireless sector for many years to come. Table 4.3 illustrates Nokia's dominance of the global handset market in the middle of 2002. Motorola, the nearest competitor to Nokia, had less than half the sales volume for the same period.

Without Nokia's influence, the design paradigm for the modern mobile phone might never have shifted from Fordist-type thinking (i.e., 'one size fits all') into

**Table 4.3**   Mobile phone sales figures for 2002

| Company | Sales Q3 (2002) (000s) | Global Market Share (%) |
|---|---|---|
| Nokia | 37,447 | 35.9 |
| Motorola | 15,030 | 14.4 |
| Samsung | 11,063 | 10.6 |
| Siemens | 8,145 | 8.4 |
| Sony/Ericsson | 4,999 | 4.8 |
| Others | 27,572 | 26.4 |
| **Total** | **104,256** | **100** |

*Source*: Ray Le Maistre (2002) Nokia Extends Handset Lead, *Unstrung*, 26 November.
http://www.unstrung.com

what Dan Steinbock refers to as a 'segmentation' strategy that capitalized in selling the mobile as an object of self-expression:

> In the early 1990s, Motorola was the Ford and Nokia the General Motors of the mobile industry. Like GM in the 1920s, Nokia segmented the markets to capitalize on its strengths and to exploit Motorola's weaknesses. The customer base has exploded from business to consumer markets. Driven by the marketing concept, the marketing mix shifted toward the consumer . . . New mobile device models proliferated. Continuous product introductions and the new design language coincided with Nokia's move from geographic segmentation to customer segementation and value-based segmentation. These shifts went hand in hand with the move from narrow business markets to broad consumer markets.[14]

At the centre of this segmentation strategy was industrial designer, Frank Nuovo. Nuovo is an Italian-American industrial designer from Monterey, California, who began working as a consultant for Nokia in the early 1990s, after having worked as a designer for the automobile industry in America.[15] He eventually became vice-president in charge of design for Nokia and later started his own company, Vertu, which now sells exclusive luxury designer phones that retail for thousands of dollars.[16] Based out of Nokia's home in Helsinki, Nuovo cultivated a rich combination of influences in design thinking to create an aesthetic and functional approach to the mobile phone:

> At Nokia, the breakthrough design was the classic 2100 cell phone of 1994. The phone's size was actually increased to give it an elliptically shaped top and rounded keypad, in hopes 'it would be friendly, like a companion, not a little, square, hard box,' said Frank Nuovo, vice president and chief designer at Nokia Mobile Phones, who led Nokia's seventy member design team. 'Putting a brick up to your face was not something I thought would be good.' Nuovo saw Finnish design as unique. It was based on a very utilitarian approach but with an appreciation of beauty. His background was in the automobile industry, where styling is considered very emotional. That approach, he believed, would work well with Finnish function and form.[17]

Nuovo's influence has made an important contribution to the popularity of second generation service and today we can see his hand in transforming the mobile phone from a utility object to an elegant, user friendly fashion item.[18] In the late 1990s Nokia also launched an ingenious marketing campaign to associate its phones with Hollywood celebrities:

In April 2000, Nuovo's sleekly designed Nokia phones arrived in Hollywood ... The 'first fashion phone' [the Nokia 8860] appealed to the exclusive yet rapidly expanding membership of the 8860 club in which *Vogue* [magazine] listed Lauryn Hill ... Tom Cruise, Nicole Kidman, Janet Jackson, Barbara Walters, Minnie Driver, Paul Newman, Tom Hanks ... [and] Steven Spielberg ... Many of these celebrities provided the stage for a carefully orchestrated marketing campaign in which opinion leaders encouraged the use of Nokia phones among their fans. Hence, cameos of the 8860 appeared in everything from *Sex and the City*, a suggestive TV show, to *Hanging Up*, a recent Diane Keaton movie. In addition Nokia gave its 8860 phones as gifts to all the presenters at the Emmy Awards. The 8860 was preceded by the 8210, which was introduced in Members of Paris during Fashion Week. 'That's our haute couture phone', said Nuovo, who described the objective of his design team as 'humanized technology'. For him, the goal was to meld style and reliability.[19]

To take things even further, Nokia also recognized and capitalized on the highly self-expressive nature of mobile phones by creating a new and highly profitable market in accessories. Interchangeable coloured faceplates, personal ringtones and downloadable icons were first introduced by Nokia and became extremely popular because they allowed people for the first time to be creative with this technology by customizing their phones according to their own preferences and tastes. Nokia also included games and other non–phone functions on their handsets, recognizing that such features would tap into the 'segmentation by lifestyle' marketing that has characterized the personal communications revolution.

Nokia also went beyond the aesthetics of its hardware to radically rethink the user interface design of the mobile phone. Previously handsets tended to require customers to remember special key codes and to work with small and unfriendly screen displays in order to access the features and functions. Drawing extensively on human centred design practices, Nokia designers greatly simplified the user interface, making it easier for everyone. As one Nokia designer put it,

> Technology can be pleasurable if it gives the user a sense of control, or if its use attests to a high degree of skill. Pleasure can also be evoked by aesthetic appearance or positive associations that attach to a technical object.[20]

**Figure 4.4**   Nokia phones from the 1990s

*Source*: Nokia

*Notes*: Examples of Nokia's revolutionary approach to mobile phone design during the late 1990s. From left to right: the 6100 series, a low cost model for first time mobile phone owners with interchangeable faceplate; a range of coloured faceplates for the 3200 series handset; the 8800 series is designed for a higher end market to appeal to the more fashion conscious mobile phone customer (the world's 'first fashion phone').

**Figure 4.5**   Clearnet Canada's marketing campaign in the 1990s

*Source*: not known [TELUS?]
*Notes*: Second generation mobile phone operators launched marketing campaigns based on organic, natural forms that complimented the shape of the popular Nokia handsets. This image was used by Canadian mobile carrier Clearnet in the late 1990s

In a sense, Nokia's segmentation by lifestyle approach has been to the previous generation of mobile phones what the graphical user interface (GUI) of Microsoft's Windows was to the command line programming of the old DOS computer systems.

The marketing of the mobile phone has also been helped along with new retail strategies aimed at conveying a sense of user friendliness to consumers who might otherwise be wary of a wireless device. In particular, it was the new entrants in the mobile phone sector that adopted simple and fun names like 'Orange', 'Fido' and 'T-Mobile' as a way of making the mobile more approachable for the average consumer. Advertising campaigns stayed away from emphasizing the technology as such, to focus on lifestyle and to depict the mobile phone as a way to connect with friends and family in a hectic world. Some marketing campaigns even adopted organic forms and themes to complement the rounded shapes of the new Nokia phones.

### 4.8.2   The popularity of prepaid

The digital technology of the second generation networks also permitted mobile operators for the first time to launch prepaid or 'pay as you go' service plans. Before this business model was introduced, mobile phone service plans tended to be based on a monthly contract that required customers to make a significant financial commitment to one operator. For many potential customers, it was this contract and associated credit check that discouraged them from acquiring service. The new digital cellular systems, however, enabled mobile operators to measure telephone calls in such a way that air time credit could be pre-sold in standard increments or 'top-ups' such as $10 or $20. In effect, the prepaid business model offers something not unlike a mobile payphone, where the customer pays in advance for credit which it then debited as it is used.

Today prepaid service represents a major share of the global mobile phone market, and is especially popular in less developed countries where personal incomes are low and cost control is a major concern for customers. In fact, prepaid is widely regarded as *the* innovation that has enabled the widespread adoption of the mobile phone in places with historically low telephone penetration like Africa and South America. While this is generally applauded as a step toward improving the digital divide, some observers are more circumspect about the long range implications of prepaid on cultural development:

> The problem [of prepaid] can be summarized as one of apparent success in achieving short-term regulatory benchmarks for telecom access, but at a cost which may impinge future network access and development; and which may be further exacerbating divides between rich and poor at a national level.[21]

The view reflected in this remark is that while prepaid appears at first glance to be a silver bullet for achieving higher penetration of telephone service in developing communities, it could allow policymakers to skirt more difficult questions concerning the regulation of universal service obligations as a public good.

Even in the advanced economies of the world, however, prepaid has also assumed a significant share of the total market for mobile phone service. Recent figures from the Organization for Economic Cooperation and Development (OECD) show that as a percentage of total market share, the prepaid model makes up about 40 percent average in the OECD countries, dipping to about 2 percent in Finland and South Korea and peaking above 90 percent in countries like Mexico and Italy. Industry forecasts suggest that the market is not set to decline either, with one report forecasting that prepaid will achieve almost two-thirds of the global wireless market by 2009 – which translates to over a billion customers.

This optimism has been tempered, however, by growing concern in some countries that prepaid services are a potential threat to safety and security. The anonymity that is possible with prepaid service is seen to be an aid to terrorists and criminals needing to coordinate their activities through mobile phones. In response to this perceived threat, a number of countries including Norway, Germany, Switzerland, South Africa, Australia, Singapore and Malaysia have passed laws that require customers to provide identification when activating a prepaid account. Whether such measures will be implemented more widely and how this might affect the adoption of prepaid remains to be seen.[22]

## 4.9   The beep heard around the world

Among the surprises of digital cellular was the widespread adoption and use of the short messaging service (**SMS**) that had been included in the GSM standard. Ironically, it has been suggested that if the SMS concept had been subjected to closer scrutiny by the GSM development teams it might never have been implemented at all because nobody at the time could imagine how it might be widely used.[23] Another perspective on the early development of the short message service also suggests that its popularity was completely unanticipated by the GSM developers, who saw it as a way to give the phone a simple radio paging feature:

> There is some debate within the mobile communications industry as to the exact history of SMS but the product would appear to have been originally designed as a one-way messaging service that would be a replacement for pagers. Targeted at business users, it was envisaged that call centres would mediate the messages and that people would not originate them in text

format through their own mobile, but would dictate them to the call centre instead.[24]

The basic Short Message Service implemented in the GSM standard is a store and forward system that permits small amounts of text (160 characters) to be sent to and from a mobile phone using the control signal over the GSM air-link. As noted in the quote above, the designers of the GSM standard saw this as a way of providing one-way pager functions for the mobile operators, such as voice mail notification or customer updates. However, once the public began to realize the potential of SMS to send messages from phone to phone, the popularity of this feature erupted in Europe and South East Asia, especially in places like the Philippines where it was seen as an inexpensive (and fun) alternative to voice calls.

No one is quite able to explain why SMS has become so popular but it is more than likely that part of its appeal is simple economics. According to one version of the story, text messaging was a service adopted by customers using prepaid (pay as you go) mobile phone service. Prepaid customers considered text messaging an economical alternative to voice calls because it is relatively cheap and quite manageable in terms of keeping track of costs. In some places, SMS was even offered free as an enticement to new customers.[25] A process of positive feedback, or what is sometimes called a virtuous circle, eventually developed to make text messaging an incredibly popular alternative – in some cases even a substitute – to

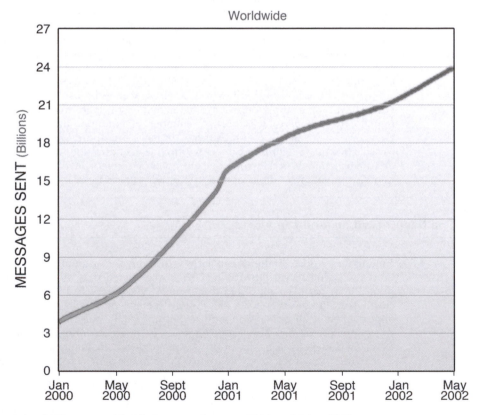

**Figure 4.6**   SMS use worldwide between January 2000 and May 2002

*Source*: GSM

traditional voice calls. Today, the exchange of SMS messages provides a sizeable revenue stream for mobile operators in many parts of the world.

Today there are now billions of SMS messages sent every month. Figure 4.6 from the GSM Association, tells the story of its meteoric rise to popularity. As can be seen in this chart, the worldwide surge in adoption saw the use of text messaging quadruple from just over 6 billion messages per month in May 2000 to some 24 billion per month two years later. At that time the GSM Association expected that some 360 billion text messages worldwide would be sent during 2002 (almost a billion per day).

A further two years later, in 2004, the Mobile Data Association in the UK would report about 2 billion messages being sent per month in that country alone, with peak days like New Year's 2005 when 133 million messages were sent. The Mobile Data Association also draws attention to the fact that text messaging may be impacting the market for greeting cards too, noting that '92 million text messages were sent by Britons on Valentine's Day 2005, compared to the estimated 12 million cards sent'. Although the figure is by no means a valid comparison (not all of those SMS messages were Valentine's greetings), it does draw attention to the growing importance of text messaging for interpersonal relations. For instance, Rich Ling reports on the use of SMS among young lovers as a prelude to the traditional telephone call:

> Since the message is not a physical object, such as a note, you need not meet the other in order to deliver the text message, nor do you need to engage an intermediary to play Cupid. You need not call the home of the person and perhaps meet skeptical parent being granted permission to speak to the potential new paramour. If the 'other' responds positively, you can further develop your interest via texting before, perhaps, going over to more synchronous interaction.[26]

Of course the obvious hindrance to text messaging in the early days was the cumbersome process of entering letters using a standard telephone keypad. Yet, despite the inconvenience of the multi-tap method for entering text into a phone, SMS usage continued to surge in popularity. Seeing a business opportunity in this keypad problem, a Seattle-based company called Tegic developed and filed a patent for a software algorithm that would later become the 'T9' predictive text application now standard on many mobile phones. With the predictive text input now installed on mobile handsets, the frustrating and time consuming task of entering letters using a telephone keypad was solved. Experienced users are reported achieving 30–40 words per minute with SMS.[27] However, before the T9 system was invented many enthusiasts developed their own SMS shorthand based on a similar system used for instant messaging and email. Glossaries of SMS shorthand were even put together for the novice 'texter'.[28]

Eventually SMS went commercial and value-added services began to appear when operators and third party entrepreneurs realized that a variety of information services, ringtones, logos, and even Internet chat could be offered. To use value-added SMS, a customer composes a text message that includes a request code and sends it to a special telephone number, or 'short code'. A server located at the SMS portal receives the request code and replies to the mobile phone with the desired information. The reply can take the form of an SMS message with requested information, or it might be a ringtone or small graphic sent via the SMS channel. In the late 1990s when this commercial prospects of SMS became apparent, a company originally based in Finland called 'Zed' was established as a personal message portal to provide content for local mobile operators in a number of countries. Today, Zed is only one among a large number of SMS portal services

**Figure 4.7**   Zed Philippines portal (screenshot)

*Source*: Zed Philippines, http://smart.zed.com

that offer a rich variety of novelty items to mobile phone customers. In many cases local operators are offered a revenue sharing agreement with the content provider as an incentive to carry the service. Premium SMS service can be seen as an initial foray into the world of *m-commerce* (mobile commerce), with the wireless sector using it in part to begin experimenting with business models for delivery of more sophisticated content over wireless networks.

### 4.9.1   SMS in North America

One glaring exception to the SMS success story was for quite some time in North America. While the rest of the world was adding SMS to its repertoire of everyday life, Canadians and Americans were *not* texting one another. If it was such a windfall for the mobile carriers elsewhere, then why was it not being promoted in these two countries? Whereas, one could find full-page adverts in newspapers and magazines across Europe and Asia for SMS-based ringtones and logos, such a thing was a rarity in North America during this period. What was the difference?

Part of the reason in this case does in fact appear to be technical. In particular, it was related to the fragmented standards caused by the combination of CDMA, TDMA and GSM operators in North America. Unlike in Europe, which is almost completely blanketed with the GSM standard, Canada and the US are a patchwork of different air-link standards. One of the barriers to SMS adoption has been simply that these different networks did not support interoperability for text messaging. Although CDMA and TDMA networks do offer their own versions of short messaging, the ability to send messages from one operator's network to another was seriously limited. For example, until only a few years ago a Verizon customer in the United States could not send a text message from his or her phone to a friend using Cingular phone service. As a result, the growth of SMS in North America was stifled in part by a lack of a common gateway between domestic networks.

In December 2001, the Cellular Telecommunications Industry Association (CTIA) began working with US mobile operators to develop a solution that would enable *inter-carrier* text messaging. The solution was unveiled at a conference in Orlando, Florida, in March 2002.[29] In April 2002 the Canadian mobile carriers established the first common inter-carrier SMS gateway in North America, making it possible to send messages between GSM and CDMA networks. The Canadian Wireless Telecommunications Association (CWTA) reported in November 2002 that, 'since the introduction of inter-carrier text messaging, the volume of messages sent by Canadians has increased by 98 per cent'. Clearly the gateway made a difference but the amount was still relatively low compared with other countries. For instance, the CWTA has reported since that Canadians are sending about three million text messages per day, which is still far less than the volume of messages that were being sent in many European countries during the late 1990s. At that time countries such as the UK, with about twice the population of Canada, were seeing in excess of three times the volume of messages, in the order of 20 million per day.[30]

In January 2003, the CWTA and the American-based CTIA announced that a cross-border version of the inter-carrier SMS gateway had commenced operation, unifying the North American text messaging market for the first time.[31] The innovation that solved the North American interoperability problem is a protocol known as SMPP, or 'short message peer to peer protocol', which is an open industry standard designed to simplify integration of mobile networks including GSM, TDMA, CDMA and PDC. Work began on the protocol as far back as 1997 and today it is widely deployed in the mobile sector, with ongoing development coordinated through an industry group referred to as 'The SMS Forum'.

Later that year, in October 2003, the CTIA announced it was to launch *common short code* capability for mobile phones in North America. As in other countries, this would assist in the growth of premium rate SMS services by allowing customers to place requests by sending short messages to service providers with a five-digit short code rather than a full telephone number.[32]

## 4.9.2 Textual politics

In addition to being a new way to initiate and maintain personal relations, text messaging has also gained a reputation as a form of political communication. This reputation dates back to an event in 2000, known as 'People Power 2' that occurred in the capital of the Philippines, Manila, when text messaging was used to mobilize people for the mass demonstration – a demonstration that eventually led to the Philippine president's removal from office. People Power 2 is often cited as a symbol of the democratizing potential of SMS and a unifying element in what has been called 'Generation Text'.

The link between SMS and politics remains strong in the Philippines, and its use was expected to be widespread in the electoral campaign in 2004 as a means to distribute news and rumours among voters. Reuters, for instance, reported in a story dated March 2004, that 'By the time Filipinos go to the polls on May 10 to elect a president and 17,000 other officials across the archipelago, many mobile phone owners will have received hundreds of messages aimed at influencing their decisions at the polling booth'.[33]

In Spain the mobile phone played a dual role in the events surrounding the election of 14 March 2004. A few days before, terrorists had used mobile phones to detonate bombs placed in Madrid commuter trains, killing 202 people. A massive wave of political unrest broke across the country on the eve of the election, with text messages being used covertly to coordinate mass demonstrations that were supposed to be banned in the 24 hours preceding the vote. Reports in the media claim that on the day before the vote, SMS traffic was up 20 per cent above normal, doubling to 40 per cent higher on election day. Many of those messages it appears were intended to mobilize demonstrations and counter-demonstrations. In the end, election turnout surpassed that of previous elections, suggesting that text messaging may have played a key role in shaping the future of Spanish politics.[34]

Howard Rheingold, who has written about the political power of the mobile phone, refers to this as a 'technology that amplifies collective action', enabling relatively spontaneous gatherings and quick dissemination of political messages to large numbers of citizens.[35] Politicians themselves have recognized this potential too, with SMS even being incorporated into campaigns in the 2004 US presidential election, and in an initiative launched by MTV and Motorola called 'Rock the Mobile Vote' which was intended to get young people to the polling stations. Despite this potential, however, writer Douglas Rushkoff was sceptical about MTV's peddling of politics in this way, fearing that 'solicitation through cell phones of instant responses to complex issues – worse, in a context of cool, hip marketing – will do more damage to America's democratic process that good'.[36]

## 4.10   A strange attractor

Sceptical opinions like that given by Rushkoff are worth considering, especially given the tendency of the press and other media toward sensationalism. But even if it turns out from empirical research findings that SMS is far less a genuine political tool than the media has led us to believe, there is still wisdom in the sceptic's point of view. Reflecting on the mobile phone and its cultural impact, George Myserson writes: ' . . . because the mobile is going to be so important, the ways in which ideas are associated with it is also important'.[37] In other words, public perception of SMS and the mobile phone as a political tool is an important development in and of itself because by this very fact it will continue to influence the co-evolution of politics, culture and technology.

The second generation of mobile phones launched a personal communications revolution and forever changed our perception of the black box with an antenna stuck on top. Today we are even hard pressed to find the antenna on our mobile phone. Certainly the development of digital cellular was important in this revolution, in part because it improved spectral efficiency through new multiplexing methods. Improved spectral efficiency meant that operators could offer services to a large customer base at reasonable prices and tap into new segments in consumer markets. In addition to this important technical innovation, the influence of design and marketing in the mobile phone sector has been equally important. Firms such as Nokia and its design team led by Frank Nuovo realized the value of associating mobile communications with lifestyle and emotional appeal. As a result of these efforts, the mobile phone is now widely accepted as a deeply personal object, and one that is well suited to the idiosyncrasies of self-expression in the (post)modern urban context. In a sense the mobile phone has become a kind of 'strange attractor' of aesthetics, digital technology and emerging communication practices. Perhaps nothing makes this more apparent than the world of personal *data* communications and mobile entertainment that would evolve from text messaging.

## 4.11    Further reading

Jon Agar's (2003) *Constant Touch: a Global History of the Mobile Phone* (Icon Books) presents a highly readable history of the development of GSM and second generation mobile phones, with a European emphasis. To get a sense of how the personal communications revolution was being perceived during its heyday it is informative to look at a special issue of the *Economist* entitled 'The world in your pocket', published in October 1999. Articles are archived on the web at: http://www.economist.com/surveys/displayStory.cfm?Story_id= 246137

For a corporate history of Nokia see Dan Steinbock's (2001) book, *The Nokia Revolution* (AMACOM). Steinbock's (2003) book, *Wireless Horizon* (AMACOM), also provides a good history of the second generation mobile phone. The often overlooked role of marketing in mobile communications is examined in Steinbock's most recent (2005) book, *The Mobile Revolution: The Making of Mobile Services Worldwide* (Kogan Page). *The New Yorker* (26 November 2001) includes an article on Frank Nuovo and his work for Nokia entitled, 'The phone guy'. The article is also available online: http://www.michaelspecter.com/ny/2001/ 2001_11_26_nokia.html

Dave Mock's (2005) book, *Qualcomm Equation* (AMACOM), presents the corporate history of Qualcomm and its role in the development of the CDMA standard. At least two management books have been published on Japan's accomplishments with second generation mobile phone service: *DoCoMo – Japan's Wireless Tsunami* (AMACOM, 2002) and *The i-Mode Wireless Ecosystem* (John Wiley and Sons, 2003).

Rich Ling's (2004) book, *The Mobile Connection* (Elsevier), examines the social impact of the mobile phone on society and includes among other things an insightful chapter on the social practices associated with text messaging. George Myerson (2001) has applied the ideas of two famous philosophers to the mobile phone and published it in a small book entitled, *Heidegger, Habermas and the Mobile Phone* (Icon Books). Paul Levinson (2004) traces the cultural history of the mobile phone as a new medium of communication in his book *Cellphone* (Palgrave).

# 5 The multitask gadget

We are the first generation of humans carrying powerful personal computers in our pockets.

(Justin Hall 2004)

## 5.1 Introduction

The personal communications revolution may have been launched with the advent of digital cellular but this was to be only the beginning of the story. The 'killer application' of voice telephony was soon complemented by text messaging, which was in effect an early form of *data* service. Developers of the GSM system might have been surprised by the fervent adoption of the short messaging service (SMS) among the population but they were also thinking ahead. Following the initial deployment of second generation networks in the 1990s came the halfway generation – sometimes referred to as 2.5G – that would enable more advanced mobile data services such as picture messaging and simple email and Internet services well before the full range of '3G' services was expected to arrive on the scene. This was seen as a transition phase but has since become an important development unto itself because it again changed the mobile phone – this time from a voice-centric device for talking, into an increasingly data-centric device for multitasking. Mobile operators and consumers soon discovered that new features such as multimedia messaging, downloadable games and mobile Internet access would change forever *again* our relationship to the telephone.

This chapter introduces the world of 2.5G services, highlighting key technical terms and concepts. Another important topic in this chapter is the definition of mobility and the difference between wide area networks and local area networks (discussed later in the book). The chapter also considers some of the early air interface standards and applications that were developed to provide mobile access to more advanced data services, including access to the Internet. These techniques are still important because they provide a bridge between digital voice and digital data services in the 2.5G period and a foundation for the transition to third generation mobile phones.

## 5.2 Defining mobility

When using the term 'wireless' communications it is often necessary to make conceptual distinctions to avoid confusion in meaning. For instance, not all wireless systems are necessarily *mobile* wireless systems and national band plans will usually make a clear distinction between 'fixed' wireless and 'mobile' wireless services when allocating frequencies.

Fixed wireless systems include traditional broadcast television, direct to home satellite service, and the microwave backhaul networks that move telephone traffic from individual cell-sites to the gateway switching centre. For these types of services, the transmitters and receivers are permanently fixed in one geographic location and do not usually move from place to place. Traditional over-air broadcast TV, for instance, requires a large antenna and transmitter site that is strategically positioned to ensure regional coverage. At the other end of the signal, the television receiver (even though it might be portable) is also strategically placed in a living room, kitchen or bedroom without too much movement. Point to point microwave links are another example of a fixed wireless network because these need to be permanently located and aimed so that each radio site can 'see' its companion. If the sites are moved or misaligned, then radio contact is lost.

Mobile wireless systems, on the other hand, include mobile phones, pagers, Family Radio Service (walkie-talkies) and some satellite phones. These radio systems are designed for situations where the handset is expected to be in motion during use. But this is a very basic distinction and could be further refined. After all, what does 'mobile' *really* mean? Does it mean we can use it anywhere in the city? Does it mean we can use it while driving down the highway in the car or on the bus? Does it mean we can use it in another city or country? Does it mean we can use it anywhere in the house?

These questions about mobility are not as finicky as it might seem, if only because it is necessary to think about such things when designing wireless products and services. For instance, application designer Johan Hjelm offers a very specific definition of mobility to guide his own work:

> If you can't pick up the device and walk out of the building while maintaining contact and continuing to use the applications you were using, it is not really mobile.[1]

With this very narrow classification, Hjelm is setting a standard for what we might call *true mobility*, which is a designation that can be set on a continuum of possibilities, as depicted in Figure 5.1.

Fixed                                    Mobile

**Figure 5.1**   The fixed–mobile continuum
*Source*: SFU Study Guide

A laptop computer with wireless Internet or email capability does not conform to Hjelm's definition of true mobility. It would be awkward (and unsafe) to pick up a laptop and to try and continue to use it while walking around a room or on the street. You certainly *could* do it but the device is clearly not designed for that kind of application. Moreover, the wireless technology used by most laptops – known as 'Wi-Fi' – is not really designed to hand-off the signal from one base station to the next. The situation with a wireless enabled laptop is therefore best described as one of 'portability' in order to distinguish a middle ground somewhere between wireless devices that are not quite fixed but that are also not truly mobile. The fixed–mobile continuum can therefore be modified slightly to include this important distinction (see Figure 5.2).

Fixed                    Portable                    Mobile

**Figure 5.2**    The fixed–portable–mobile continuum
*Source*: SFU Study Guide

While the focus of this book is on *mobile* communications, in later chapters it does discuss wireless systems that are more properly defined as *portable*, such as Bluetooth and Wi-Fi. A precise meaning of the term 'mobile' is therefore quite important for understanding the unique features of digital cellular as compared with other types of wireless networks: first, it determines how we measure the usability and viability of applications that a wireless network supports. For instance, applications designed for desktop computers are not necessarily well suited to a mobile phone. Second, the choice of terms is closely associated with the type of wireless network that is required to support the device. Wireless local area networks (LANs) are especially good for using a portable laptop computer in the office or the home, but not especially good for the roaming requirements of a mobile phone. The usability issue is not for this book, but knowing some basic distinctions in wireless data networking is the first step toward understanding different types of data services introduced in this chapter.[2]

### 5.2.1    WANs and LANs

Wireless networks are not all created equal. Some provide roaming coverage for entire cities, some for entire countries and some for the globe. Others provide limited coverage to a single building or a room within a building. Still others provide smaller coverage that extends to only a few metres.

The term wireless **WANs** refers to **Wide Area Networks**, which simply means a large zone of coverage. It is possible for a WAN to include any type of radio network that was described in Chapter 3 – single site, point-to-point or cellular – but for the purpose of this book the term will refer only to wide area *cellular* networks used by mobile phone operators.

Cellular WANs are extensions of the Public Switched Telephone Network (PSTN) and network operators face many of the same complicated business requirements of their counterparts in the wireline telephone business. These include meeting certain regulatory requirements with the national government (such as providing access to '911' emergency services), reconciling international payments for handling long distance calls, and a number of other issues with other operators related to roaming agreements, interconnection and so forth.

Today most cellular WANs support national and international roaming for voice services (with some limitations related to technical barriers between GSM and CDMA). The same freedom of mobility is not necessarily true for all mobile *data* services, which are relatively new in many countries. While customers may find that roaming with mobile data services is possible throughout their home country, when crossing the border the reality might be very different in terms of coverage and cost. In some cases, foreign coverage for mobile data services is poor and when it is available the cost can be outrageous.[3] While we can refer to cellular WANs as systems that have global roaming capabilities, it is important to remember that this refers primarily to voice services. At present, mobile data coverage using cellular WANs is far less certain when it comes to international roaming even though this will likely change in the near future.

One reason to describe the cellular WAN concept is to highlight an important distinction with data services that are available over wireless LANs or *Local Area Networks*. Wireless LANs are also commonplace today but they provide a much smaller range of coverage and use different air interface standards. Wireless LANs do not (yet) support the seamless hand-off of a cellular WAN and they are more suited to 'portable' devices and applications rather than truly mobile devices, such as a mobile phone. The book turns to look more closely at wireless LANs in Chapter 7 but for now the focus remains on cellular WANs.

## 5.3   Short Message Service

Among the simplest and yet most popular mobile data applications available today is the Short Message Service (SMS), which is the same as 'text messaging' described in the previous chapter. While this service is more appropriately called 'messaging' rather than wireless data per se, we will cover it briefly here because it was the precursor to more advanced services.

As noted in the previous chapter, SMS was first created as part of the GSM standard and is now part of the CDMA standard as well. Text messaging using SMS is a form of **store and forward** messaging similar to older style paging systems. Store and forward means that messages, once composed, are first stored on a central server and then forwarded to the customer when there is available capacity in the network. As a result, it is not 'instant messaging' in the strict sense of the term because SMS can be subject to delays on a busy network. SMS messages are transmitted over control channels that are used for call set up information between a mobile phone and the network. These channels have a limited amount of capacity and the basic GSM-based SMS message is limited in size to 160 bytes, which is equivalent to about 160 characters. SMS transmissions can also be used to deliver ring tones, advertising and SIM-card updates from the mobile operator to the customer's handset.

---

### Over 26 million text messages sent backing Live 8

More than 26.4 million people from around the world sent SMS yesterday in support of the Live 8 campaign to cancel the debts of the poorest countries, setting a world record, reports The New Zealand Herald.

The previous record for the most text messages sent on a single day for a single event was around 5.8 million for an episode of *American Idol* where viewers vote for the winner.

'I think it would be fair to say we're getting texts messages from people from Albania to Zimbabwe', said Ralph Simon, coordinator of the SMS campaign in Philadelphia, adding that lines would be open until the end of July. Western Europe probably accounted for the most messages.

'This shows how you can make an imprint with your thumb, which becomes your voice which becomes a call to end world poverty', he said.

---

**Figure 5.3**   Live 8 campaign and SMS

*Sources*: http://www.smartmobs.com/archive/2005/07/03/over_26_million.html
http://www.nzherald.co.nz/index.cfm?c_id=5&ObjectID=10333974

The profitability of SMS messages comes from the fact that they typically cost a customer about the same as a one-minute voice call. A one-minute voice call, however, uses about 300 times more network capacity than an SMS message. The net result for the mobile operators is that SMS is a very lucrative service, particularly because it has become so immensely popular in many parts of the world.

### 5.3.1    EMS and MMS

The popularity of SMS encouraged the development of more advanced messaging services using the same method. During the late 1990s, Nokia and other mobile phone vendors introduced **Enhanced Messaging Service (EMS)**. Nokia's version of EMS is sometimes called 'Smart Messaging'. EMS is based directly on the SMS design – a store and forward system that uses the air-link control channel to transmit messages to and from the handset – but included enhanced features such as the ability to transmit small monochrome graphics and to chain together several 160 character messages into a longer message.

More recently, another form of messaging has become available in certain parts of the world. **Multimedia Messaging Service (MMS)** is a far more sophisticated service for GSM networks to provide added features that could not be easily supported with the control channel technique used by SMS. Multimedia Messaging was officially launched in Europe in 2002 and many new handsets available on the market are now MMS capable. MMS offers the ability to display and send colour graphics, including small digital images and short video clips. The built-in camera that comes with many mobile phones today can take advantage of this new feature to send images to other mobile phones or email addresses. MMS also accommodates short audio clips and more sophisticated text messaging capabilities. Unlike EMS, however, MMS requires the mobile operator to upgrade their messaging infrastructure and develop a new billing structure to charge their customers for the service.

A further challenge, from the user's perspective, is that interoperability between MMS services is not guaranteed. What this means in practice is that the probability of using MMS to send pictures or sounds to your friends will depend on the destination network, the features of the MMS gateway server, the configuration of your correspondent's mobile phone, and the services they have subscribed to. Phone manufacturers and service providers recognize the challenges this represents to widespread adoption of MMS and have been working on solutions to solve interoperability problems. Ultimately the interoperability of MMS between service providers depends on the introduction of a new air-link standard for mobile phones that is capable of transmitting and receiving mobile data.

## 5.4    Wide area mobile data

A wide area mobile data network is similar to that of a mobile phone network in that we can identify three basic segments: the air-link, the backhaul and the gateway. At the air-link segment, a data-capable mobile handset connects by radio waves to a base station. Mobile data networks have special equipment located at the base stations to separate voice and data traffic into different network pathways. General Packet Radio Service (GPRS), for instance, is a mobile data service that requires the installation of a Packet Control Unit (PCU) at the base station. The base stations might also use a special backhaul network for the data transmissions that eventually connects through a gateway to the Internet.

### 5.4.1  Circuit switching and packet switching

A basic technical distinction between mobile data networks is whether they are **circuit-switched** or **packet-switched**. As a rule of thumb, all analogue and early 2G digital PCS networks provide circuit-switched data services. Newer technologies, such as 2.5G and 3G networks will also offer packet-switched service. Here are two basic definitions of these terms:

- *Circuit-switched* is 'a type of network that temporarily creates an actual physical path between parties while they are communicating'.
- *Packet-switched* is 'a type of network in which small discrete units of data are routed through a network based on the address contained within each packet'.[4]

Circuit-switched data services are like using a home telephone and a modem to connect to the Internet. It is first necessary to dial a phone number to establish a connection. Once connected the line remains open until the session is over and the customer decides to terminate the call. Circuit-switched services are usually charged for by the amount of time that the customer remains connected to the network. This means that a longer call, even if very little data traffic is actually passed across the connection will cost more than a brief session where lots of data is transferred.

Packet-based data services are sometimes called 'always-on' connections. This term is used because data is transmitted in separate packets rather than as a single continuous connection both the network. As a result, a mobile phone can send and receive data in discrete bursts without the need to maintain a continuously open connection with the network. This eliminates the need to establish a dedicated circuit, which means that more users can share the data connection. The packets of data contained in each burst will find their proper destination with address information contained in them. Packet-switched services are typically billed by the quantity of data traffic that a customer transmits and receives from their mobile device, usually measured in kilobytes or megabytes.

Some mobile operators provide unlimited data, especially in the home or local territory of the customer, in order to encourage use of these services. However, this once again raises a problem of scarcity – this time with bandwidth rather – because it creates a situation in which a small number of heavy data users could degrade the quality of service for more casual data users. The tradeoff that operators face is, on the one hand, to encourage customers to use a new service and to create positive feedback to grow it further through customer interest and the resulting revenue stream. On the other hand, the operators also want to derive as much revenue from their bandwidth as possible, which means effectively charging per byte. However, such a pricing strategy could drive away potential users who might be reluctant to experiment with a service that uses an unfamiliar pricing mechanism. One solution that operators adopt in light of this challenge is to place a cap on the amount of 'free' data that can be transferred, thereby striking a balance between incentive and fair use of the scarce resource of network bandwidth.

### 5.4.2  A mobile data network

Beyond the air-link segment, the rest of a mobile data network is designed around several support nodes that locate and authenticate data traffic, much like the Mobile Switching Centres do for voice traffic. In a GPRS system, these are called Serving GPRS Support Nodes (SGSN). Data traffic will then travel over the

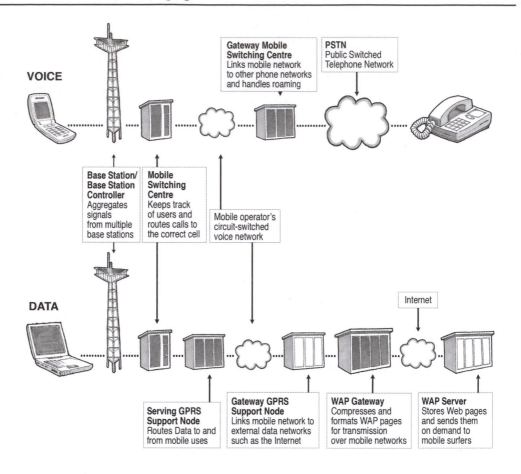

**VOICE**

**Gateway Mobile Switching Centre**
Links mobile network to other phone networks and handles roaming

**PSTN**
Public Switched Telephone Network

**Base Station/ Base Station Controller**
Aggregates signals from multiple base stations

**Mobile Switching Centre**
Keeps track of users and routes calls to the correct cell

Mobile operator's circuit-switched voice network

**DATA**

Internet

**Serving GPRS Support Node**
Routes Data to and from mobile uses

**Gateway GPRS Support Node**
Links mobile network to external data networks such as the Internet

**WAP Gateway**
Compresses and formats WAP pages for transmission over mobile networks

**WAP Server**
Stores Web pages and sends them on demand to mobile surfers

**Figure 5.4**   Mobile data network architecture
*Source*: *SFU Study Guide*, p. 51; see also Dornan (2002): 217

mobile carrier's internal packet-switched network (also called an 'Intranet') and to a gateway, where it will then be sent over the Internet to its destination.

For example, when a customer is looking at a website on their 2G mobile phone, the data will pass through a special gateway operated by the service provider to provide a link to the Internet. Somewhere out on the Internet will be the server that provides the data that the customer has requested through their mobile handset. This arrangement is similar to the **client/server model** that most regular website traffic. In both cases, a computer of some type (either a desktop computer or the mobile phone) acts as a 'client' that makes requests over a network to a 'server'. The server fulfils this request by sending web pages or other information back over the network to our mobile device. The gateway is the point of interconnection between mobile operator's network and the Internet.

As with the previous chapter on 2G mobile voice service, this chapter is focused on the wireless component of the network – the last mile – rather than the rest of the elements, although they are of course important. Also with the previous chapter on 2G, we find that there are several different air-link standards for mobile data services over cellular WANs.

## 5.5    Air-link standards for data

The most basic way to have mobile data access is by using a mobile phone as a modem, just like one would use a telephone at home for making a dial-up connection to the Internet. In this arrangement the customer connects their computer to a mobile phone using a data cable, infrared port or Bluetooth connection. The mobile phone then provides the air-link between the computer and the Internet using a standard dial-up connection.

This type of configuration will work for both circuit-switched and packet-switched services. In the circuit-switched configuration, the customer dials-up an Internet Service Provider (ISP) much like standard dial-up modem service. Of course the drawback to this method is that the user is usually billed for every minute of connection time whether or not they are actually exchanging data. The download speed available with this kind of configuration tends to vary between 9.6 and 14.4kbps (kilobytes per second), which by today's standards is the same as a very slow modem. When billing by time this slow speed means long calls that could cost a great deal of money to the customer. In some cases compression software can be installed on the computer to improve the speed.

### 5.5.1    HSCSD

An improved version of the circuit-switched modem method is available on some GSM networks. Known as **High Speed Circuit Switched Data (HSCSD)**, this service is based on a minor upgrade to GSM networks that can chain together four 14.4kbps circuits at the same time, increasing the potential speed to something like a 56K modem. Essentially HSCSD works by concatenating two or more telephone calls to increase the capacity for data transmission.

HSCSD was developed in 1997 but released commercially in 2000. The GSM Association reported that by 2002 it was available in 27 countries worldwide. While this was a promising start and while this technique does improve the performance of circuit-based data connections, HSCSD also increases power

---

**Nokia 7280 Call Management Data Features**

- Phonebook with up to 1000 contacts with multiple entries per contact
- Calendar with notes and reminders
- Alarm clock
- To do list
- HSCSD and GPRS for high-speed data connectivity capable
- XHTML browser (WAP 2.0) 1, 2, 12
- SyncML for daily synchronization of daytime and night time phones
- Capable of synchronizing your phonebook, calendar and to do list with your PC
- Capable of sending and receiving data via Bluetooth wireless technology or via infrared

**Figure 5.5**   Technical details of a mobile phone, showing HSCSD capability
*Source*: http://www.westcoin.com/nokia7280.html

consumption of the mobile phone and RF exposure to the user because it is like making two or more phone calls simultaneously. As a result, it also increases costs because the user must pay as much as eight times the cost of a regular call, making it rather expensive for many customers to consider using.

### 5.5.2   GPRS

A more recent alternative to HSCSD is a packet-switched upgrade to GSM networks called **GPRS (General Packet Radio Service)**. GPRS is an 'always-on' service, which means that the customer does not have to dial-up their service provider each time the mobile phone is transmitting or receiving data. This is comparable in some ways to having high-speed Internet access at home, where the connection is active as long as the computer is operating. According to the technical specifications, GPRS is capable of up to 115kbps but this will depend on the local mobile operator and how they have decided to implement the service. In many cases, speeds will average around 56kbps, which is equivalent to a high-speed dial-up modem but well below the speeds for wireless Ethernet, cable or ADSL service. However, because GPRS is a packet-switched service, the billing system is likely to be based on the amount of data traffic transmitted and received rather than for connection time.

GPRS is a relatively simple upgrade to existing GSM networks and is the first step in the upgrade path toward 3G. At the customer end, many new handsets are now equipped with GPRS and new data cards for laptops and PDAs are available on the market.

### 5.5.3   1XRTT

The CDMA-based version of GPRS is known as **1XRTT** (1 eXtreme Radio Transmission Technology). Mobile operators that have deployed CDMA networks provide mobile data services using the packet-switched 1XRTT service. Although there is some debate, 1XRTT is purported to have a slightly better performance rating than GPRS although in practice it also is reported to remain below the theoretical limit, with 1XRTT networks providing average speeds at 64kbps. 1XRTT is also on the upgrade path to 3G, while some operators even claim it qualifies as a 3G service, though this is disputable because it does not meet all the qualifications of a 3G standard.

**Table 5.1**   Mobile data rates

| Service | Theoretical (kbps) | Practical (kbps) |
| --- | --- | --- |
| CDPD | 19.2 | 9.2 |
| GSM | 14.4 | 9.6 |
| GPRS | 115.2 | 28.8 |
| 1XRTT | 144 | 64 |

*Source*: adapted from Dornan (2002) p. 168

### 5.5.4   Slow speed data services

Despite the intense marketing campaign that has accompanied the newer packet switched services, it is important to also realize that a number of older mobile data services are still available in some places. For instance, a service called **CDPD (Cellular Digital Packet Data)** used the old analogue AMPs infrastructure to provide low speed data in most of the major cities in North America. In some parts of North America CDPD still provides mobile data access, especially in remote areas where the newer GPRS or 1XRTT services are not yet deployed.

**Mobitex** is another low speed mobile data service that was developed by Ericsson primarily for telemetry applications, such as fleet management. While it provides only about 8kbps bandwidth it nevertheless works well for certain applications that only require small amounts of data to be transferred, such as in vehicle tracking. Blackberry 900 series devices, for instance, are designed to use the Mobitex network in North America. When Palm Corporation decided to build a wireless PDA (the Palm VII), it was designed to operate using the Mobitex network in the United States operated by Cingular Wireless. In some markets, Mobitex is provided under the name RAM Mobile Data.

Similar to Mobitex is the **ARDIS** or **DataTAC** network that provides low speed mobile data. DataTAC was developed by Motorola and IBM and provided the service for the original Blackberry 800 series devices in North America.

### 5.5.5  iDEN and TETRA

In the mid-1990s, Motorola and Nextel in the United States introduced the iDEN (Integrated Dispatch Enhanced Network) service. iDEN is a unique service that is classified as Enhanced Specialized Mobile Radio (ESMR), with its own band allocation and licensing. ESMR first appeared in North America around the time digital PCS services were being licensed (mid-1990s). It provides a 'push to talk' radio service that combines the functions of a walkie-talkie type device with the networking capability of a mobile phone.

In effect, iDEN is a digital 'trunk radio' service based on a cellular network configuration and primarily designed for voice, but it also has text messaging and packet-switched data capabilities. However, the original service offered no upgrade path beyond a relatively low speed offering. For this reason, Motorola and Nextel embarked on the development of WiDEN ('W' for 'wideband') in the late 1990s as a 2.5G solution for customers wanting improved mobile data service and to compete against GPRS and 1XRTT service being offered by GSM and CDMA operators. WiDEN is a software upgrade for the iDEN that is supposed to enable up to 100kbps bandwidth for compatible phones.

In December 2004, Sprint merged with Nextel and there has been some speculation that the iDEN services will eventually be replaced by Sprint's CDMA-based network. Motorola and Nextel have suggested, however, that iDEN and WiDEN will be maintained and expanded until at least 2007, although this is not certain. Other countries have also adopted iDEN technology, including Brazil, China, Israel, Mexico and Singapore. Table 5.2 shows the 13 countries where the iDEN network is commercially available.

TETRA is another standard, similar to iDEN, and stands for Terrestrial Trunked Radio. TETRA is a European standard designed principally for use with police forces, and was designed as an open standard by the European Telecommunications Standards Institute (ETSI). TETRA is similar to iDEN insofar as both use a TDMA technique for multiplexing.

**Table 5.2**   iDEN operators worldwide

| Country | Operator | Brand name |
| --- | --- | --- |
| Argentina | Nextel Communications | |
| Brazil | Nextel Telecommunicações | |
| Canada | TELUS Mobility | Mike |
| China | Fujian Trunking Radio | Sinolink |
| Colombia | Avantel | |
| Israel | MIRS Communications | Amigo |
| Japan | NEXNET | |
| Mexico | Nextel de Mexico | |
| Peru | Nextel de Peru | |
| Philippines | Next Mobile | IMX |
| Singapore | DNA Communications | GRID |
| South Korea | Korea Telecom Powertel | |
| United States | Nextel Communications | |

*Source*: Motorola iDen International: http://idenphones.motorola.com/iden/international/
international_content.jsp?content=where&country=us

## 5.6    The first wireless web

By now, many people are familiar with HTML, also known as 'hypertext mark-up language', which are the codified tags that web browsers use to render web pages for display. While HTML is now in widespread use for Internet communications, it presents some unique constraints that make it problematic for use with mobile phones. For instance, HTML is poorly designed for the bandwidth limitations and small screens available with mobile phones. Anyone who has tried to surf the web using a slow modem knows the experience of waiting and waiting for a website to download. In the wireless world, all that waiting of course costs the consumer either for airtime or packet charges. Moreover, the limited memory capacity inside many mobile phones and their small screens are not able to fully render most conventional websites, making the results less than spectacular if not outright useless in some cases. In other words, wireless data services require some new means of tagging information that either simplify the old HTML standard or adopt a new form of markup language altogether.

In conjunction with the need for a new markup language is the need for new types of *microbrowsers* that display the content of the web page on the mobile phone. There are numerous of these now on the market, each designed to work with one or more of the markup languages described below. Many new mobile phones will come equipped with a default application like Openwave's Mobile Browser or Microsoft's Mobile Explorer, but some handsets will permit user-installed microbrowsers offered by third party application developers, including open source initiatives.

### 5.6.1    C-HTML

One of the first initiatives to modify HTML for less small information appliances was called **Compact HTML (C-HTML)**, which was created around 1998 by Japanese software company Access Co. C-HTML is a variation of HTML that removes all except the most basic forms of tags for describing text and improves the performance of wireless data services because it contains no elaborate formatting capabilities such as tables, colours or images. Each of these features might otherwise consume unnecessary bandwidth and processing power, so C-HTML has been designed based on the following four design guidelines to balance interoperability with existing standards and the constraints of mobile phones:

- *Interoperability*: C-HTML was based on standard HTML specifications.
- *Restricted power and memory capacity*: C-HTML was intended to be implemented with small memory and low power CPU devices, therefore frames and tables which require large memory were excluded from it.
- *Limited display capabilities*: Compact HTML assumes a small display space of black and white colour. However, it does not assume a fixed display space, but it is flexible for the display screen size. Compact HTML also assumed a single character font.
- *Restricted user interface*: Compact HTML was defined so that all the basic operations can be done by a combination of four buttons – cursor forward, cursor backward, select and back/stop (return to the previous page). The functions that require two-dimensional focus pointing like 'image map' and 'table' were excluded from Compact HTML.[5]

While it has not proven popular in the mobile sector in North America and Europe, C-HMTL was designed principally for the Japanese market and became the basis for a generation of NTT DoCoMo's iMode service.

## 5.6.2  Web clipping

Around the same time C-HTML was introduced, Palm Computing's parent company 3COM developed **web clipping**, a proprietary standard intended for use with the Palm VII personal digital assistant. The Palm VII was capable of connecting to the wireless Mobitex network deployed in the United States but faced similar design constraints related to processing power and bandwidth. In some respects, web clipping was similar to C-HTML in that the idea was to create a stripped-down version of HTML that would contain only the most basic elements needed to display text, menus and simple graphics. By removing all unnecessary formatting and graphics, web clipping reformats websites to suit the bandwidth and specific screen display limitations of Palm-type PDAs.

## 5.6.3  HDML

Also recognizing the need for a mobile-enabled markup language was a company called Unwired Planet (now Openwave) that developed the first version of the **Handheld Device Markup Language (HDML)** in 1996. HDML-based service was launched in the United States by AT&T under the brand name Pocket-Net, and was deployed over its CDPD network. Sprint later introduced it as the 'PCS Wireless Web', which ran over its CDMA network.

HDML was significant in part because it replaced the familiar concept of web pages with a new metaphor to describe the layout of wireless Internet sites. Rather than a single web page, HDML was based on the metaphor of cards and decks. Again, the small screen size and limited processing capability of most mobile phones at the time did not allow for an information presentation typical of most websites. The card/deck metaphor was adopted to suit the limited interface requirements. In HDML, a 'card' was defined as 'a single user interaction' which could be a short piece of information or a menu listing a set of choices. The following is an overview of the card concept, as described by its authors Peter King and Tim Hyland:

> The fundamental building block of HDML content is the card. The user [device] displays and allows the user to interact with cards of information. Logically, a user navigates through a series of HDML cards, reviews the contents of each, enters requested information, makes choices, and moves on to another or returns to a previously visited card.
>
> Cards come in one of four forms: *Nodisplay*, *Display*, *Choice*, or *Entry*.
>
> Display, choice, and entry cards contain text and/or references to images that are displayed to the user. Choice cards allow the user to pick from a list of available options, and entry cards allow the user to enter text.
>
> While it is expected that cards contain short pieces of information, they might contain more information than can be displayed in one screen full. The user [device] will provide a mechanism for the user to view the entire contents of the card. An example of this would be a user-interface that allows scrolling through the information.[6]

In the HDML standard a collection of several cards is called a 'deck'. This approach permits more efficient use of bandwidth because it allows for downloading small decks of information into a mobile phone rather than needing an over-air transmission each time a new bit of information is requested. The authors explain that the deck is roughly the equivalent of a web page:

> HDML cards are grouped together into decks. An HDML deck is similar to an HTML page in that it is identified by a URL . . . and is the unit of content requested from a server and cached by the user agent.
>
> Individual cards within a deck are identified by name and can be addressed by URL fragment. For example, the URL of 'Card1' in 'http://www.foo.com/MyDeck.hdml' is *http://www.foo.com/MyDeck.hdml#Card1*[7]

After some initial success with the HDML standard, Unwired Planet joined in an initiative with Nokia, Ericsson and Motorola to launch the Wireless Application Protocol Forum in 1998. As a result of this joint venture with the major mobile phone manufacturers, HDML would form the basis for the WAP 1.0 standard.

### 5.6.4   WAP

**WAP** stands for Wireless Access Protocol, a bearer-independent service developed by the Wireless Application Protocol Forum, which later became the Open Mobile Alliance. WAP is in fact not a single standard but a set of protocols designed to work together to resolve some of the constraints of transmitting data over cellular networks. For instance, WAP pages are written in Wireless Markup Language (WML), a derivative of HDML, but also require a host of other protocols to coordinate the signals that pass between the server, an operator's gateway and internal network, the base station and air-link segment and ultimately to the handset.

WAP is properly described as a *bearer-independent* protocol, which means that it can operate over any air-link standard, although most of the early WAP services were developed for and ran over GSM networks. When it was first introduced mobile data services were mostly circuit-based, so early WAP applications were relatively modest compared with what is possible today. In the very early days, a customer might have to dial a special phone number on their mobile phone in order to first access the data service. Once a connection was established the data transmissions were often slow and clumsy (and of course expensive). As a result, the early experience of mobile data using WAP and the other standards tended to be an expensive disappointment, leading some early adopters and the trade press to harshly criticize early WAP services.

With the advent of 'always-on' packet-based data services, such as GPRS and 1XRTT, the latest range of WAP applications can now run faster and more efficiently. The WAP Forum was renamed the Open Mobile Alliance in 2002 and has since become the standards body for the mobile communications industry. Building on the earlier version using WML, the more recent WAP 2.0 standard uses *XHMTL MP* (XHTML Mobile Profile), a subset of the widely used XML (extensible Markup Language) that is used to facilitate data sharing across different types of networked systems. An interesting development in this standard is the 'WAP Push' feature first introduced for WAP version 1.2. This feature is based on an asymmetric exchange that sends out a notification by narrowband SMS, inviting the user to visit rich content on the web:

> WAP Push is essentially an extension to SMS that enables the recipient of the WAP Push message to immediately view an online page of content in one click. WAP Push messages are binary SMS messages that contain a URL. The benefit of using WAP Push versus SMS is that for a similar cost of delivery you can reach your customers with rich multimedia WAP content such as pictures, game downloads and polyphonic ringtones.[8]

While the WAP standard has become increasingly popular with the advent of 2.5G networks and more powerful mobile phones, some observers predict that it will eventually be replaced by a next generation access standard that provides 'true' web access to mobile devices.

### 5.6.5   The protocol stack

In order to understand WAP as a set of different specifications, it is necessary to consider the world of protocol stacks, which form the basis for all data communication systems. Digital information and communication systems are built in layers, sometimes referred to as protocol stacks. A protocol is a set of rules for communication between similar devices. The WAP standard, for instance, is based on a set of protocols stacked in layers, each providing the rules necessary to enable the various functions needed when transmitting data to a mobile phone.

When data networks were first being designed and built in the 1970s and 1980s by companies such as IBM and Novell, each company tended to invent its own set of proprietary protocols. As a result, interoperability problems between different systems and pieces of equipment became a major concern for vendors and customers alike. To resolve this problem, the International Standards Organization developed a template called the Open Systems Interconnection (OSI) model. The OSI Reference Model defines a stack with seven layers of protocols. Each layer serves a different purpose within a communication system and supports the layers above and below it. The WAP standard and the Internet itself are based on the OSI Reference Model, although they do not conform exactly to its original form.

WAP, as depicted in Table 5.3, is built on a series of layered protocols, loosely corresponding to the OSI Reference Model, although this is only an approximation for illustrative purposes. The aim here is merely to show the various types of machine to machine communications that are required to enable a simple mobile data service such as WAP. The table also shows why WAP is a bearer-independent standard separate from the air-link layer used to physically transport it

**Table 5.3**   WAP protocol stack

| OSI Reference Model | WAP equivalents | Function |
|---|---|---|
| Application layer | WML (Wireless Markup Language); Wireless Application Environment | Controls how user interacts with the data |
| Presentation layer | XML (eXtensible Markup Language) | Controls how data is presented to applications |
| Session layer | WTP (Wireless Transaction Protocol) | Error control |
| Security layer | WTSL (Wireless Transport Security Layer) | Encryption |
| Transport layer | TCP (Transport Control Protocol) | Control of packet traffic |
| Network layer | IP (Internet Protocol) | Addressing of packets |
| Data link layer | Bearer service (GPRS, 1XRTT) Air-link (TDMA, CDMA, GSM) | Multiplexing scheme |
| Physical layer | Radio spectrum | Physical medium |

to a mobile phone. It also draws attention to the specific function of the wireless application environment in the protocol stack.

## 5.7   Wireless application environment

With the growth of wireless data services, the computing demands placed on mobile phones have increased substantially. Beyond the well established technology developed for mobile voice service lies an uncertain and rapidly changing world of data applications. For equipment manufacturers and mobile operators this uncertainty presents a challenge to ensure that the handset is capable of performing the wide range of tasks that a user might wish to do with it. This situation contrasts with the previous era of mobile phone technology, where the handset was in a sense 'hardwired' with a specific set of applications. This of course meant that possibilities for adding new software or upgrading the phone with different applications was not possible. In other words, each phone was shipped with all the capabilities it would ever have.

A relatively simple mobile phone configured with several default applications made sense in the early days. As noted already, the first and second generation phones had small memories and limited processing capability, perhaps with the addition of an address book and a simple game, like 'Snake'. However, in an increasingly data centric mobile communication environment, equipment manufacturers perceived that customers would want handsets with more functionality and with upgrade capabilities. The challenge in this case was to strike a balance between standard software design and interoperability that would permit multiple applications to be added to a mobile phone either during manufacturing or after it is in the customer's hands.

One solution to this challenge is to add a special operating system to the handset. Models with this feature are known in the industry as *smartphones*. By incorporating an operating system into the handset, an equipment manufacturer such as Motorola or Siemens increases its value by making it capable of handling many different kinds of applications. This is possible because the operating system abstracts the functions of the phone and presents a generic interface for application developers, similar to the system that has evolved in the computing world with the advent of Windows OS, Mac OS and the resulting boom in the software market. This ingenious system greatly simplifies software development and ensures reasonable stability and reliability for the application designers because they do not need to think about the idiosyncrasies of each specific phone model when they are designing their software. It also simplifies it for the consumer, who can expect user-friendly applications that incorporate standard practices in information and interface design.

In terms of the protocol stack, the wireless application environment lies between the presentation of the content and the hardware layers of the device, relaying instructions to and from the processing unit and the user. More specifically, the application environment is typically composed of three sub-layers: the operation system (OS), an optional layer for interpreting data called *middleware* and the graphical user interface, or GUI, which presents the content to the user.

Two major players, with two separate standards, occupy the middleware layer in mobile phone market today. The purpose of middleware is to reduce the barriers for developing mobile phone applications in order to attract a larger number of programmers and to increase the range of devices able to use the applications they develop. Middleware for mobile phones today consists principally of the J2ME standard developed by Sun Microsystems and the BREW standard developed by Qualcomm.

## 5.7.1 J2ME

J2ME, which stands for 'Java 2 Micro Edition', is an implementation of Java for small devices like mobile phones and PDAs. This middleware is designed to allow programmers to use their 'Java' skills on very small devices that may not have as much computing, memory or storage capacity as a normal computing device. J2ME is based on Java, a modern, object-oriented computing language, developed by computer manufacturer Sun Microsystems to enable a single version of an application to operate on (almost) any computer platform. In fact, the motto for Java is 'write once, run anywhere'.

Unfortunately, as Java moved from its origins in TV 'set top' boxes into the world of general computing it became more memory and processor intensive. In 1999, Sun recognized the problem of porting Java to mobile phones and other small devices and so developed J2ME. J2ME is not only a compact application environment unto itself but it is also designed to be modular so that functional elements can be removed to make it extremely small if necessary. The end result of all this development is that the popular programming language Java can now be used to develop and run applications on mobile phones with the following constraints and requirements:

- 128K to 512K total memory available with at least 256K RAM.
- Limited power; typically battery operation.
- Connected to some type of network, with the possibility of limited (9600/bps or less) bandwidth.

- User interfaces with varying degrees of sophistication down to and including none.[9]

The J2ME platform has become extremely popular and a wide variety of so-called 'midlets' are available for download to Java-enabled mobile phones. Mobile games are popular midlets, as are certain utility programs such as notepads, currency converters, instant messenging and calendars.[10]

### 5.7.2  BREW

The other major middleware initiative is known as BREW or the 'Binary Runtime Environment for Wireless'. BREW was introduced in 2001 by Qualcomm to tap into the growing market for mobile data applications that J2ME had initiated. Even though it was first aimed at the CDMA handset market, Qualcomm has in fact licensed the BREW technology to GSM-based manufacturers. Like its Java counterpart, BREW is designed to simplify application development for mobile phones and to provide consistency and compatibility between phones in order to see wider deployment and use.

### 5.7.3  GUI

The graphic user interface (GUI) is another area where, as in the case with the WAP Forum, joint initiatives have been launched to promote application development and to make it easier for customers to use applications on their mobile phones. Having a common and consistent user interface is current practice in the computing world (e.g., Microsoft enables common user interface standards through their Windows User Interface Guidelines and tools such as Visual Basic). This is now the case too in the mobile computing world, where the 'UIQ' interface layer was developed in parallel with the Symbian OS and made available to Symbian licensees. This is intended to give handset manufacturers an enhanced 'look and feel' for their smartphones without having to develop all the elements from scratch.

## 5.8  Mobile operating systems

The availability of third-party software is now widely seen as a requirement for promoting the widespread adoption of mobile data services. The creation of a common operating system – especially if it is adopted by major mobile phone manufacturers – not only simplifies the development process but it allows software developers to spread their development costs across multiple platforms and hedge their bets regarding the success of any individual phone model. As a result, the mobile operating system (OS) is another crucial consideration alongside middleware and GUI elements.

In the world of personal computers, the importance of the operating system, and the extent to which one company can come to dominate that business, is exemplified by Microsoft Corporation with its Windows operating system. IBM famously underestimated the central importance of the operating system for its personal computers at the beginning of the 1980s and eventually lost control of perhaps the most important market. Mobile handset manufacturers, reluctant to repeat that experience, have undertaken a number of initiatives first to minimize the role of the operating system and then to ensure that no one player becomes dominant in this area (or that they control the dominant player).

At present there are four major competing mobile operating systems for smartphones: Symbian, Windows Mobile, Palmsource and Blackberry. In addition, there is also an open source mobile OS based on Linux. Symbian and Windows Mobile are interesting examples to consider because they represent two very different approaches to the mobile computing platform.

### 5.8.1   Symbian

Symbian is an alliance of six major mobile equipment manufacturers (Nokia, Ericsson, Sony Ericsson, Panasonic, Siemens, Samsung). As a business strategy, the Symbian alliance is in part an attempt by handset manufacturers to retain control of the operating system market – or at least an attempt to avoid losing control of it to a third party, like Microsoft – but still gain the economies of scale enabled by a common application environment and widely available software development tools. From a marketing and technology perspective, it is also a 'phone-centric' strategy to create a richer customer experience through advanced mobile data services. In effect, strategy is based on an emerging vision of the mobile phone as a multitask gadget – a mobile computing platform that complements and extends the function of the desktop computer.

Nokia, holds about half of the shares of Symbian and is a major influence and leading developer of phones based on the Symbian OS. In fact, the Nokia Series 60 platform was designed for the Symbian OS and is among the most popular smartphone user interfaces in the world today. Part as a result of the popularity of the Series 60, Symbian has dominated the smartphone market. Figure 5.6 depicts the various shares of the market for mobile operating systems in early 2005.[11]

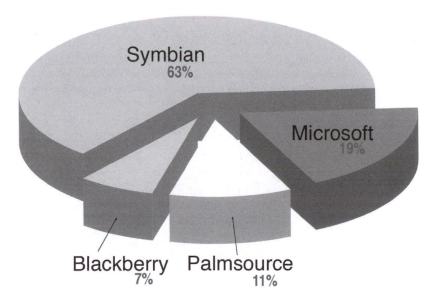

**Figure 5.6**   Mobile OS market share
*Source*: See Note 11.

### 5.8.2   Microsoft

Microsoft is the main competitor to Symbian, in part because of their dominance
in the PC industry and their deliberate move into the mobile phone sector. Their
'Windows Mobile' product is similar to 'Pocket PC' and other versions of the
Windows operating system for small portable devices, where the design philosophy is to extend the user's desktop experience and applications to the mobile
phone. This includes business productivity tools such as MS Word and Excel, as
well as other Microsoft applications.

Whereas the Symbian alliance is approaching the operating system business *de
novo* in order to vertically integrate the hardware with the software, Microsoft is
coming from a different direction. Its strategy is one of vertical *specialization* in the
OS market, using its brand name and experience in the desktop business to enter
into what could well turn out to be the fastest growing segment of computer
software and hardware.

As a result, Windows Mobile provides a scaled down but compatible version of
their desktop operating system – both in terms of user experience and from an
application development perspective. In fact, Microsoft claims there is as much as
an 85 per cent overlap between Windows Mobile for smartphones and a Windows
Pocket PC application, which reduces the problems of development and interoperability through the re-use of software code and similar GUI standards.

## 5.9   Division, convergence, emerging practices

The development of 2.5G networks and services has followed the split in the
world of digital cellular between GSM and CDMA based technology. GPRS was
introduced as the air-link to provide packet-based service for GSM mobile
phones, while 1XRTT was deployed to provide the same function for CDMA
networks. Prior to the advent of these fast data services were the various low
bandwidth data services such as the CDPD standard that was deployed on the
analogue AMPS systems in North America. In fact it was the limited functionality
but widespread availability of the Mobitex and ARDIS networks that provided the
infrastructure for Research in Motion to introduce its wildly successful *Blackberry*
device (only later did it introduce a model for GSM/GPRS networks).

While the development of air-link standards for mobile wide area data networks
has paralleled the CDMA/GSM split in the digital cellular era, there were also
important changes taking place in the upper layers of the protocol stack that
represent efforts to create an interoperable application environment for the mobile
phone. Both J2ME and BREW are part of this effort, as are other developments at
the operating system and graphical user interface layers. Perhaps this is exemplified
most plainly in development of the SMS gateway in North America to enable text
messaging between CDMA and GSM operators. Today of course the requirements are far more demanding and include mobile multimedia messaging (MMS),
downloadable Java-based applications (midlets), other forms of Internet content,
and even more sophisticated applications for productivity and entertainment.

From the perspective of the customer, the advent of 'always–on' service has also
changed the experience of mobile data services from what it was in the early days
of circuit-switched connections. It has introduced a new segment of consumers to
reasonably affordable multimedia communications and spawned new forms of
communicative practice. Music downloads and rich messaging have become part
of the functionality of the mobile phone and everyday life. In fact, the circulation

of digital images captured by mobile phones with cameras has become a concern among privacy rights advocates. But it has also inspired new and unanticipated uses for the device, such as the mobile blog or 'moblog'.

The idea of the mobile phone as a multitask gadget of social significance is perhaps best illustrated by a recent news item in a local Canadian newspaper headlined, 'Intimidation at skateboard park'. The item describes an encounter between parents and a group of teenagers at a local park, where the youths had been causing trouble and were intimidating other children. Frustrated and angry with the situation, one of the parents decided to take action:

> I asked my friend to take the kids to the park while I tried some intimidation of my own. I simply stood on the sidelines, still in shock and filled with anger and embarrassment, and pretended to take pictures with my cellphone.
>
> The teen slowly made his way back to me on his skateboard and stopped in front of me. He offered an apology saying that he did it on a dare. I calmly told him what I thought of his antics and said he really needed to apologize to the kids as the incident was quite scary too for them.
>
> The sad thing is I wanted to accept his apology, but in my heart, I doubted his sincerity as I believe he was more concerned about what I was going to do with the pictures than the ugliness of his actions.
>
> (Lundin 2005)

In this case, it was the mobile phone acting as a surveillance device that was a crucial factor in diffusing a difficult situation between concerned parents and miscreant youths. Clearly the camera-equipped mobile phone does not address, as this parent indeed recognized, the deeper roots of the problem; however, in this instance it did play an unexpected role in defusing an uncomfortable social situation. More to the point, it is only one of many possible examples of how the growing functionality of 2.5G technologies has opened our eyes to an even more ambitious vision for mobile communications with the promise of third generation cellular networks.

## 5.10  Further reading

William Webb's (2002) book, *The Future of Wireless Communications* (Artech House) is now somewhat dated but still provides an interesting technical and business perspective on recent developments in the mobile sector, including sections on standardization, radio spectrum, industry structure and user requirements. Hoffman's (2003) book, *GPRS Demystified* (McGraw-Hill) provides a technical and business perspective on this 2.5G technology associated with GSM networks.

Qualcomm's website for BREW developers contains a number of demos and white papers that might be of interest to those who are interested in the details of this middleware: http://brew.qualcomm.com/brew/en/ Similarly, Sun Microsystem's J2ME website contains a wealth of information – much of it quite technical – on this platform: http://java.sun.com/j2me/

For those curious about wireless web design, McGrath's (2000) book, *WAP in Easy Steps*, might provide a good starting point. Those interested in the possibilities of multimedia messaging might consider something such as Ralph and Graham's (2003) book, *Multi Media Messaging Service: Technologies, Usage and Business Models* (John Wiley & Sons).

*Symbian OS Explained* (John Wiley & Sons) by J. Stichbury (2004) provides an in-depth look at this mobile operating system. It will be of most interest to those who have some experience with programming in C++ code rather than the non-technical reader. The Windows Mobile website is recommended for those interested in knowing more about this operating system: http://www.microsoft.com/windowsmobile/

# 6 Let's go surfing

The biggest gamble in business history; control of a vast new medium; the opportunity, at last, to monetise the Internet: clearly, a great deal is at stake.

*(Economist)*[1]

## 6.1 A mobile information society

In October 2001, the *Economist* published a special issue entitled, 'The Internet Untethered'. In many respects this was the sequel to another special issue entitled, 'The World in Your Pocket'. Whereas the first special issue, published in October 1999, chronicled the expansion of 2G mobile networks around the world, the 2001 sequel issue was a bit different: subtitled, 'A Survey of the Mobile Internet', it forecast the next step in the convergence of the mobile phone with the Internet and an emergent mobile information society.

'The Internet Untethered' covered a number of issues related to the development of third generation (3G) mobile phone services and the introduction of broadband data services to the world of digital cellular networks. According to the *Economist*, however, the road to 3G was likely going to be a bumpy one. After all, mobile operators in Europe had spent US$billions on acquiring 3G spectrum licences before any of the technology was deployed and long before there was any certain demand for the mobile broadband offering. In short, despite the immense potential of a mobile information society, the future remained quite uncertain.

Despite the uncertainty, 3G networks and services have now been launched in a number of countries and this next generation of mobile communications is gaining market share. What is it about this next generation of mobile phone that has caused so much hype in the media, particularly in Europe, and just what will become of the Internet now that is has been untethered? The aim of this chapter is to explore these questions by examining the origin of the 3G concept, its subsequent development into a family of technical standards, and some of the social and political associated with the growth of mobile broadband.

## 6.2 The third generation

Several years before digital cellular service was launched in North America, an ambitious vision for the 'next generation' of mobile networks was taking shape at the International Telecommunications Union (ITU). However the next generation vision was *not* centred on broadband data services. Instead, the ITU in 1992 acted on the vision and initiated a project with the goal of creating a single mobile communications standard for the world. This global standard would include harmonized spectrum allocation for future mobile services, as well as provide common technical specifications for improved mobile voice and data applications.

## 6.2.1  Virtual home environment

This project, initially called, 'Future Public Land Mobile Telecommunications System' or **FPLMTS**, proposed a the idea of a *virtual home environment* that would allow customers seamless roaming around the world using a wide range of interconnected networks both terrestrial and satellite. For the time the roaming concept unto itself was an ambitious proposal. The idea of 'surfing the web' from a Palm Pilot or downloading videos to a mobile phone was not really discussed at the time because the 'web' had not yet been created and the Internet was still relatively unknown outside of computing science circles until the mid-1990s.

The ITU's concept of a virtual home environment might not have included the web but it nonetheless provided an important innovation related to the digital cellular concept that was being promoted in North America in the mid-1990s. In the FPLMTS vision, digital cellular was seen as a crucial step toward a world of 'Personal Communication Services' (PCS) that would transform the everyday world of telecommunications:

> [In this world] a telephone number or communications address is associated with a person rather than a place. A PCS system will identify the communications device closest to a person whether it is through satellite transmission, mobile cellular transmission, or fixed wireless transmission technology and then route a call direct to the person.[2]

What is perhaps most notable about the initial vision for PCS was that it was not centred solely on the mobile phone. In fact, as the excerpt suggests, the intended plan was to develop an intelligent network that would permit the user to access their home environment (telephone number, address book, preferences, etc.) wherever they were and on whatever device they might choose. If the customer were located outside on the street, calls would be routed through their mobile phone. If the customer then walked into their office, calls and preferences might be automatically forwarded to the desk telephone. In sum, this early concept made very little reference to mobile data applications and concentrated instead on the creation of a sophisticated roaming service almost exclusively for voice telephony.

In order to achieve the virtual home environment, the FPLMTS initiative expanded the 'hand-off' concept to include both **horizontal** and **vertical** domains. In the horizontal domain, the system was envisioned as providing geographical roaming across terrestrial-wide area cellular networks. To some extent, this objective has been achieved with 2G networks, as it is now possible to roam easily around much of the world using a tri-band GSM handset. CDMA is more problematic but recent developments in handset design are overcoming this roaming barrier.

On the other hand, in order to be fully realized the PCS vision would have to realize the goal of seamless roaming in the *vertical* domain. This objective has so far proven to be more of a challenge. A vertical hand-off refers to the capability of roaming between different types of networks, such as WAN to LAN, or terrestrial cellular to satellite. An example of a vertical hand-off would be a mobile handset capable of switching over to a local area network when it is carried inside a building, or switching over to a low-earth orbiting satellite network when the customer is roaming outside the range of terrestrial cellular networks. Vertical roaming is the necessary step to enable the PCS concept of intelligent routing between devices, such as a mobile phone or desktop telephone.

The difficulty with achieving real-time vertical hand-offs in practice is probably less a technical problem and more of a business challenge related to cost and customer demand. The mobile operator Globalstar, for instance, offers a multi-mode phone capable of vertical roaming between its Low-Earth Orbiting (LEO) satellite network and terrestrial 800MHz CDMA networks. Nokia and other handset manufacturers have also recently introduced mobile phones capable of vertical roaming between GSM networks and wireless Local Area Networks using Wi-Fi. British Telecom (BT) has for some time now been promising to achieve **fixed–mobile convergence** with the launch of its 'Bluephone' service that would allow customers to redirect their mobile phone through their broadband home connection. While it may be technically possible to achieve the vertical roaming feature of the PCS vision, the business case for it has yet to be proven.

## 6.2.2   IMT-2000

Once the FPLMTS initiative was underway, the initial vision for PCS was refashioned and the difficult acronym was replaced with the project name 'International Mobile Telecommunications 2000' or **IMT-2000**. IMT-2000 was chosen in part to symbolize three convergent objectives of this evolving vision for mobile communications: first, a working system would be achieved by the year 2000; second, the system would provide an optimal bandwidth of 2000kbps (2Mbps); and, third, it would operate in the 2000MHz band worldwide.

Even though the popularity of the Internet was still some years away and the range of possible data services was quite narrow by today's standards, the very first technical specification of IMT-2000 were based entirely on bandwidth. Three rates were established, each corresponding to a different type of ISDN (Integrated Services Digital Network) service that was the standard system being used for data services over landline telephone networks at that time. The data rates were established at 144kbps, 384kbps and 2Mbps (or 2000kbps). Today we can see those original data rates reflected in the evolutionary standards for 3G, as shown below.

Again, it is vital to keep in mind that at that time (circa 1992) the Internet was not widely known outside expert academic and technical domains. A technology known as 'ISDN' – a circuit-switched data service – predominated discussions about the future of landline and mobile communications, in part because Internet Protocol (IP) was still relatively obscure. However, with the invention and adoption of the web browser in the mid-1990s, Internet Protocol suddenly shot into prominence and talk of ISDN-based solutions slipped into the background (despite its important role continuing even today). The IMT-2000 initiative retained the ISDN data rates in its standards but eventually shifted its work to developing a packet-switched architecture based on the Internet standard.

Among the first hurdles for IMT-2000 was simply allocating spectrum for a unified global service. The initiative originally called for global roaming cap-abilities through a common set of global frequency bands. Unfortunately and for many reasons, some historical and other political or economic, global spectrum allocation is a difficult objective to achieve. This certainly has been the case with IMT-2000, where the commitment to a single worldwide band for mobile telecommunications has not been achieved. In fact, the only country to actually follow the initial IMT-2000 recommendations for spectrum allocation was China. The Europeans and Japanese were already using part of this proposed allocation for

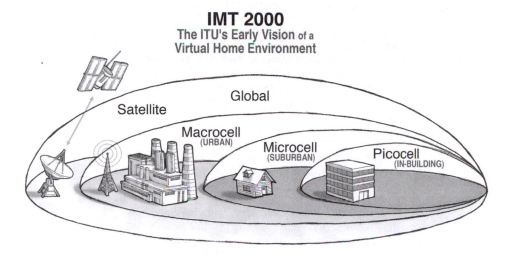

**Figure 6.1**   An early IMT–2000 concept diagram from the ITU

*Source*: http://www.tele.ntnu.no/radio/newresearch/systems/mobile_telecommunications.htm

other services, including GSM cellular service. In the United States, the spectrum bands had been already allocated for PCS or fixed wireless services.

In addition to the hurdle of globally harmonized spectrum allocation, regional interests have also created obstacles in the technical standardization of 3G systems. For instance, the European Union had an interest in promoting a GSM-based evolution to 3G, whereas the United States and certain Asian interests supported a CDMA-based development path. In the end, a number of different standards were introduced creating potential interoperability problems for global roaming on 3G networks.

Another significant challenge in the implementation of the IMT–2000 vision has been the cost of building new infrastructure. In order to achieve the broadband capabilities on a cellular network, many more base stations are required than with 2G cellular networks. The additional cost of acquiring spectrum and physical locations to install new base stations is often very high, and without a well defined 'killer application' for broadband mobile service, the business case carries considerable risk.

In spite of these obstacles and the risk involved for the investment community, the Europe Union has long regarded 3G as an important regional economic driver for the 21st century. A number of policy documents illustrate the EU's early perspective on 3G mobile services, and this is just one example:

> By the beginning of the year 2001, 63% of EU citizens had a mobile phone, the overwhelming majority of them (235 million) subscribing to GSM services. The EU telecommunications services market is now worth over €200-billion with an annual growth rate of 12.5%. Mobile communications, which increased by some 38% in 2000, already account for about 30% of the total revenues of the telecom services sector in the EU. The EU has thus become the world leader in mobile communications and its equipment manufacturers and operators are amongst the sector's most innovative and fastest growing companies.

In Europe, the 'first generation' of analogue mobile phone systems was followed by GSM (so-called 2G). Now the 'third generation' of mobile communications (3G) is coming, combining wireless mobile technology with high data transmission capacities. 3G systems promise access to Internet services specifically tailored to meet the needs of people on the move, via multimedia applications using image, video, sound as well as voice. *The convergence intrinsic to 3G of the two main technological trends in recent years, the Internet and mobile communications, is thus bound to be of great social and economic importance to the European Union.*

(emphasis added)[3]

From its inception in the early 1990s, the IMT-2000 vision gradually evolved into a series of technical standards, with the ITU World Radio Conferences working out a set of frequency allocations around the world for 3G services. However, with the growth and popularity of the Internet, the original plan focused on the 'virtual home environment' has been replaced with a distinct emphasis on the technical delivery mobile broadband data services, including video telephony. As with many visionary projects of the early 1990s, IMT-2000 found itself having to adapt to the disruptive effects of business, politics and technology.

## 6.3   3G in Europe: UMTS

In the face of competing technical standards and difficulties in allocating spectrum for global mobile services, IMT-2000 has evolved into *a family of standards* divided according to three geographic regions: Europe, North America and Japan. The European Union with its vested interest in promoting GSM technology opted for a technical system based on **Wideband CDMA** (W-CDMA) and has allocated spectrum and issued licenses in accordance with this standard. This European version of IMT-2000 is known as the Universal Mobile Telecommunications System (**UMTS**), and is often referred to as such in European Union policy documents, the European press and in everyday conversation among Europeans.

The **Third Generation Partnership Program** (3GPP) is an industry/government group responsible for overseeing the technical standardization of the W-CDMA version of IMT-2000. Members of the 3GPP include international standards organizations with an interest in developing a successor to GSM, or otherwise promoting W-CDMA. 3GPP organizational members are not just from Europe, however, as it includes participants from the United States, Japan and Korea.

**Table 6.1**   3GPP member organizations

| Country | Acronym | Organization |
| --- | --- | --- |
| Japan | ARIB | Association of Radio Industries and Businesses |
| Japan | TTC | Telecommunications Technology Committee |
| China | CCSA | China Communications Standards Association |
| Korea | TTA | Telecommunications Technology Association |
| Europe | ETSI | European Telecommunications Standards Institute |
| North America | ATIS | Alliance for Telecommunications Industry Solutions |

The UMTS Forum is a subsidiary of the 3GPP, responsible for promoting W-CDMA and its version of 3G to equipment vendors and mobile operators. The UMTS forum has classified six principle service categories for 3G networks, which help us to perceive the range of 3G services that are likely to appear on the market in the near future:[4]

- *Multimedia content*: including graphics, video clips, music, locator services, games and directories formatted especially for mobile handsets.
- *Multimedia messaging*: Any combination of photos, video clips, audio clips, graphics or text can be sent to another mobile handset, PC or other device. 'Mobile broadcasting' of media (such as news) to many terminals simultaneously is similar to cell broadcasting for SMS.
- *Internet/extranet access*: Mobile access to email, rich web content, corporate network resources, etc.
- *Instant messaging*: 'Real-time' text-based messaging via the Internet.
- *Location-based services*: LBS could allow subscribers to locate the nearest restaurant, fuel station or shop of their choice.
- *Rich voice*: Two-way real-time enhanced voice, video and other forms of data. Presence – enabling a caller to see if a contact is available or 'online' to receive calls or messages – will promote even greater usage of voice telephony. 'Push to talk' is a voice communication service similar to CB radio or walkie-talkie that provides simultaneous group communications, one way at a time, at the touch of a button.[5]

The evolution toward UMTS service is based on two phases. During the initial phase, mobile operators using GSM will upgrade their networks to GPRS service. This upgrade enables the deployment of packet-based services at improved bandwidths. By the year 2002, most major mobile GSM networks in Europe and North America had made this upgrade, despite the fact that wide area roaming is still not available in some areas.

Journalists writing in the trade and popular press sometimes referred to GPRS as a '3G' service but the term 2.5G is probably more appropriate to describe the capabilities and bandwidth of GPRS and 1XRTT. Moreover, the deployment of the first phase toward UMTS is relatively inexpensive for mobile carriers because it involves minor modifications to their existing networks and no need for additional spectrum. The next phase toward 3G within the UMTS design requires a commitment to expensive upgrades to the mobile networks and additional spectrum in the 2GHz band for deployment of Wideband CDMA (W-CDMA) infrastructure.

Before committing to W-CDMA, however, there is the possibility for mobile operators to adopt another type of intermediary service that offers a bit more than GPRS and does not require additional spectrum. **EDGE** (Enhanced Data rates for GSM/Global Evolution) could be termed a '3G' system because it achieves optimal data rates of 384kbps but some regard it as a transitory service for mobile operators while they acquire and build out their W-CDMA networks. In the case of TDMA operators in North America, EDGE is considered a 3G standard because it can be made backwards compatible with their existing networks and spectrum licences. In the case of GSM operators in Europe, EDGE remains an option for deployment while building out their full suite of UMTS but it seems that European GSM operators that have been awarded UMTS spectrum licences have decided to bypass EDGE for the time being and focus directly on the deployment of W-CDMA.

## 6.4   3G in North America: cdma2000

In North America, the evolution to 3G will progress along a different path than in Europe, in part because of the entrenched position of cdmaOne in the US and Canada. 'cdmaOne' is the term used to describe the 2G version of CDMA developed originally by Qualcomm and deployed throughout North America, Korea, Japan and increasingly in China. The upgrade path for cdmaOne does not require operators to build entirely new networks, as in the case of GSM evolving toward W-CDMA. Rather, cdmaOne will evolve into a system known as **cdma2000**, which is compatible with existing spectrum allocation and network infrastructure.

The intermediary phase for the cdmaOne upgrade is known at 1XRTT, which provides data rates roughly equivalent to GPRS. As described in the last chapter, most mobile operators in North America and elsewhere already provide 1X service over their wireless networks. Following 1XRTT, the next upgrade is to **1XEV-DO** (1xEvolution Data Optimized), recognized by the Telecommunications Industry Association as IS-856 and also referred to as the cdma2000 3G standard. The first 1XEV-DO commercial services were launched in 2002, with its first widespread appearance in North America following a few years later. As of 2005, Qualcomm has reported some 12 million users of 1XEV-DO worldwide.

There is some variation used in the terminology, and cdma2000 is also sometimes referred to as a group of standards that includes a range of 1X technologies. According to proposed upgrade paths, a system called 3XMC (Multi-Carrier) – so-called because it is based on a design that uses three 1.25MHz channels (hence, '3X') – is the purported next stage in CDMA evolution beyond 1X. However, this upgrade has a wider channel configuration than its 2.5G predecessor and would therefore require mobile operators to obtain additional spectrum for its deployment – as is the case with UMTS in Europe. At present its future remains somewhat uncertain.

Technical oversight of cdma2000 development is undertaken by a sister organization to 3GPP, called **3GPP2**. In many respects these organizations have identical roles to each other as well as similar memberships with one notable exception: no European standards development organizations are involved with 3GPP2. Organizations that participate in 3GPP2 come from the US, Korea, Japan and China. The organization in charge of promoting cdma2000 is called the **CDMA Development Group** (CDG), and it performs a similar role to the UMTS Forum.

**Table 6.2**   3GPP2 member organizations

| Country | Acronym | Organization |
| --- | --- | --- |
| Japan | ARIB | Association of Radio Industries and Businesses |
| Japan | TTC | Telecommunications Technology Committee |
| China | CCSA | China Communications Standards Association |
| Korea | TTA | Telecommunications Technology Association |
| North America | TIA | Telecommunications Industry Association |

## 6.5   3G in Japan: FOMA

With the introduction of its *i-mode* mobile service in February of 1999, NTT DoCoMo established first mover advantage in providing mobile data services for online banking, shopping, email and text messaging, restaurant guides, as well as for checking news, weather and traffic reports. In 2001, NTT DoCoMo then upgraded its *i-mode* service to 3G and unveiled a W-CDMA-based system under the brand name FOMA (Freedom of Multimedia Access). In fact, FOMA was the first commercial 3G service to be introduced in the world.

Today in Japan, there are three competing networks with mobile operator, KDDI, holding the largest 3G customer base at over 17 million subscribers, as of January 2005. Vodafone has recently acquired J-Phone and holds the smallest 3G customer base in Japan with about half a million subscribers. Whereas Vodafone has deployed a W-CDMA solution for its 3G service, KDDI operates a cdma2000 network with both 1XRTT and 1XEV-DO offerings.

Japan provides something of a laboratory for the future of 3G services, and experience from that country seems to indicate that video telephony will not be the killer application that was once thought would propel the market. On the contrary, it appears that in Japanese 3G networks, it is music downloading that is proving to be most popular among consumers. Recent statistics indicate that the market for KDDI's *Chaku-uta* mobile music service in Japan is similar to that for iTunes in the United States, with cumulative downloads reaching 150 million in the 18 months following its introduction in July 2003.[6]

## 6.6   The IMT-2000 family portrait

The chart below describes the main 3G upgrade paths as they are expected to take shape in major regions around the world. Each standard has its own organization responsible for setting technical requirements and promoting these systems. For W-CDMA in Europe the UMTS Forum and 3GPP undertake this role. For cdma2000 this role is served by 3GPP2, and for EDGE it was the Universal Wireless Communications Consortium (UWCC), which is now part of an organization called '3G Americas', which addresses the upgrade path for GSM/TDMA operators in North and South America. In the case of Japan, DoCoMo has adopted a variation on W-CDMA under the FOMA initiative.

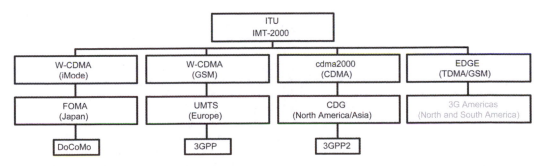

**Figure 6.2**   3G development groups worldwide

## 6.7    Stumbling blocks

Many observers in both government and industry have looked to 3G as the development that will usher in a truly mobile information society, where broadband data services achieve global roaming capabilities and the Internet is 'untethered' as the *Economist* saw fit to put it. Almost in parallel with the dot com boom of the late 1990s came the startling idea that the mobile phone might also lead to a revolution in commerce, entertainment and information services.

Unfortunately, the media hype that was behind the investment frenzy in the dot coms of the late 1990s was also at work in the telecom sector. As a result, the trade press and investors promoted early expectations about 3G that could not be immediately fulfilled. Feature articles in the media, such as *Scientific American* and *New Scientist* conveyed startling images and fantastic scenarios about advanced mobile multimedia applications and a wireless web experience that were several steps removed from the practical reality of the technology at the time or, for that matter, from a viable business case. Following the collapse of the dot com bubble and the bust in the telecom sector – in part due to spectrum auctions for 3G licences – these initial disappointments led to growing scepticism in the media about the viability of broadband mobile communications. One example of the initial disappointments in the transitionary period was with the early WAP (Wireless Application Protocol) services.

### 6.7.1    'WAP is crap'

Not long after its introduction in the commercial market the phrase 'WAP is crap' began to circulate in the media reports about mobile phones. When the company Unwired Planet (later Openwave) introduced the first micro-browser for mobile phones in 1995, the media and industry quickly oversold the wireless web experience to a willing but largely naive audience of consumers. Many customers were encouraged to imagine a wireless web experience much like that they were used to on their desktop computer. However, at the time of WAP's initial entry into the marketplace in the late 1990s, most carriers were offering slow, circuit-based data services and limited access to WAP content through their portals. Of the few data services that were available at that time, most were simply novelty-based services such as horoscopes, sports scores, or stock market reports. As one critic wrote, 'Why would people use WAP and pay high charges like 20 cents a minute for horoscopes?'[7]

In some cases, WAP was also established on a 'walled garden' model with mobile operators offering a predefined menu of content that limited customer choice. Some customers discovered that their handsets did not provide full functions or seemed to have interoperability issues with their operator's network. As a result, the first encounter with the wireless web turned out to be rather disappointing and in some cases, an expensive disappointment.

With the appearance of GPRS and 1X services in 2001, some of the restraints that had plagued WAP in its early days have now vanished. The packet-switched design of 2.5G services enable faster and more efficient use of WAP services and mobile carriers have also taken greater care to invest in their mobile portals. Content developers are learning about the constraints of a wireless environment and the needs of mobile phone users, and practical new services offerings are appearing. New models of mobile handsets are now available with the Java or BREW mobile execution environment that enables small applications to be run on the phone (see the previous chapter). This enhanced functionality of the mobile phone permits downloading and interacting with content, such as video clips and games, and enriches user experience with WAP.

Above all, perhaps the most important lesson learned from early experience with WAP is that 3G will be nothing but a set of technical standards unless innovative, compelling services are developed and supported for customers.

### 6.7.2 'The winter of handset discontent'

During the period when the media began to promote the 3G idea in news reports and magazine articles, the wireless sector was actually facing a slump in handset sales. By this time, particularly in Europe, many consumers already owned a mobile phone and the market had become saturated with 2G technology. In July 2001, for instance, *Forbes* published an article entitled, 'The winter of handset discontent' that reported on what might have been the first major downturn in mobile phone business. This slump in handset sales reflected a maturation of the wireless sector related to the success of 2G services, as the author noted:

> the mobile phone business is going through a nasty transition. Mobile phones have, for all intents and purposes, become a commodity business in which the market leaders are the ones who can best endure the pain associated with constantly shifting cycles of shortages and oversupply.[8]

Earnings forecasts and sales projections for the year 2001 had been overly optimistic and many of the major handset manufacturers, especially Nokia, Ericsson and Motorola, were faced with job cuts and significant losses on the stock markets. To make matters worse, this downturn in sales was taking place about the same time that shares in the telecom sector collapsed in the biggest stock market drop since the Great Depression, along with the crash of the dot coms.[9] While in absolute terms the mobile phone market was still undergoing phenomenal growth, in relative terms (compared with previous years) it was badly slumping and the equipment manufacturers were feeling the effect. The question lurking in the back of the minds of the analysts was whether 3G was going to arrive at the worst possible time in terms of consumer demand, or whether it would inject new life into a troubled wireless sector.

Fortunately the handset manufacturers were preparing to introduce new product lines based on 2.5G technology, such as GPRS and 1XRTT. While these weren't quite 3G in the true sense of the term, they did promise to reinvigorate the market. For instance, mobile games and downloads were introduced and promoted heavily for the Christmas 2002 season and continued into the 2003 in an effort to sell new handsets. Nokia and Sony Ericsson both introduced a new line of mobile phones equipped with cameras and Multimedia Messaging Service (MMS) capabilities, paving the way for customers to take and send digital pictures. Bluetooth became increasingly integrated with mobile phones, opening up new features that allowed handsets to communicate directly with PCs and other phones. Untapped markets also remained for the 2G handsets. North America remained a relatively immature market compared with Europe, as did the massive markets of India, China and in the developing world where there was tremendous pent-up demand for mobile phones.

With the deployment of 3G services beginning in 2003 in combination with the growing popularity of 2.5G camera phones and mobile games, a new wave of handset sales re-invigorated the marketplace. Mobile operators might have complained that delivery of 3G handsets was delayed initially but they are now widely available in countries where operators are expanding their efforts at selling 3G services to their customers.

### 6.7.3   The crash of the LEOs

The global roaming features of IMT-2000, which were to be extended by mobile satellite telephone service also ran into difficulties, as the start-up companies that could have fulfilled this role faced bankruptcy. For example, the first offering came from a company called Iridium, an initiative of Motorola, which aimed to provide low orbit satellite (LEO) mobile phone service to a global customer base. Launched in the autumn of 1998, Iridium was intended to seamless global roaming primarily for business customers. The concept was very exciting and ambitious with 66 low orbit satellites (originally 77 were planned) providing what amounted to a cellular network in the sky.

Special Motorola handsets were designed to communicate with the satellites as they passed overhead, much like a typical mobile phone communicates with a cell-site base station. The satellite network then provided the backhaul to earth receiving stations and on to a gateway connected to the public switched telephone network. The cost of launching the service was enormous (Motorola invested more than US$5 billion in it) and customers were required to use the special bulky handsets, each priced around US$1000.

Not long after operations began Iridium was forced to file for bankruptcy. Despite early optimism about the service, Iridium was not sustainable due in part to several significant, perhaps unforeseen, developments. First, terrestrial cellular services and international roaming agreements quickly expanded at about the same time as Iridium initiative was getting underway. Despite Iridium's global coverage, it seems that the bulk of its targeted business customers need phone service in urban centres where normal mobile phone coverage is generally excellent. The places where Iridium phones were most needed – deserts, oceans and remote areas – tend to be relatively small markets, especially in relation to the large sunk costs that were needed to launch and maintain a sophisticated satellite network. In other words, the market was too small. Furthermore, Iridium phones had an inherent technical drawback: customers could make calls only when in line of sight of a satellite, creating problems for customers trying to make calls from inside office buildings or when working in mountainous terrain. After Iridium declared bankruptcy a newly founded Iridium Satellite LLC, partly owned by Boeing and other investors, acquired it. The new system is now used primarily by the US Department of Defense but it remains available for those with the need and budget to pay for it.

In the same year Iridium filed for bankruptcy, a competing firm Globalstar began to offer its LEO-based mobile phone service. With a slightly smaller network of 48 satellites, Globalstar intended to market mobile satellite services to the same relatively small group of customers as Iridium. Globalstar could offer less expensive handsets and lower service charges because it used satellite technology that made greater use of ground support stations, lowering the cost of its overall deployment. However, the same line of sight difficulties plagued its services and, with the news of Iridium's bankruptcy casting a dark shadow over satellite telephone services generally, Globalstar had difficulties enticing customers to join its service. The investment community offered a sobering assessment of the situation and, by implication, of the proposed satellite component for the original IMT-2000 vision:

> It's not that there isn't a need for telephone service in remote areas where traditional landlines and cellular towers don't exist. It's just that there's little money to be made from it, especially now that mobile phone roaming has improved all over the globe. After opening its doors with grand plans for a half-million subscribers and a half-billion dollars in revenue, Globalstar

admitted last year that it had only 13,000 subscribers and only $2 million in revenue to show for it.[10]

Globalstar struggled for a few years, only to narrowly escape bankruptcy in 2003. Other investors have since acquired the assets of Globalstar and it is still possible to obtain service from these companies today. The downside is that because these systems are based on low earth orbiting satellites, their effective lifetime is limited by the life of the satellites, and when the two networks of Iridium and Globalstar satellites are eventually decommissioned it is not likely that there will be another LEO provider immediately stepping up to fill the gap. Despite the short lived promise and the US$ tens of billions invested in infrastructure and marketing, a key element in the original IMT-2000 vision has proven impossible to sustain on a large scale or, perhaps, even on a niche basis over the long-term.

### 6.7.4    The spectrum auction

Perhaps one of the biggest potential stumbling blocks to 3G resulted from the exuberance caused by the success of GSM technology in Europe. The excitement that followed from the popularity of 2G services led several of the large operators to pay exorbitant amounts of money for 3G spectrum licences in a series of auctions held in 2000. In the UK, for instance, the government collected some US$36 billion for 3G licences divided among six wireless service providers. In Germany, the biggest spender in the auction wars, four companies bid a total of US$51 billion for spectrum licences.

On one hand, the auctions did bring in enormous sums of money for the treasuries of these national governments. On the other hand, the cost of acquiring the 3G spectrum hobbled some of the most important mobile operators in these countries because of the financial burden caused by the auctions. Yet in a number of countries, the spectrum auctions that were hoped would bring in a windfall for national governments produced only a trickle of revenue, as mobile operators became aware of the folly in the UK and Germany. Still other countries, like Finland, took a more traditional approach and opted for more traditional comparative review process to issue spectrum for 3G.

In October 2000, after the biggest of the European spectrum auctions had concluded, the *Economist* reported that telecom companies were preparing to invest more than US$300 billion in order to deploy 3G services. The magazine at that time suggested it might very well be 'the biggest gamble in business history'. The risk came from the uncertain demand for 3G services in the marketplace and whether it would be a solution in search of a need, as some observers suggested:

> When equipment makers and telecoms operators try to explain how money will be made from 3G, they do little to allay the doubts of investors. The mobile phone industry is careful not to claim that handsets will replace PCs for surfing the Internet. But it claims that there will be huge interest in services that exploit what is different about the mobile phone: that it is always with you. Services based on knowing who you are, where you are, what sort of information you want and exactly when you want it, are touted as 'killer applications'. Telecoms companies even have hopes of becoming surrogate banks, as customers use mobiles as 'electronic wallets'.
>
> But there are two huge problems with this vision. The first is that time- and location-specific services are likely to be low in value. How much would you pay to be guided, say, to the nearest petrol station or to receive

personalized messages, such as updates on your share portfolio? Something, certainly, but perhaps not very much – and the money may go to the provider, not to the utility that connects him to his customer. The second is that services this simple do not need as much bandwidth as 3G provides. Yet for their investments in 3G to stack up, within seven or eight years the companies need to be earning at least half their revenues from transactions and from data traffic.[11]

Despite the scepticism it is important to remember the case of SMS text messaging, where it is never entirely clear at the outset of any innovation what the 'killer application' may in fact be, or what form it might take in the end. Nevertheless, the economic aftershock of the spectrum auctions, combined with the bust in the dot com and telecom sectors, placed a number of European mobile operators in a position where it was essential that they deploy 3G quickly and to make it palatable for as wide a market as possible.

## 6.8  Are we there yet?

In June 2005, an industry news report *3G Today* reported 147 commercial operators providing 3G services (including 1XRTT) in 66 countries around the world. The first operators to launch 3G services were in Japan and South Korea: NTT DoCoMo launched FOMA in 2001, while Korean operators KTF and SK Telecom followed with 1XEV-DO services in 2002.

The first US operator to offer 1XEV-DO service was Verizon, starting in 2003. Telecom New Zealand and Telstra in Australia both deployed it in late 2004. Canada's Bell Mobility and TELUS Mobility also introduced this type of 3G service in 2004. Other countries that have deployed 1XEV-DO include Brazil, Guatemala, the Czech Republic and Israel.

W-CDMA service was first offered in Europe in 2003 by Hutchison Telecom using their brand name '3' in countries that included the UK, Austria, Italy and Denmark. In 2004, the other large mobile phone operators in Europe, such as T-Mobile, O2 and Orange launched their own W-CDMA offerings. Cingular in the United States offered the first GSM-based 3G in North America in 2004.[12]

While 3G service is just getting started in many countries, vendors are already pushing ahead with the next leap forward in mobile data services with HSPDA, or 'High Speed Packet Downlink Access'. At the annual 3GSM conference in Cannes, France in early 2005, HSPDA was being introduced as an upgrade for 3G networks to transform them into 3.5G systems that could bring data speeds up to 14Mbps. Word at the conference was that some operators would begin deployment in late 2005 or 2006.[13]

While it looks as if 3G is now well on its way to becoming a full fledged commercial service offering, a potentially rival technology known as Wi-Fi has been quietly working its way into the consumer world of wireless data services. While Wi-Fi is better described as 'portable' rather than being truly mobile, it does provide relatively cheap and fast wireless data service that has something of a headstart on 3G services. Industry speculators see in this situation yet another possible obstacle to the adoption of 3G and have asked if we might expect to see a wireless war – *la guerre du sans fil* – between potentially rival services based on the technologies of Wi-Fi and 3G.

## 6.9   Further reading

The International Telecommunications Union (ITU) (2002) report, 'Internet for a Mobile Generation' while a bit dated now provides a good perspective on assumptions and ideas driving 3G developments. It also provides a number of international casestudies. Consult the ITU website: http://www.itu.int/osg/spu/publications/mobileinternet/index.html

For those interested in the business models being discussed for 3G services, Tommi Ahonen's (2002, 2004) books, *M-profits: Making Money from 3G Services* (John Wiley and Sons) and *3G Marketing: Communities and Strategic Partnerships* (Wiley) provide good starting points. Dan Steinbock's (2005) book, *Mobile Revolution* provides a good overview of the marketing of mobile services with lessons for 3G services. Paul Klemperer (2002) offers a post-mortem assessment of the European 3G spectrum auctions in his article entitled, How (not) to run auctions: the European 3G telecom auctions, *European Economic Review*, 46: 829–45.

The Programme in Comparative Media Law and Policy (November 2003) at Oxford University produced a background paper entitled, '3G Mobile Self-regulation' to inform a policy debate on adult content and emerging mobile multimedia services. This report is available at http://www.selfregulation.info/iapcoda/index.htm.

# 7 La guerre du sans fil

The bottom–up forces of wireless freenetting and the top–down force of 3G mobile telephony are heading for decisive conflicts over the next five years.[1]

(Howard Rheingold, writing in 2002)

## 7.1 Introduction

In French is has been called 'the war of no wires' – *la guerre du sans fil* – referring to the looming conflict between third generation mobile networks and the local Wi-Fi hotspots appearing in cities all over the world.[2] Although the technology is not entirely substitutable, Wi-Fi is regarded by some as a direct threat to the success of 3G service. This chapter is devoted to a look at this emergent Wi-Fi technology and a consideration of the ways in which it might be a contender in a wireless war with 3G. The chapter also takes up the various perspectives and scenarios about the future of mobile data services in a world where community-based 'free-netting' encounters the 'top–down force' of 3G mobile services.

## 7.2 3G versus wireless LANs

It is first important to recognize that while 3G and Wi-Fi both are methods for providing wireless broadband data, they are not directly substitutable technologies. 3G is a 'true' mobile service according to Hjelm's definition, previously introduced in Chapter 5:

If you can't pick up the device and walk out of the building while maintaining contact and continuing to use the applications you were using, it is not really mobile.

The mobility aspect of 3G comes from the fact that it is a direct evolution in digital cellular service based on a wide area network infrastructure that is capable of providing real-time hand-offs between cells and roaming across geographical regions and across international borders. 3G service also represents an extensive business proposition because it requires mobile operators to obtain new spectrum and special radio authorizations; to build out expensive new infrastructure; and to develop and market new data services that require customers to upgrade their mobile phones.

Wi-Fi, by contrast, is not 'really mobile' when measured against Hjelm's criteria. It is more accurately defined as a *portable* wireless service based on local area network architecture, which means the reach of any specific access point is limited at best to about 100 metres (300 feet). Wi-Fi users can 'roam' only to the extent that they might find another wireless local area network within the vicinity that they can use, but this is not the same as the hand-off capability under the central control of a wide area cellular network system.[3] In addition, Wi-Fi providers do not normally need to obtain radio licences and do not need to build a large network of infrastructure to support the service – in a coffee shop, for instance, a single Wi-Fi antenna and one broadband connection to the Internet might suffice to serve a large number of customers.

As a commercial service, 3G offers integrated circuit-switched voice and packet-based data, with downlink bandwidth for data service achieving 2Mbps under ideal conditions. Wi-Fi, on the other hand, is capable of packet-based data service only – including, of course, the prospect for digital **Voice Over Internet Protocol (VoIP)** – but with a much higher bandwidth of 11Mbps or better in the case of the newer systems. 3G terminals will likely cost hundreds of US dollars to purchase, while Wi-Fi cards and base stations are mass market items, affordable for a large number of consumers. Monthly 3G service may be relatively costly for most customers, whereas Wi-Fi service is available for free in many locations.

Perhaps most importantly, Wi-Fi is widely available today and already well deployed in many major urban centres. The widespread adoption of authentic 3G service, especially in North America, will still be several years away. Even in Europe and Asia, where 3G is expanding much faster, the 'war of no wires' continues to remain a concern for the mobile operators that have made such heavy financial commitment to their spectrum licences and infrastructure for 3G networks.

## 7.3   Hotspots and radio bubbles

Part of Chapter 5 was devoted to presenting the difference between Wide Area Networks (WANs) and Local Area Networks (LANs) in order to make a distinction between 2.5G digital cellular networks and other wireless data systems. This chapter considers important distinctions within the LAN category of wireless networks in order to identify key technical differences between 3G digital cellular networks and 'Wi-Fi' systems.

To begin it is necessary to recognize that the term *Local Area Network* (LAN) has a specific meaning that refers to a network designed to provide coverage throughout a relatively small geographical area, such as an office complex, a campus or a cafe. In any of these cases, the air-link segment for a wireless LAN provides a much smaller zone of radio coverage than a typical wide area cellular network. To take the distinction even further, the term *PAN* (Personal Area Network), is a term that has been coined recently with the development of a technology called Bluetooth, which is described in more detail in Chapter 9. The important point to note here, however, is that PANs are designed to provide an even smaller zone of coverage than LANs, such as a desktop, a living room or a small workspace. For example, a PAN based on Bluetooth technology might provide wireless network coverage for the immediate area surrounding a desk or PC computer, or within the confines of an automobile, to enable several devices to communicate with each other.

To differentiate between these zones of coverage, the terms **hotspot** and **radio bubble** are helpful. Wireless LANs provide hotspots of coverage within an office building or across a campus. By contrast, we can think of wireless PANs as providing a small radio bubble of coverage that extends to several metres or less. In both cases the user must physically enter the hotspot or the radio bubble in order to connect to the network as contrasted with the apparent ubiquity of cellular WANs in most cities. It is also important to note that both LANs and PANs are not necessarily mutually exclusive. In fact, Wi-Fi and Bluetooth both create opportunities for developing applications that operate in conjunction with wide area cellular networks. One simple example is the use of Wi-Fi or Bluetooth to link a nearby mobile phone to a special SMS application on a desktop computer. In this case the hotspot or radio bubble, as the case may be, creates a very small wireless network that allows the user to type messages into their mobile phone by using the computer's keyboard and to view incoming text messages on the computer's screen.

A final distinction in wireless networks is also worth mentioning but will not be discussed at length in this book. The appearance of a technology called WiMAX has given rise to a new form of wireless network known as a **Metropolitan Area Network** or MAN. WiMAX systems are based on a standard known as IEEE 802.16 and provide wireless broadband access with radio coverage measured in square kilometres, somewhere between a LAN and a WAN. WiMAX provides a form of 'fixed' wireless access that is growing in popularity as an alternative to DSL or cable modems for delivering broadband data services to homes and offices. The European competitor to WiMAX is known as HIPERMAN, which stands for High Performance Radio Metropolitan Area Network.

The term MAN is interesting because it was also used for Metricom's *Ricochet* network, which has been described as a unique type of cellular digital network. The Richochet concept was based on shoebox sized radio repeaters mounted on streetlights to provide small hotspots of coverage. Unlike Wi-Fi, however, the radio repeaters in the Richochet network were capable of making hand-offs like a regular cellular network, thereby providing city-wide roaming for users. Metricom used this system to offer medium-speed mobile data services in city centres and business districts in about 20 American cities during the 1990s. Unfortunately Metricom went bankrupt in 2001 but another firm later purchased some of its assets and a Richochet-like service was resurrected in a few American cities such as San Diego and Denver, Colorado.

## 7.4   What is Wi-Fi?

Wi-Fi is a trademarked term, owned by the Wi-Fi Alliance, to describe the **IEEE 802.11** family of technical standards developed by the Institute of Electrical and Electronics Engineers (IEEE) for wireless LANs. There are a lot of variations on IEEE 802.11 standard including the following:

- *802.11a* provides transmission of data up to 54Mbps in the 5GHz band. This standard uses an orthogonal frequency division multiplexing encoding scheme (OFDM) unlike the frequency hopping spread spectrum used by 802.11.
- *802.11b* (the original Wi-Fi standard) provides a data transmission at speeds of up to 11Mbps in the 2.4GHz band; 802.11b uses only DSSS.
- *802.11g* provides transmissions over 20Mbps in the 2.4GHz band.
- *802.11e* is similar to 'a' and 'b' versions of 802.11 but includes support for 'quality of service' (also known as 'QoS' in the telephone business), an important feature for voice over IP applications.
- *802.11n* is a new initiative announced by the IEEE in early 2004, with the aim

of increasing bandwidth to 100Mbps. Development of the standard is expected to be complete by late 2006.[4]

Of this suite of standards, IEEE 802.11b was the first to gain mainstream popularity and it has emerged as the common standard for small office/home office (SOHO) applications. In fact, a large number of wireless LANs found in North America and other parts of the world use the 802.11b standard, although 802.11g and 802.11a are becoming more common. A typical wireless LAN system based on the 802.11 standard will have two key elements:

Each device using the network will require a *wireless card*. Some devices, such as laptops, come equipped with built-in 'aircards' or 802.11b radio and antenna. The network will require at least one **wireless access point**. The access point will in turn require a source of electricity and is placed in a strategic location to ensure good radio coverage within a home or office space.

In certain cases, a central wireless access point may not be needed to create a LAN because the IEEE 802.11 specifications permit two distinct operational modes: 'infrastructure' or 'ad-hoc'.

**Infrastructure mode** requires all data traffic to pass through a central wireless access point that transmits by radio to the wireless cards in devices such as laptop computers or PDAs. The access point is usually connected to the Internet through a gateway service provided by cable, ADSL or the Ethernet infrastructure in the office or on campus. This topology is not unlike a network designed around a single cell, with the access point serving as the 'base station'.

When operating in **ad-hoc mode**, the 802.11 specification permits direct radio transmissions between two or more devices without the need for a central access point. Ad-hoc networks will give point to point access for local devices but will *not* provide access to the Internet or other wide area service unless one of those devices is also interconnected to gateway (e.g., DSL or cable modem).

### 7.4.1   The Wi-Fi alliance

In an effort to build awareness of the benefits of wireless network access, a group of equipment manufacturers formed the Wi-Fi alliance. The term Wi-Fi in fact derives from 'Hi-Fi', which is the jargon used in selling high fidelity audio equipment. In addition to marketing Wi-Fi to consumers, the Alliance puts considerable effort into testing and certifying equipment as being compliant with the 802.11 family of technical standards. The aim of the testing and certification initiative is to ensure that 'Wi-Fi' equipped computers and handheld devices will work with any other terminal, access point or base station that calls itself Wi-Fi compatible. According to the Alliance's website, it has certified over 1500 products since the introduction of the program in spring 2000. The program itself is divided into three distinct categories corresponding approximately to the **air-link**, network and content layers:

- *Wi-Fi products based on IEEE radio standards*: 802.11a, 802.11b, 802.11g in single, dual-mode (802.11b and 802.11g) or multi-band (2.4GHz and 5GHz) products.
- *Wi-Fi wireless network security*: WPA (Wi-Fi Protected Access) and WPA2 (Wi-Fi Protected Access 2).
- *Support for multimedia content over Wi-Fi networks*: WMM (Wi-Fi Multimedia).[5]

### 7.4.2   Centrino

Intel corporation announced in early 2003 the introduction of a new brand called 'Centrino'. Centrino combines Intel's existing chip technology with Wi-Fi capabilities. The idea is by no means new – wireless notebook computers and Wi-Fi have been around for some time – but the publicity and presence created by the Centrino brand is a good indicator of the increased efforts of the computing industry to enter the profitable wireless LAN market by building strong and recognizable brands.

In fact, Intel's efforts have included the promotion of 'Centrino-compatible' wireless hotspots, which some analysts interpret as a strategic effort at branding the Wi-Fi market through the creation of public access points that will boast the Centrino logo. Co-branding efforts are likely to follow too, as Intel has already signed deals with a hotel chain, Marriott International, and a mobile carrier, T-Mobile USA, to promote the Centrino label. There are already numerous sites identified and validated by the Centrino brand, and the number is expected to continue to grow in the near future.[6] The efforts by Intel may also be interpreted as an attempt to merge wireless LAN technology with the highly successful 'Intel Inside' campaign that it launched in order to market their CPU (central processing unit) and prevent it from becoming a commodity item indistinguishable from the processors developed by other firms.

### 7.4.3   Apple Airport

'Airport' and 'Airport Extreme' are Apple's brand names for its implementation of the 802.11b and 802.11g systems. Airport Extreme is based on 802.11g and is compatible with 802.11g systems and is backwards compatible with 802.11b systems. Apple has been very aggressive in promoting wireless through its Mac line of computers and they were one of the first laptop manufacturers to offer an integrated wireless aircard in all their systems. More recently, Apple was the first computer manufacturer to include a wireless aircard in all of its notebook computers as a standard feature.

### 7.4.4   HiperLan and HomeRF

Beyond the confines of the IEEE family of 802.11 standards there is are fact other wireless LAN standards, including the European HiperLan1 and HiperLan2, as well as Home RF.

HiperLan is inspired in part by GSM and European governments that have dedicated spectrum for its development in the 5GHz band, but it has faced an uphill battle following the success of Wi-Fi. In fact, the original HiperLan specifications never resulted in any equipment being manufactured, leading some critics to dub it 'hype' LAN. HiperLan2 is similar to 802.11a but it provides a more robust technique for quality of service guarantees for users, which could be important for delivering voice over IP service. In terms of reaching the marketplace, however, HiperLan2 remains well behind IEEE 802.11. As a result, Wi-Fi vendors are now lobbying European governments for access to the dedicated HiperLan spectrum so that 802.11 systems can be deployed using it.[7]

HomeRF is another specification that provided potential competition to Wi-Fi technology. Like HiperLan, HomeRF also arrived on the scene when 802.11 had begun to achieve rapid adoption by the consumer market, thus creating obstacles in the form of network effects and economies of scale. 'Network effects' refers to the dramatic increase in the perceived value of a technology or service when it is adopted by a large number of people. For instance, the more that people adopt Wi-Fi and install 802.11 access points, the more valuable that specific standard becomes in terms of providing ubiquitous access for consumers and economies of scale for equipment manufacturers. A relative newcomer like HomeRF runs into an interoperability problem because most customers will have Wi-Fi cards installed in their computers. As the network effect takes hold of the industry so does an economy of scale in the manufacturing process, which then drives down the prices of Wi-Fi cards and systems, creating a virtuous circle and positive feedback loop that favours the 802.11 standard over its competitors.[8]

Even with the positive feedback loop favouring the Wi-Fi standard, a system like HomeRF could have had certain advantages in the marketplace. For instance, the security provisions for HomeRF and its built-in support for voice telephony could be seen as positive attributes in certain consumer settings. Nevertheless, the Home Radio Frequency Working Group, a group of more than 100 companies that had developed a specification (Shared Wireless Access Protocol (SWAP)) for the HomeRF system, was disbanded in early 2003.

## 7.5 Two cultures of networking

An interesting backdrop to *la guerre du sans fil* is a reflection of significant differences in the culture of networking between the telecommunications engineers and computer programmers. This cultural divide predates modern mobile communications and extends way back to the earliest days of data networking as observed by historian Jane Abbate in her book, *Inventing the Internet*:

> The first battle over data network standards flared up between the telecommunications carriers and the computer manufacturers. ... The carriers saw data communications as simply an extension of telephony ... [and] assumed that most customers would use the network to access a computer from a terminal – which, like a telephone, is a fairly simple device. They did not expect most customers to engage in computer-to-computer interactions over the public data networks. As things turned out, the 'telephone model' of computer networking did not fit well with the way computer users actually wanted to use networks.[9]

While much has clearly changed with the advent of the Internet, many critics of 3G still perceive a gap between the world of the telecom engineers and the computer networking culture behind the development of Wi-Fi technology. These differences are perhaps most evident in debates about appropriate business models for providing wireless broadband access. For instance, 3G networks and services are based on a highly centralized, vertically integrated model that had evolved from the traditional telecommunications approach. Customers are expected to pay for a monthly service bundle that would include both traditional voice as well as new enhanced data applications. These applications might include multimedia messaging, mobile commerce and transactions, mobile video conferencing, multimedia downloads, and mobile Web surfing perhaps within a 'walled garden'. A major challenge for 3G operators, however, is that this business model may not be appropriate for many customers and that the enhanced applications, such as video calling, are still uncertain in terms of consumer demand.

Wi-Fi technology, while it might not be 'mobile' in a true sense, does provide cheap access to an already existing range of 'proven' Internet services, such as websites, file sharing, email, instant messaging and even voice telephony with

VoIP. Another important difference is that the 3G concept is based on a business model adopted from the telecommunications world, whereas Wi-Fi has emerged from the computer networking community, which has bred into it an ethic of openness by way of the end to end (e2e) principle that eschews strong vertical control mechanisms within data networks.[10] With the entry of telecom operators in the Wi-Fi business this ethic of openness has come under fire from commercial interests.

On the one hand, the telecom sector has tended to promote a commercial model that seeks to control access to the Wi-Fi networks and to make it a pay per use service, much like any other telecom service including 3G. On the other hand, this presents a challenge to the community access model that initially emerged among W-Fi enthusiasts and that emphasizes open access to applications and services across the network. Both models are currently being used in the provision of Wi-Fi in various cities around the world, but the fundamental difference in principles behind each has created an internal battle among advocates of public Wi-Fi access.

All models proposed for public Wi-Fi systems do the same basic thing: they provide wireless distribution points for high-speed Internet access. These distribution points are usually situated in high traffic areas where people are likely to want to use the Internet, such as airports, hotel lobbies, coffee shops, libraries, and university campuses. The Wi-Fi service provider arranges for a high-speed Internet connection to the location where the wireless LAN is to be installed. The connection is usually provided by DSL, cable or a specialized high-speed connection purchased from a local internet service provider (ISP). The Wi-Fi provider then installs one or more 802.11 wireless access points in the location to achieve the desired coverage.

Where the commercial and community models differ, however, is in the way that access to the Wi-Fi system is granted to the general public. With the commercial model, users wishing to access the Internet are required to pay for the service on a per use basis. This might be based on a single monthly fee or a per minute/per hour basis. In order to implement this system, some kind of software control is often used to limit access to the Wi-Fi access point, such as a password protection. Commercial Wi-Fi providers might even offer 'turnkey' systems to proprietors of cafes, airports, hotels and other public gathering places to make the initial set-up simple and cheap.

### 7.5.1  Commercial Wi-Fi strategies

A dominant strategy has yet to emerge within the commercial Wi-Fi model in part because there are many means and motivations for providing such a service.[11] Some organizations regard the provision of wireless Internet access as a business in itself, others see it as an additional product line for their business (e.g., telecom operators), still others feel that it is an amenity that enhances a pre-existing customer experience (e.g., sitting in a coffee bar), and finally there are those who consider it a means of meeting the needs of customers unable to take advantage of 3G wireless services. Table 7.1 lists a few of these business models, which are described in more detail below.

A number of large commercial operators now provide Wi-Fi access on a tariffed basis to the public. Initially these services were run by 'Wi-Fi only' organizations, such as FatPort in Canada, or Boingo in the United States. The Fatport example is typical of the wireless service companies that were into the market early as a Wi-Fi only business. It established a collection of local hotspots starting in Vancouver, Canada, and then expanded into a national provider of Wi-Fi service with

**Table 7.1** Commercial Wi–Fi strategies

| Business model | Organization | Strategy |
| --- | --- | --- |
| Stand alone Wi–Fi business | Take 5 | Provide the service 'for free' as part of the normal amenities to a coffee shop, just like air conditioning. |
| Single hotspot | Whotspot | Charge for use, by the month, day or hour. Software and services for managing this are available from companies like Fatport and Whotspot. |
| Network of hotspots | Fatport | Charge for use, by the month, day or hour. Add value by creating a network so that people can use the service in other locations in the city, country or internationally. |
| Partnerships | Fatport | Allow other organizations to single nodes or networks, using your technology, billing systems and other 'back end' services. Negotiate reciprocal access agreements to increase the value of your own network. |
| Reselling/aggregation | Boingo | Build your network of Wi–Fi 'hotspots' entirely through partnerships. Create custom software for access and security and handle all the billing and customer service yourself but purchase data access on a wholesale basis from other providers. |
| Mobile add–on | T–Mobile | Provide Wi–Fi services as a network of hotspots but use your mobile phone customers and billing system as a way to both reduce back office expenses and keep customers; enhance the value of your service. |
| Telco add–on | Telus | Similar to the above, but from a telephone company perspective, and sometimes tied to ADSL or other high–speed services. |

hundreds of hotspots located across the country. Along the way they have partnered with a large number of organizations ranging from individual hotels and coffee shops, to restaurant and hotel chains, even to regional telecom operators. The commercial model pioneered by Fatport has included a revenue sharing scheme that provides an incentive for business owners to participate by installing a hotspot on their premises.

More recently, mobile operators themselves have decided to become involved in the commercial Wi–Fi business. T–Mobile, for example, has partnered with a number of firms to install hotspots for Wi–Fi access in hotels and coffee bars. It is also deploying its own 3G networks in a number of countries while continuing to manage extensive 2G coverage. The value proposition for T–Mobile's customers is an integrated billing concept, where a single account provides access to a number of different types of wireless networks. With the advent of more sophisiticated mobile phones, the technical barriers of vertical roaming will soon be overcome to provide a seamless integration of Wi–Fi with wide area digital cellular.

As of summer 2005, commercial Wi–Fi access was available in over 100 countries offered by over 350 providers running 100,000 hotspots. The United

States, with over 27,000 reported wireless locations leads the world as the nation with the most Wi-Fi coverage. London and Tokyo are leading cities with over 1000 commercial wireless locations reported for each. The top three types of location were hotels and resorts, restaurants and cafes.[12]

### 7.5.2   Community Wi-Fi strategies

With the community model, a Wi-Fi provider first obtains a high-speed Internet connection much in the same way as a commercial provider but then offers the wireless access to the public for free or a not for profit basis. This model also includes several strategies. In some cases, members of a local community install and operate the wireless LAN on a cost-shared, not for profit basis. One of the more famous community Wi-Fi networks is located in metropolitan New York City. 'NYCwireless' is based on the community model and has a mandate to promote open wireless hotspots in public spaces including parks, coffee shops and building lobbies. In addition to providing public access, NYCwireless also partners with public and other nonprofit organizations to bring broadband wireless Internet to underserved communities.

Community Wi-Fi networks often associate themselves with affiliations of community wireless networking projects advocating and supporting the deployment of so-called freenetworks. While no single definition of 'freenetwork' exists, the website FreeNetworks.org offers a good working definition of the term:

> A freenetwork is a network in which anyone with the proper equipment can send and receive data from any point in the network to any point in the network without paying transit fees. This does not mean that a freenetwork cannot be connected to other networks which charge for transit ... however while exchanging data within the bounds of the freenetwork there shall be no cost for transit or peering other than the cost of the required equipment.[13]

Community wireless networks are also benefiting from a technology development called 'mesh' networks. A limiting factor in any community wireless network has been the expense of the backhaul connection. Backhaul refers to the connection between the wireless access point and the Internet gateway. In order to expand the coverage of a community network, additional access points need to be deployed. If all of them require access to an Internet gateway the cost quickly becomes prohibitive. A mesh network reduces the need for the number of backhaul connections because the wireless access points can operate in ad-hoc mode to link to the nearest neighbouring access point, thereby extending the network with each additional node. This configuration increases the coverage zone while reducing the need for additional Internet gateways each time a new node is added. As a result, a community network can grow cooperatively, and inexpensively, with shared nodes located on community members' balconies and rooftops.[14] MIT's 'roofnet' project is a recent example of how this technology can be deployed in a community.

The community access model is not without its problems, however. In particular, the freenet movement introduces certain property rights questions regarding network access and the rights of customers to share their access to the Internet by means of a wireless LAN. For instance, many user agreements for broadband Internet service stipulate that customers are not permitted to share their service with any third party. It is not always clear whether such agreements apply in the case where Wi-Fi coverage might 'accidentally' stray beyond the property line of the subscriber and happens to allow neighbours to have wireless access to the Internet.

In fact, the practice of locating and marking open hotspots in public spaces has developed in response to the ambiguity concerning property rights and wireless networks. The practice that has evolved is known as 'wardriving'.[15] Wardrivers are people using Wi-Fi equipped computers to seek out open hotspots and who make their findings known to the public by posting them on websites and listserves. Of course, some of the owners of these open Wi-Fi access points are often unaware that others can use them to access the Internet. Some owners may not care or might have deliberately set up their access points to permit public access, and this form of 'informal community networking' is a significant, albeit erratic and unreliable, source of network access. In other cases, the owners might be quite alarmed to discover that strangers are able to surf the Internet for free by using their Wi-Fi access point. However, a point of distinction ought to be made in this respect between free-riders who use open Wi-Fi hotspots to simply check their email and those who might use them as an opportunity for malicious activities that involve hacking corporate networks or a home computer.

Despite the growth of community Wi-Fi networks and freenetting over the years, some observers have recently observed that the practice of wardriving may soon vanish as commercial access points become more commonplace and as Internet service providers file legal action to discourage unauthorized sharing through wireless access points. ISPs that provide Internet gateway service to customers might consider community access Wi-Fi as a form of bandwidth piracy, even though owners of Wireless LANs may or may not be aware that others are using their access points for free. This begs the question as to what reasonable limitations can be placed on the use of wireless access points in such situations.

## 7.6   Beyond Wi-Fi

While innovations such as HomeRF and HiperLAN might have faltered on the success of Wi-Fi it seems that competing or complimentary wireless standards continue to be developed. In early 2005 a number of alternatives or extensions to Wi-Fi and 3G appear to be on the drawing board. Most of these are in very early stages of development, which means that the standards have not been finalized and that interoperability of equipment is not yet assured. Much of the work is being done by individual firms at this stage, such as the 'iBurst' system from Array-Comm, Flarion's 'RadioRouter' (recently chosen for implementation in Finland, using spectrum in the 450MHz range), Navini's 'Ripwave' and Samsung's WiMAX/Wibro. Table 7.2 summarizes some of the newer technologies and their capabilities.

## 7.7   User experience

Aside from the technical features and capabilities of wireless LANs, there are important differences in user experience between the Wi-Fi and 3G technologies. These can be categorized into performance, form factors, interference and security.

**Table 7.2**  Emerging wireless broadband technologies

| System | ArrayComm | Flarion | IPWireless | Narini | Samsung |
|---|---|---|---|---|---|
| Access scheme | iBurst TDMA/FDMA/SDMA | RadioRouter Flash OFDM, Flash-OFDM Flexband | IPWireless UMTS TD-CDMA | Ripwave MC-SCDMA | WIMAX/Wibro OFDMA |
| Spectrum | 5 or 10 MHz TDD | 2 x 1.25 MHz FDD, 2 x 5Mhz FDD (three 1.25Mhz carriers), 2 x 5Mhz FDD (one 5Mhz carrier) | 5 or 10 MHz TDD 2 x 5 MHz FDD 2 x 10MHz FDD | 5 MHz TDD | 10 MHz TDD |
| Per user throughout (DL/UL) | 1 Mbps/345 kbps (5MHz bandwidth) | 1.5Mbps/500kbps, 2.5Mbps/90kbps, 6.0Mbps/2.5Mbps | 1.5 Mbps/512 kbps MHz bandwidth) | 2.0Mbps/1.0 Mbps (max) for standalone and outdoor modem. 1.0 Mbps/5 Mbps (max) for PCMCIA | 3 Mbps/1 Mbps |
| Available customer devices | • PCMCIA<br>• standalone Ethernet/USB modem | • PCMCIA<br>• desktop modem<br>• chipset<br>• Wi-Fi/FOFDM AP | • PCMCIA<br>• standalone Ethernet/USB modem<br>• chipset<br>• IPWireless/Wi-Fi gateway<br>• VoIP Integrated Access Device<br>• Handset, from Feb 05 | • PCMCIA<br>• standalone Ethernet/USB modem<br>• outdoor modem | no commercial product yet PCMCIA, handset in '05. |
| Mobility | <80 kmph | <300 kmph | <120 kmph | Limited low speed mobility until WIMAX 802.16e | <120 kmph |
| Standardization affiliation | 802.20 | 802.20 | 3GPP UMTS TDD | 802.20 & WIMAX 802.16e, ATIS 0700001 | WIMAX 802.16e |
| Commercialization (limited selection) | PBA, Australia, WBS, South Africa; 8 ongoing trials | Trial by: Nextel, North Carolina, US; CellularOne Texas US; Vodafone, Japan; Telstra, Australia; T-Mobile Netherlands); OCTO (Public Safety), Washington DC, US. | Woosh Wireless, NZ; UK Broadband (PCCW); Maxis, Malaysia; Sentech, South Africa; AirData, Germany 15 ongoing trials: Optus, Australia; Nextel, USA; Orange, France; Hutchison, HK & Italy. | IBAX, Italy; Unwired; Australia; >11 ongoing | none yet Successful trial with Wibro systems & prototype terminals in Dec. 04. Commercial launch In Q1/06. |

*Source*: IDA Singapore, A quick snapshot of wireless broadband access technologies today, 25 February 2005.
See http://www.ida.gov.sg/idaweb/media/PressRelease_LeadStory_Main.jsp? leadStoryId= L146&versionId=3

### 7.7.1 Performance, service and reach

A number of factors are important to consider in terms of performance requirements for wireless data services. Speed of course is important but quality of service (QoS) may be more important, particularly for real-time applications such as Internet telephony. QoS factors can be more strictly controlled in a 3G service environment because the operator has greater control over their network and can thereby ensure that high value subscribers and services are granted priority access and bandwidth on demand. By contrast, Wi-Fi systems do not feature the end to end control of a telecom network and therefore make it much more difficult to control for quality of service. Security will also be more robust in a 3G network as compared with a Wi-Fi environment because of sophisticated encryption and access control.

### 7.7.2 Form factor issues

3G handets will be designed to accommodate different environmental conditions than what might be considered for most Wi-Fi systems. For example, power consumption and resource management may be more advanced with 3G systems that depend on small mobile handsets using batteries and with relatively modest computer processing capabilities. The integrated interface design of 3G terminals will likely be more amenable to true mobility than many Wi-Fi systems, which may be more appropriate for portable applications such as deep web browsing and extensive file management. Alternatively, the advent of hybrid 3G/Wi-Fi systems may enable applications running on a device to use 3G networks in some specific instances when mobility is the primary concern, or conversely switch over to Wi-Fi when the need arises for higher bandwidth services.

### 7.7.3 Interference and discrimination

Aside from the considerations already discussed, consumer regulatory concerns are somewhat different between Wi-Fi and 3G systems. For example, Wi-Fi operates in 2.4GHz or 5GHz, licence-exempt bands. This has made for relatively inexpensive consumer equipment and has contributed to its rapid growth in sales. Unfortunately, it also means that the popularity of Wi-Fi systems may lead to increasing interference in these bands as more and more wireless LANs are deployed. Interference will reduce quality of service in Wi-Fi systems and lead to problems with running real-time applications such as voice over IP or video/audio streaming. In cases where multiple Wi-Fi networks are creating interference problems with one another it is not always clear who might be at fault or whether there is any legal recourse for the parties involved.

The architecture of Wi-Fi systems ultimately requires a point of interconnection with the Internet backbone. In some cases, this creates a bottleneck where the operator of a Wi-Fi system may need to contract with the large telecom operators to obtain access to the Internet through their broadband facilities. This is similar to the situation where you need to buy either a DSL or high-speed cable service as a first step in setting up a wireless LAN at home. However, commercial or community Wi-Fi operators may face discrimination from these operators when trying to obtain high-speed backbone service. The operators, many of whom are affiliated with wireless carriers might regard the Wi-Fi operators as direct competition to their 3G investments and use their bottleneck control over high-speed backbone access as a means to protect their investment. It is not always clear how regulatory bodies might choose to respond to such a case.

### 7.7.4   Security

With wireless standards now leading the field of development in telecommunications and computing, the issue of security is of paramount importance
yet it often remains ignored by users of wireless systems. Among the major problems is the 'leaky' quality of Wi-Fi systems, where coverage tends to stray beyond
the confines of the specific location of intended use. There have been stories of
people using Pringles potato-chip cans as makeshift antennas to hone-in on Wi-Fi
access points, looking for open network access using software such as NetStumbler
or Air Sniffer.

To counteract the leakiness of Wi-Fi systems, data encryption techniques have
been designed for the 802.11 standard. The most common of these is known as
**Wireless Encryption Protocol** (WEP). WEP can be activated to provide some
measure of security for 802.11b systems by using 40/64bit and 128bit encryption
key lengths. However, once it is enabled the data speed over the air link may be
reduced by half or more. WEP has received criticism concerning its robustness as a
security measure and, moreover, offers security only for the air-link segment of
the transmission and does not provide the end to end coverage of a **Virtual
Private Network** (VPN). It also does not provide a firewall between the wireless
device and the Internet or corporate LAN.

More recently, WEP was superseded by WPA ('Wi-Fi Protected Access'),
which is an interim security measure adopted by the Wi-Fi Alliance while a
definitive wireless security standard was developed. That standard, 802.11i – also
known as WPA2 – was finally approved in June 2004 and is now available in a
broad range of wireless cards and access points. With the adoption of an Advanced
Encryption Standard (AES) block cipher, the 802.11i security protocol is considered a significant advance on previous security measures.

## 7.8   Remember IMT-2000?

A curious thing with the growth of WANs and LANs – typified by 3G and Wi-Fi
– is how these technologies have evolved along separate development paths in
spite of the original IMT-2000 vision. Today's discussion about the need for
greater interoperability among devices seems incongruous when we consider that
the concept of a Personal Virtual Environment and vertical roaming across networks was the central focus of discussions a decade ago. What happened to the
original vision and how could it be that this question of interoperability continues
to haunt this domain?

One possible answer lies with the fact that when the Internet became popular so
did the concept of data networking based on Internet Protocol. IMT-2000 was
originally established on a different set of assumptions about technical development – assumptions that stemmed largely from the world of the telecom engineer.
With the arrival of the web around 1994, the world of the computer programmer
suddenly entered the picture to challenge the assumptions made about telecommunications networking in a way it had never done before. Packet-based
switching and Internet Protocol (IP) became the new focus for attention, often at
the expense of the circuit-switched ISDN approach that formed the basis for the
original IMT-2000 vision.[16] In effect, the sudden injection of the Internet into the
IMT-2000 vision challenged many of the fundamental assumptions held about
how communication networks are best designed and commercialized. With
hindsight, it now appears that the Internet – an innovation born of a computing

culture and *not* a telecom culture – probably contributed to the fragmentation of the IMT-2000 vision, producing several forks of innovation (e.g., 3G and Wi-Fi) each targeted to a unique niche in the world of wireless data.

As noted already, we can regard Wi-Fi as a product of the world of computer networking, whereas 3G is a product of the more traditional telecom world. So what does this mean for the IMT-2000 vision of a unified communication system? In some important ways, this history reflects the influence of a cultural divide in wireless data sector. On the one hand, 3G can be seen as direct extension of the telephone network, designed as a top–down, vertically integrated, and carefully planned operation ultimately under the control of the operator. On the other hand, the Wi-Fi model is an extension of the computing world, where computing intelligence resides at the edges of the network in the computers themselves. As a result computing networks tend to be open and subject to minimal central control or planning other than that needed to ensure proper routing of packet data from place to place.

Wi-Fi was developed outside and independent of the telecom industry and under a very different set of conditions intended to promote innovation and learning among programmers. Today with the continued growth of the Internet and its embodiment in the IMT-2000 initiative, it is plausible to suggest that a technology developed outside the scope of IMT-2000 might have in fact undermined the once-unified vision for a series of vertically integrated wireless networks under the control of incumbent telecom operators.

Rather than seeing IMT-2000 evolve along a well-ordered and integrated path as might have been imagined in the mid-1990s, we find ourselves today with a patchwork of technologies that approximate individual elements of the IMT-2000 vision but that do not always work well together. The reality seems to be a collection of fragmented technologies, business models and networks that include low earth orbiting satellites (LEOs), wide area cellular systems, Wi-Fi hotspots, and Bluetooth radio bubbles. Ironically, the IMT-2000 objective might now be closer than ever, achieved albeit by a rather roundabout route; after all, the individual technological components are now available but the more difficult task of uniting them into an interconnected network of networks remains to be done. Perhaps it is revealing that the final barrier toward unification is not a technological hurdle but instead one that is legal, political and economic.

Certainly one of the most significant barriers to a unified world of WANs, LANs and PANs is access to radio spectrum. As we look toward a future filled with ever more sophisticated wireless devices and networks, the growing demand for access has prompted radical new visions for spectrum management.

## 7.9   Further reading

For those interested in establishing a community Wi-Fi network of their own, Rob Flickenger's (2003) book, *Building Wireless Community Networks,* 2nd edn (O'Reilly) is an invaluable source of information. Security related issues of Wi-Fi networks are described in depth in *Wi-Foo: The Secrets of Wireless Hacking* (Addison-Wesley, 2004) and *WarDriving: Drive, Detect, Defend, A Guide to Wireless Security* (Syngres, 2004).

Howard Rheingold's book, *Smart Mobs*, examines the impact of computing culture on the development of wireless networking culture, including the growth of community networks. The JiWire website provides a database of wireless hotspots in countries all over the world, as well as industry news and developments in commercial Wi-Fi sector: http://www.jiwire.com/ NYCwireless website contains information about the community Wi-Fi movement and its activities: http://www.nycwireless.net

# 8    Bandwidth bonanza

Almost everything you think you know about spectrum is wrong.
(Werbach 2002)

## 8.1   Introduction

Recent years have seen a tremendous growth in demand for access to radio spectrum to support a vast range of new mobile and wireless communications systems. The burgeoning popularity of wireless data networks, such as those supported by Wi–Fi and 3G radio technology, is a case in point. As one might expect, demand far exceeds supply in some frequency bands and this has prompted a fundamental reassessment of spectrum policy, especially in the United States where the issue has been the subject of impassioned debate about innovation and the Internet, led by intellectuals like Lawrence Lessig.[1] Academics and policy-makers are now taking a hard look at long held assumptions about radio spectrum and the way it is allocated, allotted and assigned for use. Some have even claimed that new digital radio technology will enable a 'bandwidth bonanza' and over-come the problem of spectrum scarcity forever. Yet in order for this technological potential to be released it is argued that changes must be made to the command and control model of spectrum management that has prevailed worldwide for almost a century.

This chapter introduces the basic contours of the spectrum management debate by examining the most prominent arguments falling under the *property rights model* and the *open spectrum model*, as well as some of those falling somewhere in between the two models. The debate is complicated – both technically and politically – and some of it is deeply rooted in the American constitutional tradition, so one must be careful about making sweeping generalizations with regard to the framing of the issues and their applicability to other countries. Nonetheless, the spectrum debate points to a historically contingent relation between technology, society and the physics of radio, particularly when it comes to defining the problem of unwanted interference.

## 8.2   Tragedy of the commons

Spectrum scarcity and the problem of unwanted interference has long been the basis for government controlled band plans and radio licensing schemes. The rationale for this 'command and control' model of spectrum management is often explained with reference to Garrett Hardin's essay entitled, 'The tragedy of the commons'. In 1968, Hardin was a professor of biology at the University of California when his paper was published in the journal, *Science*. It examined the problem of human overpopulation on the environment.[2]

In presenting his analysis, Hardin observed that if any type of valuable resource is accessible to everyone without any kind of regulation or managed oversight, it will quickly be consumed to the point of exhaustion because each individual in the community will seek to maximize his or her own interests in the resource without regard to others. This applies especially to the use of land or water but could equally apply to radio spectrum. The 'tragedy' of the commons is that even though there might be an abundance of a resource, it will tend to be squandered through the inevitable self-seeking behaviour of individuals who have access to it. Therefore, according to Hardin, the imposition of rules and coercive mechanisms are justified in order to balance individual liberties against the wider societal value of a shared resource. Without such mechanisms in place, the value of any common resource will be inevitably lost for both individuals and the community.

The early history of radio is a case in point: in the years before government involvement in spectrum management, radio operators often complained of interference problems caused by neighbouring operators with powerful or poorly designed transmitters. Eventually, the situation became so bad that some frequency bands were rendered unusable. Here was a tragedy of the commons unfolding, with a once abundant resource squandered through improper management. To restore balance to the situation, governments decided to intervene to control access to the radio resource with spectrum allocation and licensing regimes. The tragedy of the radio 'commons' was averted through a management strategy that could (usually) resolve interference problems among users. However, even this government led solution has received criticism, most notably by one economist who argued that it was an inefficient and wasteful model for managing spectrum.

### 8.2.1 The Coase Theorem

Criticism of the traditional 'command and control' model dates back to 1959, when economist Ronald Coase published a paper challenging the Federal Communication Commission's spectrum management in the United States.[3] Coase, who was later awarded a Nobel Prize for his work in economics, is credited with first presenting a 'property rights' model for spectrum management. In his paper he claimed if radio spectrum were treated like any other form of private property, the profit motive would create a market for licence holders to bargain and trade for access to spectrum. In turn this 'free market' exchange would maximize the rationality and efficiency of its use because it would best match supply with demand.

This of course contrasted sharply with the government's view at the time, which was that spectrum was *not* like private property and that its effective management would come only from expert assessments undertaken by regulatory agencies. In fact, it was such a radical idea at the time that when Coase was asked to testify before the FCC in the early 1960s, one commissioner asked him outright, 'Is this all a big joke?'[4] The very notion that radio spectrum might be managed through the granting of basic property rights was practically inconceivable among regulators. Radio spectrum had long been considered a public resource and was therefore administered in the public interest by an appointed body seen to be capable of determining what was in the public interest – the so-called 'wise man' theory of regulation.[5]

Coase's argument has since become known as the *Coase Theorem*, the essence of

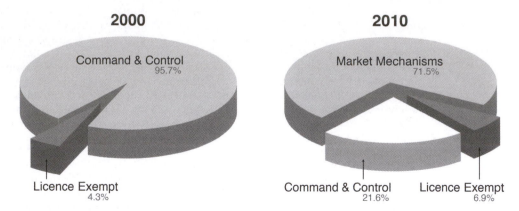

**Figure 8.1**  Ofcom's proposal for liberalizing its spectrum management policy
*Source*: http://www.ofcom.org.uk/images/consultations/sfr_nov1

which may be applied not only to spectrum but also to any kind of common resource: 'With well-defined property rights, the free market will generally allocate resources to their most efficient use so long as transaction costs are low'.[6]

The Coase Theorem provides a theoretical basis on which to establish free market governance of commons resources, and has inspired major spectrum reform initiatives in countries around the world, including the US, Canada, Australia and the UK. No longer is it considered 'all a big joke'. In fact it is now taken quite seriously as these countries and others have recently introduced auctioning and spectrum trading strategies to increase the efficient use of spectrum. The regulatory body in the UK (Ofcom), for instance, has responded to concerns about efficient use of spectrum by adjusting its policy from one based largely on comparative review to one that will grow to rely on competitive processes. Figure 8.1 indicates how this proposal would liberalize the current licensing regime by 2010, thereby making market mechanisms predominant in that country.

The Coase Theorem is established on a fundamental assumption that has fuelled debates about spectrum management since the earliest days; namely, the claim that spectrum is a scarce resource. Because radio systems are susceptible to unwanted interference it has long been argued that there is a limit to the number of radio systems that can be accommodated in any band at one time. Congestion and interference are therefore paramount concerns when allocating spectrum and issuing radio authorizations. Today, for instance, congestion is regarded as a major problem because of the sharp rise in demand for access to spectrum, especially in the frequencies that are most highly prized by wireless service providers including those in the UHF band between 470–800MHz. It is partly this perceived surge in demand that has provoked governments to introduce reform to their spectrum policy frameworks. The Ofcom spectrum framework review in 2004 was prompted by this situation:

> Spectrum has been managed in the UK for around 100 years. The general approach adopted world-wide during this period has been for the spectrum manager to decide, often in accordance with an agreed international framework, on both the use of a particular band and which users are allowed to transmit in the band. This approach was appropriate while there were relatively few uses and users and the spectrum manager could have as good an

understanding of the best use of spectrum as the market itself and hence could sensibly control all aspects of spectrum usage.

However, in recent years, as demand has started to exceed supply in some areas, this centrally managed approach to spectrum, sometimes termed 'command & control', has started to become problematic. Where spectrum is scarce the use of 'beauty contests' meant that Government had to choose between competing would-be service providers. In the US, such decisions were increasingly subject to legal challenge leading initially to the use of lotteries to overcome this problem and then eventually to the use of auctions. Other countries have followed the US lead. Auctions are useful tools in deciding who can use the spectrum, but they need to be combined with the ability to change use, which we term 'liberalization' to help decide the use that spectrum can be put to.[7]

There are three important assumptions in this statement:

1  spectrum is a subject to a condition of *limited supply*;
2  to address this condition it must be *assigned* in an efficient and equitable manner; and
3  in some cases the *market* is the best mechanism for ensuring efficiency and equity for access to spectrum.

The Ofcom statement is consonant with the Coase Theorem and leans toward a property rights model of spectrum management. In such a model licence holders are permitted to lease, sell or otherwise make available their block of spectrum in a more flexible manner and respond more effectively to real market demand. This contrasts with the traditional command and control model in which the government carefully determined the type of wireless service that any licensee was permitted to operate.

## 8.3  Scarcity in question

Despite rising demand caused by mobile phones and other wireless services, the assumption of a limited supply of spectrum does not apply equally across the entire range of frequency bands. For instance, some analysts have suggested 'well over 90 per cent of the airwaves go unused at any time' and that there are in fact large portions of spectrum allocated for services that have never been developed or deployed, thus wasting the potential value of these bands.[8] A case in point is the spectrum allocated for digital cellular phone service in North America, some of which was acquired from unused blocks of the UHF band that had been originally assigned to broadcasters in the 1960s. UHF is a band that was allocated for over-air TV channels 14–69 (consuming some 330MHz of bandwidth) at a time when cable TV was less prominent and when satellite TV was non-existent. In part because of the subsequent success of cable and satellite penetration, the UHF band has never carried more than a few channels. Needless to say, the potential of the band has been underutilized at the expense of other potential services. Figure 8.2 shows how the demand for spectrum to support North American digital cellular service (1.9GHz) and Wi-Fi systems (2.4GHz) is in sharp contrast to the surrounding bands currently assigned to other services.

Findings from studies done on the actual use of spectrum suggest that the scarcity issue may be something of a misconception – that in fact there is considerable spectrum available if it were only accessible to potential users. For those

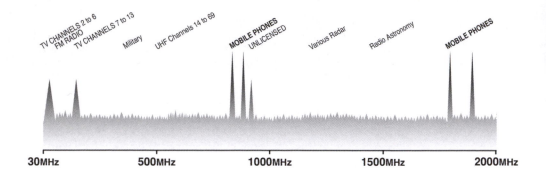

**Figure 8.2**    Spectrum use in the PCS and Wi-Fi bands

*Source*: Forbes.com 'Dead Air', 25 November 2002. Retrieved April 2003. Available at http://
www.forbes.com/forbes/2002/1125/138_print.html

who advocate the private property model of spectrum management, the solution
to this situation is to find a way to use the available frequencies more efficiently
and to provide an incentive to encourage the use of underutilized bands. The
Coase Theorem suggests that if governments were to liberalize the assignment
procedures, such inefficient uses of this resource would disappear because licensees
would have a vested interest and the necessary legal right to offer these bands to
those bidders that valued it the most and that would, by implication, put it to the
best use.

A more radical viewpoint on privatizing spectrum comes out of an FCC
Working Paper published in 2002.[9] In this proposal, the US regulator would hold
a 'Big Bang Auction' where all current licensees could put all or some of their
spectrum allotments on the market. The FCC would then put all other available
bands on the auction block and bidding would be open to anyone for any
combination of bands. If licensees choose to accept a bid, they would receive the
money for it, and not the FCC as is the current arrangement. All spectrum entered
into the Big Bang Auction would be granted private property rights with certain
technical restrictions; however, use of the bands would not be determined by the
FCC. After the conclusion of the Big Bang, spectrum management would devolve
to become largely a matter for private enterprise in the hands of individuals and
corporations rather than the government. While it is not likely to happen in the
future, the Big Bang Auction proposal does indicate how attitudes have changed
since Coase's ideas were first presented to the FCC in the late 1950s.

## 8.4   Open spectrum

In contrast to the private property model is another view sometimes called the
'open spectrum' approach. Advocates of this approach have placed their faith in
technological innovation to resolve the tragedy of the commons. One notable
supporter of the open spectrum approach is David Reed, an information systems
designer with the MIT Media Lab, who played an important role in contributing
to the original architecture of the Internet with the 'end to end' principle.[10] The
end to end (E2E) principle is important in this case because Reed argues that it

should be the basis for a reformed spectrum management policy. Instead of 'dividing [spectrum] into disjoint frequency bands and coverage areas' to resolve the interference problem, governments should recognize that the next generation of intelligent digital radios could make the interference issue all but disappear. Reed's claim is part of a far more ambitious vision, where wireless networks will flourish in much the same manner as the Internet and where innovations in radio technology will make it difficult to plan spectrum allocation as it has been done in the past. Reed forecasts a ubiquitous networked society of wireless personal communications devices and information appliances:

> [These] will be densely deployed, owned by users, small businesses, and corporations, and will be deployed in an unplanned, ad hoc manner. An important characteristic of such devices will be their mobility. Devices carried by a user or carried in a vehicle will be mobile as a result of people moving, whereas appliance devices will be moved just as furniture is moved – as workplaces and home are rearranged. Communication reconfiguration resulting from mobility will be the norm – it would be unacceptable to the owners of these devices to buy new devices merely because one crosses an artificial spectrum boundary.[11]

This is a vision of a world in which all kinds of devices have the capability to be networked through a wireless connection. Here it is possible to detect something like the IMT-2000 initiative, but extended far beyond telephones to include any kind of potential information technology. If such a vision were ever to be realized, spectrum would of course be in extremely high demand, even if it were only for relatively small networks, such as LANs or PANs. A future of densely packed wireless networks therefore would require bountiful access to spectrum and flexibility for these networked devices to switch between frequencies and air-interface standards when necessary. If such access were forthcoming it would open up the possibility of a new form of wireless architecture known as the mesh network.

### 8.4.1  Mesh networks

Another term for network architectures – such as point to point, single site, and cellular – is 'topologies'. A full mesh network is based on a topology where each node in the network is connected directly to each of the others. A partial mesh topology is also possible when most but not all nodes are connected to all the others. Figure 8.3 shows a schematic of a full mesh network with each node shown as a sphere and connections as lines. These connections could of course be either wired or wireless.

In Reed's view, the mesh network is an important topology for emerging wireless systems because it creates what he calls 'cooperation gain'. With wired networks, mesh topologies are expensive to build because cables need to be placed between each node and all the other nodes in the network. This is labour intensive, consumes a lot of cable and is therefore an expensive design. With wireless systems, however, there is no cost to run cable and set up time can be very fast.

Cooperation gain is the idea that the presence of more radio devices can actually *increase* the carrying capacity of spectrum provided that the devices can communicate with one another. In a wireless mesh network each device acts as an open transceiver and is therefore capable of receiving messages designated for its user but also relaying messages to other devices. The more devices there are, the more pathways for any radio signal to travel. More pathways mean greater carrying

## Mesh Network

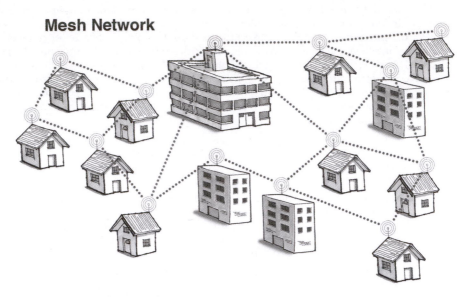

**Figure 8.3**   A full mesh network concept

capacity, as Reed remarks: 'there exist networked architectures whose *utility increases* with the density of independent terminals'.

According to this formulation, dense mesh networks could dramatically increase the value of wireless networks while at the same time lowering the power requirements for individual terminals and, perhaps most significantly, *reduce* demand for spectrum in some bands. In sum, overall efficiency gains are achieved by an 'adaptive network architecture' enabled by intelligent radio devices. Others also see the potential in this concept for wireless networks:

> In a network architecture called a mesh, each RF receiver also acts as a transponder, retransmitting data sent by other devices in the network. In other words, every new device uses some of the network's capacity but also adds capacity back. Because a device in a mesh no longer needs to send information all the way to its ultimate destination (such as a cell tower), it can use less power. That allows the network to add more devices without any noticeable increase in interference. The approach resembles the distributed architecture of the Internet, in which every router can move traffic along an efficient path.[12]

The vision challenges many of the assumptions made about radio spectrum and interference but it depends on a major breakthrough in radio technology that, in theory, will eliminate most of the problems with unwanted interference.

### 8.4.2   Smart radios

The realization of the adaptive network architecture depends on the development of 'smart' radio systems. In particular, it will require many small radios to operate in any given geographical area without interfering with each other and the only practical way to achieve this arrangement is to do two things: keep the power output of each radio very low and to re-use a range of frequencies as much as possible. One technology that appears to be well suited to such requirements is already available in the form of spread spectrum that enables many users to transmit on the same frequency, in the same place, and at the same time. Spread spectrum, as you may recall is the basis for CDMA, Wi-Fi and Bluetooth systems. Wideband CDMA, the basis for Europe's third generation UMTS systems, is also based on a spread spectrum design.

The unique flexibility and potential of spread spectrum systems comes from the fact that they multiplex signals using pseudo-random codes, either by frequency hopping or direct sequence.[13] In effect, this means that several unique channels can share the same band of frequencies without interference because the receivers at the ends of the network are intelligent enough to filter out unwanted signals based on the codes assigned to each unique transmission. (If this is unfamiliar, you might review the passage on multiplexing and CDMA from Chapter 4.)

The latest breakthrough in spread spectrum technology is the *ultra-wideband* (UWB) concept. UWB systems are designed to transmit across an extremely large stretch of spectrum but with very low power output. The typical bandwidth spread of a UWB system is an astonishing 2000MHz, which is purported to be 'more than the bandwidth used by all existing cell phones, broadcast media, and wireless LANs put together'.[14] The extremely low power output of UWB systems means, however, that they can share spectrum with other devices without causing significant interference. This feature also means they are most suited to LAN or PAN applications rather than wide area networks where higher power outputs are required.

Figure 8.4 shows the relative power outputs required for narrowband versus spread spectrum systems. Note how much spectrum the spread waveform requires but how 'quietly' it operates in the environment. David Reed and other UWB proponents claim that smart transceivers should enable the dense deployment of low power spread spectrum systems without creating significant interference problems.

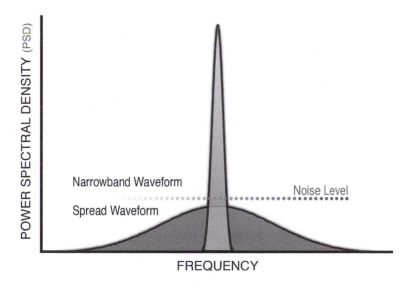

**Figure 8.4**   Comparison of narrowband versus spread spectrum systems

*Software defined radios* (SDR) represent another leap forward toward adaptive wireless networks. Almost all radio systems today are designed to operate within specific bands of frequencies. Many North American mobile phones, for example, are designed to operate only in 800MHz and 1900MHz bands. These phones will not operate in places like Europe where spectrum in the 900/1800MHz bands is reserved for mobile phone service. In other words, the phones are *tuned* to specific frequencies, outside of which they will not operate. It is possible to make mobile phones that are tuned to more frequencies and this is the case with many new models, but there are real limits in terms of cost and engineering constraints. Software defined radios, however, solve this problem.

A software defined radio consists of a programmable digital transceiver. This programmable feature means that some of the most fundamental characteristics of a radio system – such as the air-link, operating frequencies, channel coding and encryption techniques – can be easily changed or modified with a software application. Software defined radios are extremely flexible compared to current radio systems and in the future could be altered easily and inexpensively by downloading and installing new software on an as needed basis. For example, an SDR mobile phone could be programmed to work anywhere in the world simply by installing software that would adapt its operating frequency and air-interface standard to local conditions. In other cases, multipurpose radios could be designed for many different types of uses:

> In principle, a software radio originally used for cellular telephony could, for example, download new software and begin to receive broadcast television signals, or, more likely, access a network that uses a new cellular transmission protocol. Even more sophisticated 'cognitive radios' would work cooperatively, analyzing other nearby radios and adapting on the fly to avoid other transmissions.[15]

The 'cognitive radio' idea takes SDR one step further to imagine the development of sophisticated intelligent radios capable of detecting other radio transmissions in their environment and then adapting their output to operate in the quiet spaces between those existing transmissions. The result, if successful, would be a very efficient use of spectrum with little need for strict control over frequency assignments – in effect, an 'open spectrum' commons could be enabled through these new technologies.

### 8.4.3   Spectrum and democracy

Yochai Benkler and Lawrence Lessig are two of the leading American voices in the open spectrum debate. In 1998, they co-authored an article for the *New Republic*, entitled 'Net gains'. Written partly in response to a wave of spectrum auctions that were taking place in the US at about that time, Benkler and Lessig claim that new spread spectrum technologies could very well render obsolete the constitutional basis for spectrum management in the United States and possibly in other countries. Echoing David Reed's views, they claim that new innovations in radio technology will make possible a world of shared use spectrum and, as a result, eliminate the need for government to act as an arbiter of this natural resource. More to the point, they suggest that current auctioning and licensing of spectrum would in fact violate the American First Amendment (i.e., the right to freedom of expression) if spread spectrum were to make shared use spectrum viable:

> Our argument is straightforward: the FCC regulates speech. It says that, if you want to speak on 98.6 FM in Boston, you must get a license (or buy

one). If you speak on 98.6 without a license, you will have committed a crime. The FCC will prosecute you and seize your transmitter. All this despite the fact that the First Amendment to the Constitution says, 'Congress shall make no law ... abridging the freedom of speech.' What gives?[16]

Keep in mind that legal systems differ widely around the world and that the authors are presenting a deliberately polemical viewpoint to spur on a policy debate. Nonetheless, Benkler and Lessig make an important point regarding new technologies:

> If the engineers are right – if the efficiency of an architecture of spread-spectrum wireless technology were even roughly equivalent to the architecture of allocated spectrum – then much of the present broadcasting architecture would be rendered unconstitutional. If shared spectrum is possible, in other words, then the First Amendment would mean that *allocated* spectrum – whether licensed or auctioned – must go. And, if allocated spectrum must go, then so must the government's giveaways and sales to private industry. If we are right, the government can no more auction the right to broadcast in Boston than it can auction a license to print a newspaper there.
>
> (emphasis added)[17]

While the article refers to 'broadcasting' as such, it could equally apply to most wireless services, including personal mobile communications, much like David Reed's vision entails.

Benkler and Lessig present the case for open spectrum on political grounds, drawing on technical developments to support it. In effect, they argue that recent breakthroughs in radio technology undermine the rationale for strict government management of spectrum. In other words, the politically sensitive issue of determining the right of specific users to 'speak' over the airwaves is made on the grounds of spectrum scarcity. When something like spread spectrum technology eliminates the scarcity it also, according to Benkler and Lessig, undermines the political authority of a government body to issue exclusive licences to use those airwaves.

A problem with their argument in that article, however, is that shared spectrum already exists in many bands. Most countries, for example, distinguish between primary and secondary users who share certain bands on the condition that secondary users must not interfere with primary users. For example, amateur radio is designated as secondary use in a number of bands. In other cases, governments have created licence-exempt bands, such 2.4GHz where technologies such as Wi-Fi and cordless phones share the spectrum without need for a strictly controlled licensing regime.[18]

Benkler and Lessig are no doubt aware of this and have likely overlooked it to make a larger point. It is important, however, because it calls attention to the difference between spectrum 'allocation' and spectrum 'assignment'. As was described in Chapter 2, 'allocation' is an activity that designates categorical uses for spectrum and not the actual granting of rights to use that spectrum. Governments allocate various bands as licence-exempt, which means that the *assignment* of exclusive authorizations to individual users in these bands is forborne. Benkler and Lessig are critiquing the government controlled authorization procedures – an issue of assignment and not allocation per se. This makes a significant difference if we recall that allocation is not unlike property zoning, where some properties are better suited to certain uses because of their inherent qualities.

In this light, it is more difficult to make the case that the role of government in spectrum allocation is obsolete, or unconstitutional for that matter. As one example, consider high power or very specialized radio systems that are not suited to spread spectrum technology and that provide important public service or industrial functions. These include military, public safety, aircraft navigation, or other scientific and industrial radio systems. Even in a world of plentiful spread spectrum technologies, one could still argue that the role of government in spectrum allocation remains important for 'zoning' purposes, especially at the international level, where coordination between countries is a complex and extremely important undertaking.

This specific interpretation of their argument opens the door for a more pragmatic viewpoint that says the government could allocate a certain portion of 'open spectrum' and still maintain the right to auction exclusive rights in other bands to the highest bidders. In fact this is the situation today in many countries, where the governments have adopted a combination of assignment methods and conditions of licence.

## 8.5    The middle ground

In contrast to the more radical interpretations of the property rights or open spectrum models, a number of voices in the debate have assumed a more prag-matic position that is likely to reflect the reality of policy reform over the next few years. Among those voices, one has come from the open spectrum side of the debate with Kevin Werbach's call for a new wireless paradigm to guide policymaking:

> Despite its radical implications, open spectrum can coexist with traditional exclusive licensing. There are two mechanisms to facilitate spectrum sharing: unlicensed parks and underlay. The first involves familiar allocated frequency bands, but with no user given the exclusive right to transmit. A very limited set of frequencies has already been designated for unlicensed consumer devices, such as cordless phones and wireless local area networks, but more is needed. The second approach allows unlicensed users to coexist in licensed bands, by making their signals invisible and non-intrusive to other users. Both open spectrum approaches have great value, with the specifics depending on how technology and markets develop. Both should be encouraged. The risks are minimal, while the potential benefits are extraordinary.[19]

Working from the private property model as a starting point, economists such as Gerald Faulhaber and David Farber also advocate a mixed licensing policy that includes a provision for open spectrum. This pragmatic position is critical of the false dichotomy established by the techno-optimists who envision a world of total open spectrum and the free market economists who subscribe solely to the Coase Theorem. Nevertheless, like others on both sides of the debate Faulhaber and Faber are also critical of the current approach to spectrum management:

> Despite the recent moves toward more market-based spectrum allocation, the dominant mode of managing the spectrum is administrative fiat. Perhaps the closest analogy to the US's current approach is that of GOSPLAN, the central planning agency in the former Soviet Union. GOSPLAN drew up plans for every sector of the Soviet economy, determined how much of each scarce input was required for each industry and each factory, and then issued

orders to each factory as to how much it was to produce and to whom it was to be shipped. GOSPLAN was subject to intense lobbying by powerful factory bosses regarding quotas and shipments, and allocations were politi- cally mediated. While the FCC only controls the electromagnetic spectrum, it has operated in a very similar manner, and subject to the same political pressures. It should be no surprise that both GOSPLAN and the FCC pro- cesses have had similar results: woeful inefficiencies and wasted resources.[20]

To resolve the perceived wasteful practices of the so-called GOSPLAN model of spectrum management, Faulhaber and Farber proposed a strategy for policy reform that would 'release both the power of the market and the power of the new sharing technologies to improve the efficiency of spectrum use'. The strategy is based on two distinctions within a property rights model.

The first of these distinctions is described as 'fee simple ownership with non- interference easement'. The second is described as 'pure fee simple ownership'. In both cases, private ownership of spectrum is permitted; however, in the former distinction, a non-interference easement condition would mean that any radio transmitter 'could use this [privately owned] spectrum, but only on condition that [it] not *meaningfully* interfere with the owner's right to clear broadcast'. This regime would create an open spectrum commons for low power, non-interfering spread spectrum or agile radios within a wider private property rights model. Enacting such a regime would require some form of enforcement and Faulhaber and Faber propose an interesting technology-based solution:

> [It] would require that UWB and agile radio emitters transmit a unique identifier (similar to identifiers built into computer network interface cards) and frequency owners could monitor and record violations. Penalties could be assessed much as traffic violations are handled; it is likely that third-party collection agencies would arise to handle these violations on behalf of owners. Such monitoring would result in costs to owners. Fines for violations could recompense owners for these expenses.[21]

The second distinction of 'pure fee simple ownership' would provide for *exclusive* use of spectrum bands. The operator of any radio transmitter using these bands would be required to pay the owner – government or private – for access to that allotment of spectrum. Payment schemes might include a long-term contract or a short-term lease arrangement, or perhaps in the case of agile radio systems the possibility of a 'spot market' in spectrum on a pay per use basis. This is a far more complicated arrangement but Faulhaber and Faber argue that the transaction costs of a spot market for spectrum need not be onerous: owners would need some means of monitoring use of spectrum as well as broadcasting their price to potential customers. Third-party brokers might be called upon to manage this arrangement, much like the current system used to manage royalty payments for the music industry.

## 8.6 Frontier thinking

While it is probably not realistic to expect that governments will ever do away completely with their role in managing the radio spectrum, Ronald Coase's idea for introducing limited private property rights is now taken quite seriously in many countries. Similarly, the open spectrum model will continue to attract the interest of regulators, especially as ultrawideband (UWB) systems and software-defined radios become commercially available on a large scale. In the long run, a pragmatic combination of the three models – command and control, property rights and open spectrum – will be needed in future if governments are to enable the bandwidth bonanza needed to meet an ever rising demand for spectrum. However, new possibilities for mesh networking and 'cooperation gain' will continue to challenge old assumptions about spectrum scarcity and radio interference, encouraging a kind of frontier thinking when it comes to envisioning future possibilities for mobile communications. This will be especially significant as we move into a world that could soon be permeated by billions of tiny wireless personal area networks.

## 8.7   Further reading

Jonathan Nuechterlein and Philip Weiser provide a helpful overview of spectrum policy and the wireless sector in the US in chapters 7 and 8 of their (2005) book, *Digital Crossroads: American Telecommunications Policy in the Internet Age* (MIT Press). Lawrence Lessig's (2001) book *The Future of Ideas* (Random House) devotes a chapter to the idea of creating a spectrum commons. A more extensive argument is presented by Kevin Werbach in his report, *Radio Revolution: The Coming Age of Unlicensed Wireless* available at http://werbach. com/docs/RadioRevolution.pdf Other articles on mesh networks and spectrum policy can be found at Werbach's website: http://werbach.com/

Thomas Hazlett's view on spectrum policy reform is outlined in the working paper, 'The wireless craze, the unlimited bandwidth myth, the spectrum auction faux pas, and the punchline to Ronald Coase's "big joke": An essay on airwave allocation policy' (January 2001). The paper is available in PDF from the AEI Brookings Joint Center website: http://www.aei.brookings.org/publications/index.php?tab=author&authorid=7

For an international perspective on the open spectrum debate, the Open Spectrum Foundation website provides links to reports and a variety of sources of information from around the world: http://www.openspectrum.info/

# 9 | Into thin air

The most profound technologies are those that disappear. They weave themselves into the fabric of everyday life until they are indistinguishable from it.

Mark Weiser[1]

## 9.1 Wireless, wireless everywhere

In 1991 a computer scientist by the name of Mark Weiser published a paper in *Scientific American* entitled 'The computer for the 21st Century'. Weiser and his team at the Xerox Palo Alto Research Center (PARC) in California had in 1988 begun to invent a new generation of computing systems, and this article introduced a mass readership to a different way of thinking about computing. It described the historical transition from large mainframe computers of the 1960s and 1970s, to the stand-alone desktop personal computer (PC) of the 1980s and 1990s, and then presented a future vision of networked computing appliances. This emerging form of computing was presented as an integrated system of advanced computing devices and intelligent interface design, combined with anytime, anywhere, data communications.

Weiser coined the term *ubiquitous computing* to describe a world 'in which each person is continually interacting with hundreds of nearby wirelessly connected computers'. At that time wireless networking was primitive but today, with technologies like Wi-Fi and Bluetooth, the possibility of 'anytime, anywhere' data communications is entering the realm of commercial reality. The combination of microcomputing technology with pervasive wireless networks could radically alter our relationships to people and things in the near future. Take, for example, Philips Electronics' *Phenom* project, which uses ubiquitous computing to create 'an environment that is aware of the identity, location and intention of its users, and that eventually [will be] capable of butler-like behavior'.[2] Or perhaps consider a public space, where people use their mobile phones to leave 'virtual messages' to tell stories about things that have happened in that place.[3]

On the one hand, these possibilities offer a compelling vision of innovative services, efficient transactions and human-centred technologies for future societies. On the other hand, they also raise fundamental questions about privacy, public safety and environmental impact. This chapter will begin with a discussion of some of the main enabling technologies of the ubiquitous computing idea. It will then look at some persistent and emerging concerns for mobile communications today and in the near future.

## 9.2    Arrival of the personal area network

Personal Area Networks are one of the core enabling technologies for the ubiquitous network society. The PAN permits a micronetworking environment of wireless devices in the immediate workspace (or playspace) of the user, and it will bring wireless devices into new relationships with our bodies and in our interpersonal relationships. A few years ago, the PAN concept was restricted by technological limitations that affected the degree to which wireless devices could be used effectively in a mobile environment. Today, with the advent of technologies like Bluetooth and RFID, an increasing integration of WANs with LANs and PANs is a certainty.

### 9.2.1    Red before Blue(tooth)

Prior to the creation of the Bluetooth standard for personal area networks, the world of wireless PANs was dominated by devices that used an *infrared* or 'IR' airlink. Many people will be familiar with IR technology without realizing how widespread it has in fact become:

> If you watch TV, chances are you've been 'beaming' or using Infrared devices for most of your life. The commands from the remote control to the TV travel on infrared light waves instead of through a cable. Actually, the first TV remote control was developed by Zenith Radio Corporation in 1950 and was named 'Lazy Bones'. A few years later the first wireless TV remote controller 'Flashmatic' was introduced. The first remote controls included buttons that turned the TV on and off. By the early 1980s, the industry incorporated infrared, or IR, remote technology into the devices. Today, remote controls are made for many other consumer electronics products, including VCRs, cable and satellite boxes, and home audio receivers.[4]

**Infrared devices** operate in several frequency bands just below visible light, somewhere between $10^{12}$ and $10^{15}$ Hz.[5] Today IR-enabled devices are one of the most widespread wireless data technologies having been installed in millions of consumer products (despite the fact that it is hardly ever used in many of these products). In the mid-1990s when the Internet inspired a surge in demand for personal computers, device manufacturers were looking to develop a standard that would enable wireless data networking between computers and peripheral devices such as printers and personal digital assistants. In 1994 the Infrared Data Association (IrDA) was formed as a non-profit organization to promote IR technology and to ensure interoperability between devices. The organization's acronym is often used synonymously to describe the technology. IrDA has been evolved into several versions, ranging from 115Kbps for the original 'SIR' standard up to 16Mbps for the VFIR standard.[6]

According to proponents of IrDA technology, infrared devices do have some unique advantages, such as low power consumption; secure transmissions because of the narrow beam of IR transmissions; and the fact that they are relatively free of licensing requirements and regulations. Yet IrDA technology has not been widely adopted for wireless data networking. Part of the problem has been attributed to early difficulties with interoperability between devices and also the fact that IR transmitters must be carefully aligned to establish a stable connection. Anything more than 30 degrees out of alignment and the connection will likely fail. As a result of this limitation, users often have to fuss with their laptop and PDA or phone by placing them on a smooth, stable surface and to ensure the IRDA transceivers are correctly aimed and unobstructed before a data connection can be established. As one might imagine, this is a serious constraint in many mobile situations except in those instances of brief, very close range communications. Nevertheless, a large number of mobile phones and other portable computing devices still include IrDA among their features, in part because it is relatively inexpensive to build in to most devices. Although it does not appear at the moment that IrDA will ever be widely adopted for general purpose mobile PANs, it will likely remain an important wireless technology for specialized applications. For example, the narrow directional beam of IrDA transmissions makes them less susceptible to unintended interception and could be a secure option useful for wireless point-of-sale payment systems such as vending machines.

### 9.2.2   King Bluetooth

A much more flexible standard for PANs is the new air-link standard known as Bluetooth. Bluetooth uses low power transmissions in a licence-exempt band to create a small radio bubble that solves the finicky line of sight requirements of IrDA technology. Recognizing the potential for a single wireless PAN standard, a special interest group was formed in 1998 among five major electronics manufacturers with interests in mobile computing, including Ericsson, Nokia, IBM, Intel and Toshiba. The name of the special interest group was taken from the 10th century Danish king Harald Blåtand, which translates into 'Harald Bluetooth'. King Bluetooth made his mark in history by uniting Denmark and Norway under Christian rule, so his name was considered appropriately symbolic for a technology that was created to unify the world of mobile phones, peripheral devices and other accessories including 'hands-free' kits. The first specification for Bluetooth was released in 1999 and other firms such as Motorola, Microsoft, Lucent and 3Com soon joined the special interest group. Mobile phones and other devices equipped with Bluetooth began to appear on the market in 2002–03.

The Bluetooth chip is essentially a radio transceiver that operates in the 2.4GHz band for very short range digital voice and data applications. Bluetooth uses spread-spectrum frequency hopping (somewhat similar to CDMA) with a full-duplex signal up that can 'hop' up to 1600 times per second across 79 discrete RF channels. Bluetooth devices are very low power, emitting about one milliwatt, which limits their transmission range to about ten metres. Up to eight Bluetooth devices can be connected to each other, with one device acting as a 'master' and the others as 'slaves'. This arrangement forms a **piconet**. The Bluetooth specification also permits devices to perform a bridging function between piconets to form a **scatternet**.[7]

Because they are relatively inexpensive, Bluetooth chips are now installed in a wide variety of electronic systems for both half-duplex or full-duplex communications. In half duplex mode, Bluetooth can transmit up to 721Kbps of data in one direction, and 57.6Kbps in the other, or 432.6Kbps in each direction. In full duplex mode, Bluetooth can send data at 64Kbps. This is slower than a typical 802.11b or 802.11g Wi-Fi link but it is nevertheless adequate for certain types of applications, such as hands-free headsets. In response to some of the drawbacks of the first generation of Bluetooth, a new version called Enhanced Data Rate was developed and released in late 2004. Bluetooth version 2.0 offers much higher data rates (2Mbps) and will gradually come to replace the original standard.

Bluetooth devices operate in the same frequency band as Wi-Fi devices but emit lower power transmissions and use a different encoding scheme that helps to avoid interference problems. At one time a debate raged about whether Bluetooth

**Table 9.1**  Bluetooth paired devices

| Paired devices | Applications |
| --- | --- |
| Mobile phone + headset | Wireless headset for mobile phones |
| Mobile phone + mobile phone | Multiplayer games; phone book and data sharing |
| Mobile phone + PDA | Synchronization and file sharing between devices |
| Mobile phone + PC | Synchronization and file sharing between devices |
| Mobile phone + landline phone | Automatic call forwarding or message retrieval |
| Mobile phone + Point of purchase | Mobile commerce and payments terminal |
| Mobile phone + automobile | Wireless key and alarm system |
| PDA + refrigerator | Grocery list update |
| Video projector + digital camera | Wireless projection of images |
| Digital pen + PDA | Handwriting capture; digital imaging (drawing) |
| MP3 player + headset | Wireless headset for music |
| Eyeglasses + PC | Augmented reality vision |

would fade from use as Wi-Fi chips became more energy efficient and cheaper but it seems that a balance has been reached in the electronics world, possibly because of ready access to inexpensive chip sets and a growing market for specialized peripherals such as Bluetooth headsets. Many laptops and PDAs on the market today will include both Wi-Fi and Bluetooth as standard features.

The original intent of the Bluetooth initiative was to develop a technology that would enable simple PANs to be created between mobile phones, personal computers and their peripheral devices. Today, however, Bluetooth is now being considered for use in such diverse applications as automotives and household appliances. Table 9.1 lists a number of standard Bluetooth applications plus a few innovative ideas for piconets. Some of these more adventurous ideas are in fact already available; for example, Nokia has released both a Bluetooth pen and a Bluetooth-enabled video projector. LG Electronics is considering Bluetooth for its Digital Network Home (DNH) concept that promises to create an 'interhome appliance network'.[8]

### 9.2.3  Mobile social software

An interesting development is a growing 'peer to peer' (P2P) use for Bluetooth devices. This type of P2P application is chiefly found in new Bluetooth-enabled mobile phones that have the computing power and memory capacity to take advantage of more advanced software. In addition to file sharing and music sharing, a more common application is using a Bluetooth-enabled phone to interact with other phones in the immediate proximity. In some cases, owners of Bluetooth-enabled phones will deliberately enable the 'discoverable' mode on the device, allowing it to see and be seen by other similar devices nearby. Small software applications have even been developed to increase the likelihood of connecting with a desirable or suitable person by creating categories of interest or other information. Some companies have launched business concepts based on this phenomenon, although it is not entirely clear whether or not this is simply a passing trend or if it will have long-term viability. So-called 'mobile social software' (or 'MoSoSo') was in its early stages in 2005 but has been spreading in major urban centres such as London, New York and Singapore.[9]

In addition to the P2P possibilities, there are also commercial possibilities for Bluetooth-enabled piconets to distribute advertising messages, vendor coupons, targeted information and even to stream music to mobile phones. For example, when a customer enters the premises of a business or shop, their mobile phone could automatically receive a complimentary ringtone, a digital image or a short music clip via Bluetooth. The benefits of this type of business communication model is that – unlike SMS – Bluetooth messages can be sent to phones without knowing the telephone number of the device, provided that it is in discovery mode. This enables businesses to put information directly inside the device that people trust and carry with them everywhere. The message can later be retrieved, shared with friends or exchanged for goods or services like a coupon. For advertisers and even government agencies trying to reach a younger demographic that does not read newspapers or magazines, the mobile phone and Bluetooth may become an effective means of distributing digital information.

## 9.2.4   RFID

Radio frequency identification (RFID) is another short–range wireless technology that is contributing to the emergence of a ubiquitous network society. However, RFID is somewhat different from IrDA and Bluetooth inasmuch as it is a method of remotely storing and retrieving data instead of a technology to enable wireless networks. A basic RFID system consists of small tags that each contain a tiny antenna designed to respond to radio signals sent from an RFID transceiver. The RFID transmitter in turn is connected to a computer that will translate the data from the tag into useful information for the user. There are four different kinds of tags commonly in use: low frequency tags (125 or 134.2kHz), high frequency tags (13.56MHz), UHF tags (868 to 956MHz), and microwave tags (2.45GHz).

RFID tags can also be classified into passive or active types. Passive tags have no power supply and can be extremely small, in some cases less than a square millimetre and paper thin. The incoming radio signal from the RFID reader induces an electrical current in the antenna of a passive tag, providing just enough power for it to transmit a response. Active tags, on the other hand, have an internal power source and are therefore larger and more expensive to manufacture. One advantage of an active tag system is larger coverage area and greater memory capacity than passive tags. Whereas an active tag RFID system might have a range similar to Bluetooth (up to ten metres), a passive tag system is usually limited to a range of one metre or less.

At present RFID tags are still too expensive to deploy as broadly as some analysts have anticipated, but they are already widely applied to consumer products or in the transportation industry where they can be affixed to containers or pallets of goods for inventory control. In fact WalMart, which is the largest retailer on the Earth, has set 2006 as the deadline when all of its suppliers will be required to affix RFID to products bound for WalMart's warehouses. As the price of RFID tags continues to drop with larger volumes of production it is conceivable that they will soon be embedded in most manufactured products.

Beyond inventory control, RFID systems are also appearing in the consumer market as a form of smart card technology. Typically these smart card devices look like a credit card but contain an embedded RFID tag that contains a unique identifying code linked to a customer account. When purchasing petrol, for example, the customer has only to wave the card over the reader on the gas pump, and the transaction is completed with the customer account debited accordingly. Credit card companies are also looking to use RFID technology to create cards that do not need to be swiped but instead can transfer card information merely by passing close to the card reader.

Some of the more sophisticated applications for RFID include tags embedded in passports, tags sewn into children's backpacks (for monitoring attendance at

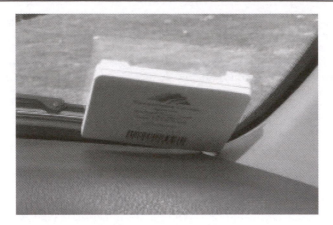

**Figure 9.1**  RFID transponder used for electronic toll collection
*Source*: http://en.wikipedia.org/wiki/Image:FasTrak_transponder.jpg

school) and tags surgically inserted under the skin of house pets and wild animals for registration and tracking. Implantable tags are also being used with human beings to prevent identity fraud and provide a secure means of storing medical records. A company in the United States called Verichip offers an 'FDA-cleared human implantable RFID microchip' for use in medical and security applications.[10] It has been reported that the Baja Beach Club in Barcelona, Spain uses Verichip product to identify its VIP customers, who can use it to pay for drinks.[11] In the United States, the State Department announced in 2004 that RFID technology would be included in new passports but has since retracted this initiative when concerns were raised that the ability to remotely read the passports could make US citizens targets for terrorism or kidnappings. A revised plan has proposed that some type of shielding be added to the cover of the passports in order to restrict access to the RFID tag inside.

Concern about unwanted surveillance with RFID tags has prompted a number of groups to speak out against the technology. The group Consumers Against Supermarket Privacy Invasion and Numbering (CASPIAN), for instance, claims that retailers will use RFID tags to track customers and their purchasing habits without gaining their consent. A statement on the CASPIAN website highlights the concerns of such groups:

> RFID [will] expand marketers' ability to monitor individuals' behavior to undreamt of extremes. With corporate sponsors like Wal-Mart, Target, the Food Marketing Institute, Home Depot, and British supermarket chain Tesco, as well as some of the world's largest consumer goods manufacturers including Proctor and Gamble, Phillip Morris, and Coca Cola 29 it may not be long before RFID-based surveillance tags begin appearing in every store-bought item in a consumer's home.
>
> According to ... Proctor and Gamble, applications could include shopping carts that automatically bill consumers' accounts ... refrigerators that report their contents to the supermarket for re-ordering, and interactive televisions that select commercials based on the contents of a home's refrigerator.
>
> Now that shopper cards have whetted their appetite for data, marketers are no longer content to know who buys what, when, where, and how. As incredible as it may seem, they are now planning ways to monitor consumers'

use of products within their very homes. RFID tags coupled with indoor receivers installed in shelves, floors, and doorways, could provide a degree of omniscience about consumer behavior that staggers the imagination.[12]

Concerns of groups like CASPIAN might be somewhat exaggerated but public anxiety over unwanted surveillance and RFID remains a barrier to the adoption of the technology and an important issue for both government and industry to resolve.

The ultimate contribution of RFID to a ubiquitous network society is yet to be determined but some early indications that the widespread adoption of the mobile phone means that it is a prime target for both RFID tagging in its own right and as a device that could be made capable of reading RFID tags embedded in other objects. With its well developed user interface and network connectivity, today's mobile phone could be transformed into a consumer-grade RFID reader. In fact, researchers in both Japan and Korea have demonstrated systems that can 'RFID-enable' a mobile phone and give it the ability to identify products on a shelf, seek out consumer information and comparative pricing from remote databases, track purchases and even pay for products purchased.

RFID technology is also a component of a much larger vision in wireless LANs and PANs, providing a means for computing devices to 'learn' about the people and objects in their proximity and make decisions to accommodate them. A simple example of this is a new TiVo remote control described in a recent patent application that presents a custom channel list depending on the individual holding the remote control at any given moment. The remote control is able to adapt to each individual because of an RFID tag embedded in a bracelet or ring that is worn by the user. This is an example of how ubiquitous computing can be employed to create a world of 'ambient intelligence'.

## 9.3    Emerging issues

While Mark Weiser's team was working on the 'ubiquitous computing' vision at Xerox PARC in California, the European Union was also promoting a similar concept for its research and development agenda. The term adopted within the European setting is 'ambient intelligence' but it seems to share most of the same features as Weiser's ubiquitous computing scenario.

### 9.3.1    Ambient intelligence

In 2001 the European Commission issued a report entitled, 'Scenarios for ambient intelligence in 2010', and this document has since become a formal point of departure for a number of research and development initiatives in countries of the European Union. The report defines ambient intelligence in a way that is similar to Weiser's idea for ubiquitous computing:

> The concept of Ambient Intelligence (AmI) provides a vision of the Information Society where the emphasis is on greater user-friendliness, more efficient services support, user-empowerment, and support for human interactions. People are surrounded by intelligent intuitive interfaces that are embedded in all kinds of objects and an environment that is capable of recognizing and responding to the presence of different individuals in a seamless, unobtrusive and often invisible way.[13]

From a technical point of view, the Ambient Intelligence concept shares features with the original IMT-2000 initiative, and with the advent of 3G mobile networks we are now beginning to glimpse the wider implications for society of the convergence in technology and services set into motion by that initiative. Ambient intelligence, however, takes this evolution one step further by presenting a world of not only human to human communications over wireless networks, but also one that includes human to machine as well as machine to machine communications. The ambient intelligence concept imagines a world where wireless networks and RFID-type chips literally permeate (some might say 'pollute') the environment. Howard Rheingold refers to this possibility as 'the era of sentient things' and suggests it could open up a new world of mesh networking and automated information exchange between humans and objects:

> Information and communication technologies are starting to invade the physical world ... Shards of sentient silicon will be inside boxtops and dashboards, pens, street corners, bus stops, money, most things that are manufactured or built, within the next ten years. These technologies are 'sentient' not because embedded chips can reason but because they can sense, receive, store, and transmit information ... Odd new things become possible. Shirt labels gain the power to disclose what airplanes, trucks, and ships carried it, what substances compose it, and the URL of a webcam in the factory where the shirt was manufactured. Things tell you where they are. Places can be haunted by intergenerational messages. Virtual graffiti on books and bars becomes available to those who have the password.[14]

In order for such 'odd new things' to become possible, wireless networks will have to become even more pervasive than they are today. This is, after all, an imagined future of a world in which all types of objects are outfitted with a radio transceiver and where public and private spaces are littered with invisible radio transceiver devices for sending and receiving bits of information. Rheingold foretells a major shift in human communications from the advent of ambient intelligent networks:

> A new media sphere is emerging from this process, one that could become at least as influential, lucrative, and ubiquitous as pervious media spheres opened by print, telegraphy, telephony, radio, television, and the wired Internet.[15]

In making this point, he is drawing attention to the fact that these new developments will affect businesses, governments, content producers, consumers, social networks and even our ways of thinking about the world. With so much at stake, Rheingold and others have started to recognize that there are urgent questions about the impact of ubiquitous wireless networks on society. Some of the most urgent questions concern the issue of privacy rights and unwanted surveillance, fears about the effects of radiofrequency energy on the human body, and about the emerging market in age-restricted content flowing over mobile communications devices.

## 9.3.2   Privacy, surveillance and safety

When a mobile phone is active it communicates constantly with the nearest base station, indicating whether or not it is available to take calls and transferring information such as short text messages, voice mail indications and even time of day and network status messages. The cell coverage area in an urban 2.5G or 3G network is often quite small, so even without resorting to special location tracking technology such as GPS (geographic positioning system) it is usually possible to trace a mobile phone to a specific geographical location within a few blocks, almost instantly, provided that authorities are given access to the mobile operator's network data.

This situation leads to public ambivalence over the location tracing capability of mobile devices. On the one hand, the feature is rather helpful in cases of emergencies where the caller is unable to provide their location details to the operator. With recent developments in 'wireless E911', location details can now be provided from the mobile network so that emergency responders can more quickly arrive on the scene and begin to administer assistance.[16] In fact, many people purchase their mobile phone for public safety reasons, with the thought that it will help them to be found during a critical situation.

On the other hand, this persistent location tracking on a wireless network means that people fear it might also be used for covert state or commercial surveillance. This has led to interest in the problem of 'location privacy'.[17] Location privacy is a public policy issue that has emerged with the appearance of location aware mobile phones and the advent of location-based services for public safety and commercial purposes. Unfortunately, the media has tended to spread misconceptions about mobile phones and location privacy with dramatic but not entirely accurate headlines:

> That dinky little Nokia in your pocket could be your undoing if you're up to no good.
>
> (UK, *The Inquirer*, March 2003)

> Big Brother's here, on your cellphone
>
> (India, *Economic Times*, May 2003)

> Cellphones: No place to hide
>
> (*ZDNet News*, July 2002)

Contrary to what might be portrayed in these kinds of media reports, location information by itself is not very useful until it is linked with other types of information about the phone user. A major debate in the issue over location privacy is therefore about the use and disclosure of location information and the requirement to gain customer consent to do so. It is this linking of information sources – location data with customer information – that is the necessary step in providing commercial services that adds commercial value to otherwise raw location data generated by a mobile phone:

> knowledge of the user's location is only part of the problem. Depending on where, when, how, with whom, and why customers are navigating in physical space, their needs will vary ... Even if the LBS [location-based services] provider was able to push information or advertising with great reliability to these customers, they might have an extremely difficult time figuring out what the customer is doing or want at that location in real time ... There is an urgent need for sophisticated mobile marketing techniques based on detailed knowledge of customer profiles, history, needs, and preferences. Information existing in customer databases developed by retailers like Amazon.com, for example, can be used in parallel with location-based information.[18]

Optimist forecasts have placed the market for such location-based services at a staggering US$32 billion in Europe alone by 2005, with a global reach of 680 million customers. While this may be an unrealistic forecast, the point here is that much of the value proposition for these services will rely less on the provision of location data *qua* data and more on the ability of service providers to establish linkages across multiple databases containing customer details. The terms and conditions by which a customer provides consent for doing so remains an important, if unresolved, policy and regulatory question in most countries today. In a world of ambient intelligence, the issue of privacy and consent will likely become more complicated and more crucial for the success of commercial services.

### 9.3.3    Health and mobile phones

With the proliferation of wireless devices and networks there is also public anxiety over the health effects related to mobile phones and the placement of cell-site transmitters in local communities. Health-related concerns raised by public health officials and community groups fall into three general categories:

1  mobile phones as a cause of traffic and other types of accidents;
2  the environmental impact of mobile phones and their components when improperly disposed of in landfills; and
3  perhaps most controversial among these are the effects of long-term exposure to radiofrequency (RF) energy from mobile phones on the human body, especially on children.

The most apparent health and safety issue relating to mobile phones is their role in causing traffic and other accidents. For instance, the number of cases of pedestrians being struck by cars and buses while talking on the phone has risen markedly in recent years, leading to public safety campaigns targeted at pedestrians and motorists in the UK, Singapore and elsewhere. Drivers in many jurisdictions are either forbidden from using a mobile phone or must use a hands-free kit when operating an automobile. Of course any law that only requires drivers to use a hands-free kit assumes that *holding* the phone is the primary distraction factor that leads to traffic accidents. There are, however, research findings that suggest the act of *talking* on a mobile phone is a significant enough distraction factor to render the driver 'impaired' to a degree not unlike that caused by alcohol consumption.[19] Moreover, the popularity of text messaging can create very dangerous situations such as the tragic case in Colorado where a cyclist was struck and killed by an automobile driven by a teenager who had drifted into the bicycle lane while attempting to drive and 'text' at the same time.[20]

Another health worry related to mobile phone use is environmental damage that results from their manufacture and disposal. Any product as widely manufactured as the mobile phone – there are reportedly over 2 billion handsets in the world today – will inevitably have an impact on the ecosystem because, like all electronic goods, they contain heavy metals and other toxic contaminants. If not disposed of properly these contaminants will leach into local landfills and rivers with deleterious impacts on people, animals and plants. Sadly, the disposal of electronics is often relegated to countries where environmental and worker safety standards are less strict than in North America or Europe. According to a report issued by Greenpeace in 2005, the issue of 'E-waste' is a serious problem in countries like the Philippines:

> Recent statistics point to a surge in computers, mobile phones, and ultimately E-waste, in the country. Shipments of personal computers [for disposal] to the Philippines were estimated to reach 426,521 units in 2004 alone, and is projected to reach close to half a million units by the end of the year. Meanwhile, the number of cellular phone users was recorded at 18 million in

2003 and at its current projected rate of increase is expected to reach more than 25 million units by end 2005 . . . Because of the lack of proper measures for E-waste disposal in the Philippines, the discarded technology is inciner-ated, dumped in landfills, or end up with backyard recyclers, exposing workers, poor communities, and the environment to poisonous heavy metals such as lead, cadmium, mercury, chromium, and halogenated substances such as brominated flame retardants (BFR), and polyvinyl chloride (PVC).[21]

In addition to industrial accidents and environmental damage, there has been a persistent, if not controversial, public concern about health effects of exposure to RF energy from mobile phones and cellular base-station transmitters. As one might imagine, this issue is important to both public health officials and to the mobile phone industry, which has a lot to lose if such a link were ever con-clusively established. Public anxiety over the health effects of transmission towers is especially acute when cell-sites are located on or nearby neighbourhood schools and playgrounds. Compared with first generation analogue phones, most digital phones today are relatively low power devices and hence much more difficult to link to any definitive physiological effects. However, the fact that many people, including children, are heavy users of mobile phones does lead to apprehension that it could cause brain, bone or skin cancer over the long-term.

Findings from a range of epidemiological studies on the health effects of mobile phones usually focus on either of two possible hazards: thermal effects and non-thermal effects. Studies on the thermal effects are concerned with *dielectric heating* of the surface of the head or other body part that comes into contact with the mobile phone and the subsequent health effects of these local, but minute, increases in temperature. Studies into the non-thermal effects consider the effects of RF energy on DNA as well as other biological functions of the body. In both cases, a key measurement is the rate at which the human body absorbs radiation, or the Specific Absorption Rate (SAR). Regulatory authorities in many countries have established maximum SAR limits for mobile phones as a precautionary measure.

According to a 2004 report published by the Royal Society of Canada, studies conducted by organizations such as the American Cancer Society, the British Medical Association, and the Australian government share similar findings:

> All of the authoritative reviews completed within the last two years have concluded that there is no clear evidence of adverse health effects associated with RF fields. At the same time, these same reviews support the need for further research to clarify the possible associations between RF fields and adverse health outcomes that have appeared in some reports.[22]

The 'adverse health outcomes that have appeared in some reports' refers to a few studies that have suggested possible links between mobile phone use and non-thermal effects such as brain cancer and the alteration of enzyme activity in cellular tissue. The World Health Organization (WHO) with its International Electro-magnetic Fields Project, as well as other organizations such as the Mobile Man-ufacturing Forum and the International Commission on Non-ionizing Radiation Protection (ICNIRP), continue to study this issue and provide updates for the scientific community and general public.

### 9.3.4   Age restricted content

Almost as soon as multimedia content began to arrive on mobile phones so too did age restricted content such as pornography and gambling. The market for such content is potentially very lucrative and its foothold in the mobile industry is

already well established. Industry reports forecast a future adult mobile entertainment market in the billions of US dollars, and in April 2005 *Wired* magazine
reported on a licensing deal struck between a leading adult film studio and
Brickhouse Mobile, 'one of the companies leading the charge to bring porn to
mobile phones'.[23]

The initial response by the mobile industry to this development has been to
introduce self-regulation, although government regulators in a few countries
(Australia, for example) have already taken action to protect children from gaining
access to adult material. The American trade group for the wireless industry,
CTIA, also issued guidelines for its members in November 2005 with similar
recommendations, stating, ' . . . those under the age of 18 would need parental or a
guardian's permission to receive content that carriers offer that may be sexually
explicit, excessively violent, or involve gambling'.[24]

The Irish Cellular Industry Association (ICIA) has initiated a three–part strategy
to address these concerns, which includes an industry-wide code of practice and a
test project for filtering adult content.[25] The ICIA has also developed a guide to
provide parents with key safety tips that are intended to encourage responsible and
secure use of mobile phones by their children. As part of the voluntary scheme in
Ireland, a number of mobile operators offer a 'dual access' provision that allows
both parent and child to see the account records held by the mobile operator,
including numbers called, account balances and the services available on the
mobile phone. In some cases, access to certain services may be barred on the
child's handset.[26]

## 9.4   Next, next generation mobile networks

Even before the third generation of mobile networks and handsets was in wide
use, network engineers and mobile operators began planning for yet another
generation. The next, next generation of mobile networks remains an ambiguous
concept, and details of the proposal will vary widely depending on the group that
is promoting it. Despite considerable uncertainty surrounding the definition of
'4G' it is possible to identify two common points of reference: higher data transfer
rates, and an IP (Internet Protocol)-based core layer. The following table compares the 4G concept with that of today's 3G networks.[27]

**Table 9.2**   Comparison of 3G systems with 4G concept

| 3G networks | 4G concept |
| --- | --- |
| Backwards compatible with 2G networks | Extends 3G capabilities by an order of magnitude |
| Circuit-switched and packet-switched connections | Entirely packet-switched connections |
| Hybrid of old and new network equipment | All network elements are digital |
| Data rates up to 2Mbps | Data rates up to 100Mbps |

*Source*: Georgia Institute of Technology (2003) Mobility Management in 4G Wireless Systems.
Broadband and Wireless Networking Laboratory. Available at http://users.ece.gatech.edu/~jxie/4G/
index.html

As an example of the 'blistering speeds' reached by 4G experiments, NTT DoCoMo in Japan recently reported that its 'MOTO-media' project achieved a transfer rate of 100Mbps. If successfully deployed in a commercial network, this kind of speed would allow mobile operators to deliver up to 32 high definition video streams to mobile handsets. For customers, this kind of service would make it possible to download a data package equivalent of a DVD in about one minute. To reach this goal, equipment manufacturers and mobile operators like NTT DoCoMo are testing new techniques for the air-link, such as VSF-OFDM (Variable Spreading Factor-Orthogonal Frequency Division Multiplexing) and MIMO (Multi-Input, Multi-Output). MIMO is a technique that uses transmissions from multiple base stations to improve the data transfer rate for mobile terminals.[28]

### 9.4.1   Open systems, IP and 4G

One of the more radical proposals for '4G' was presented in 2002 by Sun Microsystems, in which they called for the entire network to be based on open systems solutions and an IP (Internet Protocol) network. Sun's proposal for a fourth generation network contrasts with the proprietary and patent protected CDMA system and the circuit-switched orientation of GSM networks. In the case of voice services, for example, the technology has gradually changed from analogue to digital but it has remained largely circuit-switched even when some of the features are packet-switched. Sun's vision for 4G is a departure because it would establish an *entire network* around open standards and Internet Protocols. In so doing, the network designers could eliminate much of the cost associated with Signaling System 7 (SS7). SS7 is a routing protocol that was first implemented in the public switched telephone network in the 1970s and 1980s and retains a functional role in GSM and other mobile voice networks.[29] An IP-based mobile voice network, which has been foreshadowed by the use of Wi-Fi technology to make VoIP calls, promises more diversity in value-added voice services and a tighter integration between voice and data applications.

The commitment to non-proprietary, open systems standards is also reflected in the statements released by the Fourth Generation Mobile Forum (4GMF), which proposes a definition of '4G' that emphasizes the interoperability of air-link technologies through open systems standards:

> The [4G] vision from the user perspective can be implemented by integration of ... different evolving and emerging access technologies in a common flexible and expandable platform to provide a multiplicity of possibilities for current and future services and applications to users in a single terminal. Systems of 4G mobile will mainly be characterized by a horizontal communication model, where different access technologies as cellular, cordless, WLAN type systems, short range connectivity and wired systems will be combined on a common platform to complement each other in an optimum way for different service requirements and radio environments ... [using an] 'Open Wireless Architecture'.[30]

Sun Microsystem's 4G vision also illustrates how the evolution of mobile phone networks can be characterized as a steady transition from one designed around circuit-switched voice (1G, 2G) to one that is designed entirely with packet-switched data services for both voice and data (2.5G, 3G and 4G). Although it should be possible today to communicate using VoIP (voice over IP) with 3G or even 2.5G networks, the reality is that quality of service suffers when packet-based systems suffer delay or high packet loss. For example, the VoIP provider Skype does provide IP calling to mobile phones in Germany but the reports have been of mixed quality.

Some experts argue that in order to deliver *reliable* voice quality that matches what many telephone users have come to expect, mobile operators will need to have a network capable of a minimum of 500Kbps in both directions. A number of technologies promise this kind of bandwidth, including EVDO, WiMax and 3G but there are challenges with all of them, not the least of which is maintaining such high bandwidth when a mobile phone is being used in an automobile or on a fast train. Sun Microsystem's proposal for a 4G network would represent an evolutionary leap and could spawn a wholesale transformation in the design and capabilities of future mobile voice and digital systems.

### 9.4.2  Mobile TV

Another development that could lead to a new generation of mobile data networks stems from a growing interest in **mobile TV**, which is a new service offering provided over 3G networks in North America and Europe. For instance, Vodafone in the UK has launched a partnership arrangement with broadcaster Sky in November 2005 to offer 19 mobile TV channels that include 24-hour news, sport, entertainment and documentary programmes. To encourage customers to adopt the new service, Vodafone made it available free to all 3G customers for the first few months. Early reports from the mobile operator claimed that from a customer base of 341,000, more than one million streams of mobile TV were accessed in the first two weeks of going live.[31] Mobile TV offerings have also recently been launched in North America and elsewhere in conjunction with a company called MobiTV, which supplies content and technical support to wireless service providers.[32]

If a mobile operator wants to tap into the potential of mobile TV it has a number of choices depending on whether its 3G network is based on UMTS or cdma2000 technology (for a review of these terms see Chapter 5). Perhaps the simplest method in either case is to distribute the television using the current capabilities of the 3G network. Using this method, the mobile operator converts regular television signals to fit on to the tiny screen of a mobile phone by digitizing and compressing them. It then transmits these signals using the 3G air-link – 1XRTT or 1XEVDO in the case of CDMA networks, or by W-CDMA in the case of UMTS networks.

This method is known as 'clip streaming' and it has the advantage of backwards compatibility with existing network equipment and 3G mobile phone handsets. Unfortunately it is not an optimal method for delivering mobile TV. It does not accommodate high demand because each stream is like an additional phone call and in some situations could lead to customers being dropped as a result of network congestion. Vodafone, for instance, could find its 3G network overloaded during premier sporting events when many customers are requesting clip streams in order to tune in. Clip streaming is also disadvantageous because it is limited to a relatively slow frame rate compared with the faster frame rate of 24 or 30 frames per second for cinema and television.

The problems associated with the clip streaming method might be resolved with the development of new techniques for delivering mobile TV. At least four alternative approaches are in trials or early deployment, all attempting to resolve the problem of unicasting individual streams to each customer:

- *DMB*: Digital Multimedia Broadcasting, being developed in Korea
- *ISDB-T*: Integrated Services Digital Broadcasting, being developed in Japan

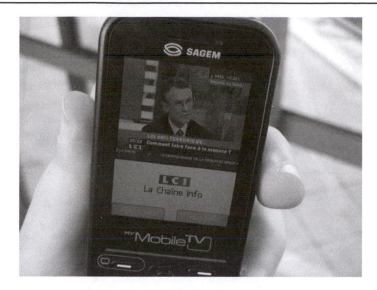

**Figure 9.2**  MobileTV

*Source*: http://www.dvb-h-online.org/Graphics/Sagem-myx8a.jpg

- *MediaFLO*: A proprietary standard, being developed by Qualcomm in the United States.
- *DVB-H*: An open standard, developed in Europe, led by Nokia.

Among these competing standards, DVB-H has received considerable attention because it is promoted by Nokia and is actively being tested in numerous cities around the world, including Madrid, Amsterdam and Sydney. DVB-H was accepted as a standard by the European Telecommunications Standards Institute (ETSI) in 2004 and is formally known as 'EN 302 304'.[33] This standard incorporates a hybrid solution, with the cellular network providing channel selection and interactivity and a digital terrestrial TV network for delivering the content. In order to address power consumption concerns, the DVB-H standard uses an innovative approach based on *time slicing*:

> Time-slicing means that the data representing a particular service is delivered to the handheld device in bursts at given intervals of time. Video and audio data (1–2Mbits), generally representing between 1–5 seconds of the content, arrives in the single burst. When the receiver is not receiving the wanted burst of data, the tuner contained in the handheld device is 'inactive' and therefore using less power. The user, however, does not notice the period of receiver activity or inactivity since the data bursts are stored in the receiver memory and played out continuously. Time-slicing could allow for up to a 95% reduction in power consumption compared to conventional [digital TV] tuners.[34]

As one might imagine, this is a complex and difficult engineering feat and presents some fundamental challenges for antenna design. The ideal antenna for the typical DVB-H frequency is much larger than a mobile phone so there is the matter of fitting it into a reasonably compact device. Furthermore this method places enormous demands on computer processing, memory and screen design in addition to the problem of managing two completely different radio interfaces. It also raises the regulatory matter of spectrum scarcity and a demand for additional frequencies in the UHF bands. In a number of countries the appearance of mobile TV will coincide with the advent of digital terrestrial TV, so industry associations such as the Digital Terrestrial Television Action Group (DigitTAG) are eager to promote the mobile phone as a new distribution channel for conventional TV broadcasters and an additional source of revenue for mobile operators.

## 9.5    Towards the u-society

In 2004 the Japanese Ministry of Internal Affairs and Communication (MIC) announced that it had adopted a new policy, one that would follow on the heels of its largely successful 'e-society' efforts. A target date of 2010 was set for the new initiative, to be called the 'u-Japan strategy', with a government-led objective of achieving a ubiquitous network society in Japan and with the secondary objective of promoting it as a model policy for the rest of the world to follow. The u-Japan concept refers directly to Mark Weiser's pioneering efforts on ubiquitous computing, and even quotes from his publications to explain that a fundamental aim of this policy initiative is the development of a 'seamless access environment for both fixed networks and wireless networks'. The policy is, of course, based on the assumption that advanced technology will soon be able to 'connect everyone and everything' into user-friendly, safe and efficient networks of people and things.[35]

Clearly there is a trend emerging here and wireless networks are at the heart of it. In the United States it is 'ubiquitous computing', in Europe it is 'ambient intelligence', and in Japan it is the 'ubiquitous network society'. In each context the vision represents what might very well be the apotheosis of mobile communications, which in some ways is quite the opposite of virtual reality. Rather than entering a computer generated world using a head mounted display, with ambient intelligence the world itself becomes a responsive environment that blurs the distinction between public and private, here and there, and now and then. To reiterate Howard Rheingold's observation, a radically new 'media sphere' could emerge before our eyes.

That might well be the case, but the primary focus of this book has been considerably more modest. It has been our intent to introduce and describe the fundamental terms and concepts of mobile communications, and to provide a glimpse into the social, economic and political influences behind the major developments in wireless technology. The book has considered electromagnetic energy as the fundamental enabler of radio communications and then later introduced the new challenges to the traditional command and control model of spectrum management. We described the early generations of mobile radiotelephony and the importance of the microelectronics revolution for making possible Martin Cooper's handheld mobile phone in 1973. In describing the impact of digital cellular networks in the 1990s, we highlighted the contribution of Nokia and Frank Nuovo in changing forever the popular perception of the mobile phone and for turning it into as much a fashion item as it is a communications device. At the same time, we explained how the mobile phone morphed into a multipurpose entertainment gadget while the industry was also stumbling toward a 3G concept that had first been formed in the pre-Internet era with the IMT-2000 initiative. We then described how Wi-Fi, wardriving and personal area networks made possible with Bluetooth devices are now drawing the world's leading industrial nations toward a fabled 'u-Society'.

Understanding technology and technological change is important not only for engineers but also for those who want to know where these developments have come from and where they might be headed. More significantly, the knowledge gained in understanding something of the technology is important for a critical engagement with social issues in a world permeated by technological change. A recent report concerned with the 'dark scenarios' of ambient intelligence makes this point quite clear: 'While the world of ambient intelligence will undoubtedly bring many benefits, trust and security should be designed into this world rather than inserted as an afterthought into an already constructed world of smart spaces'.[36]

It has been our intent with this book to provide some of the basic knowledge needed for engaging in deliberations about the design of this emerging media sphere. In this light it is perhaps most fitting to conclude with a gentle reminder from Timo Kopomaa: 'When all is said and done, it seems that mobile tele-communication is, after all, a serious business'.

## 9.6   Recommended reading

Howard Rheingold's (2002) book, *Smart Mobs: The Next Social Revolution* (Perseus) considers the future of ubiquitous computing technology and personal area networks. Chapters 4 and 8 are especially relevant to the material presented here. For technical and business perspective on PANs, Lawrence J. Harte's (2004) book, *Introduction to Bluetooth, Technology, Market, Operation, Profiles, and Services* (McGraw–Hill) is a helpful resource.

*SpyChips* (2005), by Katherine Albrecht and Liz McIntyre (Nelson Current), offers a critical perspective on the growing use of RFID technology. For more about the health effects of mobile phones on the human body, the World Health Organization International EMF Program is a good resource: http://www.who.int/peh-emf/en/index.html The US Food and Drug Administration 'Cell phone facts' website is also helpful: http://www.fda.gov/cellphones/

The Federal Communications Commission (FCC) also provides a link to an equipment identifier database that will tell you the SAR rating of most models of mobile phone: http://www.fcc.gov/cgb/sar/ For a critical perspective on the scientific work being done in this area, see the book by Dr. George Carlo and Martin Schram (2003) called, *Cell Phones: Invisible Hazards in the Wireless Age* (Avalon).

For more information about ubiquitous computing and the ambient intelligence vision there is a growing range of material. Adam Greenfield's (2006) book, *Everyware: The Dawning Age of Ubiquitous Computing* (New Riders) is one of the most recent publications on this topic. The report by the Institute for Prospective Technological Studies is perhaps the most current and complete assessment of international initiatives in this area. It is available on the Institute's website: http://swami.jrc.es/pages/index.htm A number of scholarly books have also been published in the area, including *Ambient Intelligence* (2005), edited by Werner Weber (Springer-Verlag) and *Ambient Intelligence: A Novel Paradigm* (2004), edited by Paolo Remagnino (Springer-Verlag).

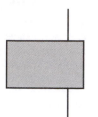

# Notes

## 1 Introduction

1 Kopomaa, T. (2000) *The City in Your Pocket: Birth of the Mobile Information Society.* Helsinki: Gaudeamus.

## 2 Radio basics

1 Guidry, M. (1995) *Violence in the Cosmos.* Department of Physics and Astronomy, University of Tennessee. Retrieved April 2005. Available at http://csep10.phys.utk.edu/guidry/violence/lightspeed.html
2 Nuechterlein, J. E. and Weiser, P. J. (2005) *Digital Crossroads: American Telecommunications Policy in the Internet Age.* Cambridge: The MIT Press.
3 Adapted from Lie, E. (2004) *Radio Spectrum Management for a Converging World* (RSM/07). Geneva: International Telecommunications Union.
4 In some cases, the function of management and licensing is divided according to different categories of spectrum users. In Canada and Australia, for example, one department handles the more technical matters related to spectrum management while a regulator is given responsibility for granting the more culturally sensitive broadcast licences that will allow certain groups or individuals to use the radio spectrum.
5 International Telecommunications Union (2005) ITU Radiocommunication Sector mission statement, available at http://www.itu.int/ITU-R/information/mission/index.html
6 International Telecommunications Union (2000) Main results of WRC-2000 (Istanbul, Turkey, 8 May–2 June 2000). Available at http://www.itu.int/ITU-R/conferences/wrc/wrc-00/results/
7 Lie, E. (2004) *Radio Spectrum Management for a Converging World* (RSM/07). Geneva: International Telecommunications Union.
8 Inter-American Telecommunication Commission (2004) Permanent Consultative Committee II: Radiocommunication including Broadcasting. Retrieved December 2004. Available at http://www.citel.oas.org/ccp2-radio.asp
9 European Radiocommunications Office (2004) ERO information. Available at http://www.ero.dk/
10 Asia Pacific Telecommunity (2005) APT Conference Preparatory Group for WRC. Available at http://www.aptsec.org/Program/APG/papg.html
11 McMillan, J. (1995) Why auction the spectrum? *Telecommunications Policy,* 19(3): 191–9.
12 Warrier, S. (1997) The Negroponte Switch, *Rediff on the Net,* 5 June. Retrieved October 2005. Available at http://www.rediff.com/computer/jun/05jhunjh.htm
13 Negroponte, N. (1997) Wireless revisited, *Wired,* 5 August. Retrieved October 2005. Available at http://www.wired.com/wired/archive/5.08/negroponte_pr.html
14 Lie, E. (2004) *Radio Spectrum Management for a Converging World* (RSM/07). Geneva: International Telecommunications Union.

## 3  Going mobile

1  The fascinating history of the early experiments in wireless can be found at Farley, T. (2004) Mobile telephone history, *Privateline.com*. Retrieved May. Available at http://www.privateline.com/PCS/history.htm

2  Farley, T. (2004) Mobile telephone history: Page 6, *Privateline.com*. Retrieved May 2005. Available at http://www.privateline.com/PCS/history6.htm

3  Agar, J. (2003) *Constant Touch: A Global History of the Mobile Phone*. Duxford: Icon Books.

4  Farley, T. (2004) Mobile telephone history: Page 6, *Privateline.com*. Retrieved May 2005. Available at http://www.privateline.com/PCS/history6.htm

5  Farley, T. (2004) Mobile telephone history: Page 7, *Privateline.com*. Retrieved May 2005. Available at http://www.privateline.com/PCS/history7.htm

6  Carpenter, D. (2005) First cell phone was a true 'brick', *ABC News*, 9 April. Retrieved 3 May 2005. Available at http://abcnews.go.com/Technology/wireStory?id=656626

7  Farley, T. (2004a) Mobile telephone history, *Privateline.com*. Retrieved May 2005. Available at http://www.privateline.com/PCS/history.htm

8  Farley, T. (2004d) Mobile telephone history: Page 9, *Privateline.com*. Retrieved May 2005. Available at http://www.privateline.com/PCS/history9.htm

9  Murray, Jr., J. B. (2001) *Wireless Nation*. Cambridge: Perseus.

10 Seybold, A. and Samples, M. (1986) *Cellular Mobile Telephone Guide*. Indianapolis: Howard W. Sams & Co.

11 Telecommunications Industry Assocation (2001) Tom Carter inducted into RCR's wireless hall of fame, *Pulse Online*, August. Retrieved May 2005. Available at http://pulse.tiaonline.org/article.cfm?id=546

12 Fransman, M. (2002) *Telecoms in the Internet Age: From Boom to Bust to … ?* Oxford: Oxford University Press.

## 4  Getting personal

1  Cutting the cord, (1999) *Economist*, 7 October 1999. Available at http://www.economist.com/surveys/displayStory.cfm?Story_id=246152

2  Myerson, G. (2001) *Heidegger, Habermas and the Mobile Phone*. Duxford: Icon Books.

3  Dornan, A. (2002) *The Essential Guide to Wireless Communications*, 2nd edn. Upper Saddle River: Prentice Hall.

4  Ibid. See also Jones Jones, R. V. (2004) *About CDMA Spread Spectrum*. Retrieved May 2005. Available at http://people.deas.harvard.edu/~jones/cscie129/nu_lectures/lecture7/hedy/lemarr.htm

5  Fransman, M. (2002) *Telecoms in the Internet Age: From Boom to Bust to … ?* Oxford: Oxford University Press.

6  Schiller, J. (2003) *Mobile Communications*, 2nd edn. London: Addison-Wesley.

7  Agar, J. (2003) *Constant Touch: A Global History of the Mobile Phone*. Duxford: Icon Books.

8  *GSM World* (2005) Live GSM networks. Available at http://www.gsmworld.com/news/statistics/networks.shtml

9  The Nokia 6340 mobile phone is a model capable of roaming on both TDMA and GSM networks. For more on GAIT see Swartz, N. (2001) Waiting for GAIT, *Wireless Review*, 1 July. Retrieved April 2005. Available at http://industryclick.com/magazine article.asp?releaseid=6735&magazinearticleid=111222&siteid=3&magazineid=9

10 *3G Americas* (2004) TDMA: Time Division Multiple Access. Retrieved May 2005. Available at http://www.uwcc.org/English/Technology%5FCenter/tdma.cfm

11 For illustration only. *Wikipedia* (2005) Figures from *Wikipedia* Largest mobile phone companies, 9 May. Retrieved 11 May 2005. Available at http://en.wikipedia.org/wiki/Largest_mobile_phone_companies#World

12 Spectral efficiency for illustration only, as quoted in Dornan, A. (2002) *The Essential Guide to Wireless Communications*, 2nd edn. Upper Saddle River: Prentice Hall, and based on a formula that divides channel bandwidth by total calls per channel, then multiplied by the number of cells per channel. Market share is quoted on the 3G

Americas website and should be regarded as an estimate only. Available at http://www.uwcc.org/English/Statistics/global_comparisons/world_subscribers_bytech.cfm

13  Samsung has introduced the first CDMA/GSM multi-mode phone, operating in CDMA at 800/1900MHz and GSM at 900/1800MHz. Verizon in the United States offers the SCH-a790 to its customers, who roam with Vodafone in GSM regions outside North America.

14  Steinbock, D. (2005) *The Mobile Revolution: The Making of Mobile Services Worldwide.* London: Kogan Page, p. 167.

15  Specter, M. (2001) The Phone Guy, *The New Yorker,* 26 November: 62–72.

16  Vertu offers two models of dual band GSM 'world' phones: the 'Signature' and the 'Ascent'. The company bills itself as 'the first luxury personal communication company specializing in handcrafted mobile phones'. (http://www.vertu.com/)

17  Steinbock, D. (2001) *The Nokia Revolution*: AMACOM.

18  For more on Frank Nuovo, see 'The Phone Guy' in the 26 November 2001 edition of *The New Yorker.* For more about Nokia's approach to human-centred design see Christian Lindholm's (2003) book *Mobile Usability: How Nokia Changed the Face of the Mobile Phone* (McGraw-Hill Ryerson).

19  Steinbock, D. (2001) *The Nokia Revolution*: AMACOM.

20  Konkka, K. (2003) Indian needs: Cultural end-user research in Mombai, in C. Lindholm, T. Keinonen and H. Kiljander (eds) *Mobile Usability: How Nokia Changed the Face of the Mobile Phone.* New York: McGraw-Hill, pp. 97–111.

21  Mahan, A (2003) Regulatory peripheries: Using prepaid to extend the network, *info,* 5(4): 37–44.

22  Privacy Rights and Prepaid Communications Services (Research Study for the Privacy Commissioner of Canada). Centre for Policy Research on Science and Technology, Simon Fraser University. (Available at http://www.sfu.ca/cprost/prepaid/) See also Gow, G. A. and Ihnat, M. (2004) Prepaid mobile phone service and the anonymous caller: Considering wireless E9-1-1 in Canada, *Surveillance & Society,* 1(4): 555–72.

23  Trosby, F. (2004) SMS, the strange duckling of GSM, *Telektronikk,* (3): 187–94.

24  Vincent, J. (2004). The social shaping of the mobile communications repertoire, *The Journal of the Communications Network* (January–March), 3: 1–5.

25  Agar, J. (2003) *Constant Touch: A Global History of the Mobile Phone.* Duxford: Icon Books.

26  Ling, R. (2004) *The Mobile Connection: The Cell Phone's Impact on Society.* Amsterdam: Elsevier.

27  Ibid.

28  see, for instance: http://www.smsglossary.com/

29  Cellular Telecommunications Industry Association (2002) CTIA demonstrates inter-carrier messaging, *CTIA Public Affairs,* 18 March. Retrieved May 2005. Available at http://www.ctia.org/news_media/press/body.cfm?record_id=1066

30  http://www.text.it/mediacentre/ (4 February 2003).

31  Canadian Wireless Telecommunications Association (2003) Canadian and U.S. Wireless Service Providers Unify North American Text Message Markets, 2 January. Retrieved May 2005. Available at http://www.cwta.ca/CWTASite/english/press releases.html

32  Cellular Telecommunications Industry Association (2003) U.S. wireless carriers to launch common short code capability. *CTIA Public Affairs,* 21 October. Retrieved May 2005. Available at http://www.ctia.org/news_media/press/body.cfm?record_id=1335

33  Baum, R. (2004) Text messages shape politics in Philippines, *Reuters,* 22 March. Available at http://www.reuters.com

34  Pfanner, E. (2004) Text-messaging the revolution, *International Herald Tribune Online,* 22 March. Available at http://www.iht.com

35  Rheingold, H. (2004) Political texting: SMS and elections, *The Feature,* 12 April. Available at http://www.thefeature.com/

36  Rushkoff, D. (2004) Rock the (wireless) vote.com, *The Feature,* 22 March. Available at http://www.thefeature.com/

37  Myerson, G. (2001) *Heidegger, Habermas and the Mobile Phone.* Duxford: Icon Books.

## 5 The multitask gadget

1 Hjelm, J. (2000) *Designing Wireless Information Services*. London: John Wiley & Sons.
2 For reading on usability issues and mobile devices see Hjelm (see Note 1) and Lindholm, C., Keinonen, T. and Kiljander, H. (eds) (2003) *Mobile Usability: How Nokia Changed the Face of the Mobile Phone*. New York: McGraw-Hill.
3 Blogger and mobile phone researcher, Joi Ito, famously incurred a bill of US$3500 during a one month trip to Europe. See *Wall Street Journal* (Eastern edition), 22 April 2004: B.4.
4 Dornan, A. (2002) *The Essential Guide to Wireless Communications*, 2nd edn. Upper Saddle River: Prentice Hall.
5 Kamada, T. (1998) Compact HTML for small information appliances, *World Wide Web Consortium (W3C)*, 9 February. Available at http://www.w3.org/TR/1998/NOTE-compactHTML-19980209/
6 King, P. and Hyland, T. (1997) Handheld device markup language specification, *W3C Note*, 9 May. Available at http://www.w3.org/TR/NOTE-Submission-HDML-spec.html
7 Ibid.
8 WAP Push (2005) *Wireless Information Network*. Available at http://www.winplc.com/solutions/wap-push.aspx
9 Nygard, M. (no date) A brief look at Java 2 Micro Edition, *Wireless Developer Network*. Available at http://www.wirelessdevnet.com/channels/java/features/j2me.html
10 For more about midlets see Midlet.org (http://midlet.org/index2.jsp) or the Open-WAP website (http://openwap.org/)
11 Orlowski, A. (2005) Smart phones boom – Symbian up, MS and Palm down, *The Register*, 26 April. Available at http://www.theregister.co.uk/2005/04/26/smartphones_q1_2005/

## 6 Let's go surfing

1 *Economist* (2001) The Internet untethered, 11 October. Retrieved June 2005. Available at http://www.economist.com/surveys/displaystory.cfm?story_id=811934
2 Chodorowicz, D. and Sciadas, G. (1998) The cellular telephone industry: Birth, evolution, and prospects, *Canadian Economic Observer*, August.
3 Commission of the European Communities (2001) *The Introduction of Third Generation Mobile Communications in the European Union: State of Play and the Way Forward* (Communication from the Commission to the Council, The European Parliament, the Economic and Social Committee and the Committee of the Regions).
4 Le Bodic, G. (2003) *Mobile Messaging: Technologies and Services*. London: John Wiley & Sons.
5 *UMTS Forum* (2003) 3G services examples. Retrieved June 2005. Available at http://www.umts-forum.org/servlet/dycon/ztumts/umts/Live/en/umts/3G_Services_example
6 3G (wCDMA, CDMA-2000, UMTS, FOMA) in Japan FAQ (2005) *Eurotechnology.com*. Available at http://www.eurotechnology.com/3G/index.html
7 Manktelow, N. (2000) One wireless viewpoint: WAP is crap, *ZDNet Australia*, 29 June. Retrieved September 2002. Available at http://zdnet.com
8 Hesseldahl, A. (2001) The winter of handset discontent, *Forbes.com*, 18 July. Retrieved May 2005. Available at http://www.forbes.com/2001/07/18/0718nokia.html
9 See, for instance, Fransman, M. (2002) *Telecoms in the Internet Age: From Boom to Bust to ... ?* London: Oxford University Press.
10 Hesseldahl, A. (2001) Disaster of the day: Globalstar, *Forbes.com*, 17 January. Retrieved May 2005. Available at http://www.forbes.com/2001/01/17/0117disaster.html
11 *Economist* (2000) The wireless gamble, 14 October. Retrieved June 2005. Available at http://www.economist.com/opinion/displayStory.cfm?Story_ID=392521
12 The examples and timeline for 3G deployment was taken from the news source *3G Today* and its June 2005 listing of 1XEV-DO and W-CDMA operators worldwide: http://www.3gtoday.com
13 King, B. (2005) Cannes demos the next fast thing, *The Register*, 16 February. Retrieved June 2005. Available at http://www.theregister.co.uk/2005/02/16/hsdpa_3g_demo/

## 7  La guerre du sans fil

1  Rheingold, H. (2002) *Smart Mobs: The Next Social Revolution*. Cambridge: Perseus.
2  The French expression is borrowed from a presentation by Eric Fleury of research group LORIA. See: http://www.loria.fr/LORIA/LORIATECH-2.old/CONTENU/AGENDA/20010301/EXPOSES/E.FLEURY.pdf
3  IEEE 802.11 does provide a soft hand-off feature like CDMA, but the successful movement from zone to zone is not necessarily assured like it is with a wide area cellular network.
4  The Wi-Fi Alliance website can be found at: http://www.wi-fi.org/OpenSection/index.asp
5  Wi-Fi Alliance (2005) *Certification Programs*. Available at http://www.wi-fi.org/OpenSection/certification_programs.asp?TID=2
6  Intel Corp. (2003) Marriott And Intel Promote Wireless High-Speed Internet Access at 400 Hotels, 27 February Press Release. Available at http://www.intel.com/pressroom/archive/releases/20030227corp_a.htm
7  Dornan, A. (2002) *The Essential Guide to Wireless Communications*, 2nd edn, p. 259. Upper Saddle River: Prentice Hall.
8  For more about network effects and positive feedback in the information and communications industry see: Shapiro, C. and Varian, H. (1998) *Information Rules: A Strategic Guide to the Network Economy*. Harvard Business School Press.
9  Abbate, J. (1999) *Inventing the Internet*. Cambridge: The MIT Press.
10  For more about the e2e principle and computing culture, see Lessig, L. (2002) *The Future of Ideas*. New York: Vintage.
11  See the following for a discussion of 'dominant designs' and emerging technologies: Abernathy, W. J. and Utterback, J. M. (1978) Patterns of Industrial Innovation, *Technology Review*, June–July: 40–7.
12  *JiWire* (2005) Wi-Fi Hotspot Finder, Product Reviews, Industry News. Available at http://www.jiwire.com/
13  This definition of 'freenet' has changed slightly in the most recent version of the Freenetworks.org website but the core meaning remains the same. The quotation was from an earlier version of the website: *Freenetworks.org* (2003) What is a freenet? Retrieved April 2003. Available at http://www.freenetworks.org/
14  MIT's 'roofnet' project is an example of mesh networking for community Wi-Fi access: http://pdos.csail.mit.edu/roofnet/doku.php
15  A pedestrian version of wardriving emerged in 2003, called '**warchalking**'. Warchalking is based on a practice developed by Hobos during the Great Depression of the 1930s, where they would use chalk marks on the sides of buildings to indicate safe places to stay or to get food or water. Although much media attention focused on the practice, it is probably safe to say that there was more talk about warchalking than there was actual practice. Given the nature of wireless networks, it is much easier to maintain an online database of open networks – or simply scan for them using software or even a device dedicated to that task – than it is to look for chalk marks.
16  ISDN: Integrated Services Digital Network 'is a type of circuit switched telephone network system, designed to allow digital (as opposed to analog) transmission of voice and data over ordinary telephone copper wires, resulting in better quality and higher speeds, than available with analog systems' (Wikipedia). At one point, prior to the Internet and TCP/IP assuming widespread popularity it was regarded as the next generation of data communications. IMT-2000 and GSM were both established with the intent of being interoperable with the ISDN model.


## 8  Bandwidth bonanza

1  See, for example, Lessig, L. (2002) *The Future of Ideas*. New York: Vintage.
2  Hardin, G. (1968) The tragedy of the commons, *Science*, 13 December. Available at http://www.garretthardinsociety.org/articles/art_tragedy_of_the_commons.html
3  For a more recent perspective see Coase, R. (1998) Comment on Thomas W. Hazlett,

Assigning Property Rights to Radio Spectrum Users: Why Did FCC License Auctions Take 67 Years? *Journal of Law and Economics*, 41, 577–80.

4   Hazlett, T. (2001) The wireless craze, the unlimited bandwidth myth, the spectrum auction faux pas, and the Punchline to Ronald Coase's 'big joke': An essay on airwave allocation policy, *AEI Brookings Joint Center*, January. Available at http://www.aei.brookings.org/publications/index.php?tab=author&authorid=7

5   Nuechterlein, J.E. and Weiser, P.J. (2005) *Digital Crossroads: American Telecommunications Policy in the Internet Age*. Cambridge: The MIT Press.

6   Ibid.

7   Ofcom (2004) Spectrum Framework Review, 23 November. Retrieved June 2005. Available at http://www.ofcom.org.uk/consult/condocs/sfr/sfr2/?a=87101

8   Woolley, S. (2002) Dead air, *Forbes*, 25 November. Retrieved April 2003. Available at http://www.forbes.com/forbes/2002/1125/138_print.html

9   Kwerel, E. and Williams, J. (2002) A proposal for a rapid transition to market allocation of spectrum: OPP Working Paper Series (No. 38), *Federal Communications Commission, Office of Policy and Planning*, November. Available at http://hraunfoss.fcc.gov/edocs_public/attachmatch/DOC-228552A1.pdf

10  The end to end principle is discussed in Rheingold's book, *Smart Mobs* on page 52; Reed's career is discussed on page 58.

11  Reed, D. (2002) Comments for FCC spectrum policy task force on spectrum policy, 8 July. Available at http://www.reed.com/

12  Staple, G. and Werbach, K. (2004) The end of spectrum scarcity, *IEEE Spectrum Online*, March. Available at http://www.spectrum.ieee.org/WEBONLY/public feature/mar04/0304scar.html

13  For more technical background refer to Dornan, A. (2002) *The Essential Guide to Wireless Communications Applications*, pp. 67–75. Upper Saddle River: Prentice Hall.

14  Dornan, A. (2002) *The Essential Guide to Wireless Communications*, 2nd edn. Upper Saddle River: Prentice Hall.

15  Staple, G. and Werbach, K. (2004) The end of spectrum scarcity, *IEEE Spectrum Online*, March. Available at http://www.spectrum.ieee.org/WEBONLY/publicfeature/mar04/0304scar.html

16  Benkler, Y. and Lessig, L. (1998) Net gains, *The New Republic*, 14 December. Available at http://www.thadk.net/ideas/lessigcopyright.html

17  Ibid.

18  It is important to note, however, that even in licence-exempt bands governments will issue and oversee equipment certification requirements to ensure that consumer products operate within required guidelines for power output and other radio emission limits.

19  Werbach, K. (2002) Open spectrum: The new wireless paradigm, *New America Foundation, Spectrum Policy Program*, October. Available at http://werbach.com/docs/new_wireless_paradigm.htm

20  Faulhaber, G. R. and Farber, D. J. (2002) Comments of Gerald R. Faulhaber and David J. Farber before the FCC Spectrum Policy Task Force, *FCC Spectrum Policy Task Force*, 18 July. Retrieved June 2005. Available at http://gullfoss2.fcc.gov/prod/ecfs/retrieve. cgi?native_or_pdf=pdf&id_document=6513282647

21  Ibid.

## 9   Into thin air

1   Weiser, M. (1991) The computer for the 21st century, *Scientific American*, September: 94–110.

2   Philips Research (2004) *PHENOM: Perceptive Home Environments*. Retrieved November 2005. Available at http://www.research.philips.com/technologies/syst_softw/phenom/index.html

3   For example, 'Urban Tapestries' is an experimental project in London that is using wireless technology 'to enable people to become authors of the environment around them'. See: http://urbantapestries.net/

4   Infrared Data Association (2004) What is infrared and Where is it used? Available at
    http://www.irda.org/
5   Infrared technologies operate in the terahertz (THz) to petahertz (PHz) frequency
    bands. At these extremely high frequencies engineers usually refer to wavelength
    instead of frequency. Several bands of infrared and optical communications are com-
    mon, including for example, 'O-band' 1260–1360 nanometres (nm); 'E-band' 1360–
    1460 nm; and 'S-band' 1460–1530 nm.
6   Dornan, A. (2002) *The Essential Guide to Wireless Communications*, 2nd edn, p. 272.
    Upper Saddle River: Prentice Hall.
7   Dornan, A. (2002) *The Essential Guide to Wireless Communications*, 2nd edn, p. 273.
    Upper Saddle River: Prentice Hall.
8   See, for instance, http://www.bluetooth.com/news/index.asp?A=2&PID=620
9   See, for instance, Dodgeball.com: Mobile social software (2005) Retrieved November
    2005. Available at http://www.dodgeball.com/
10  The nightclub's website describes the RFID-based service: 'At Baja Beach Club we
    present you a special zone designed for our VIP visitors . . . We are the first club of the
    world who offers you the veri-chip. By using an integrated chip, our VIPS always can
    identify themselves or pay for drinks without showing any identification'. The website
    also includes an interview with the proprietor about the Veri-chip system (in Spanish
    only). Available at http://www.verichipcorp.com/
11  http://www.bajabeach.es/
12  Albrecht, K. (2002) RFID: Tracking everything, everywhere. Consumers Against
    Supermarket Privacy Invasion and Numbering (CASPIAN). Available at http://
    www.nocards.org/AutoID/overview.shtml
13  Information Society Technologies Advisory Group (2001) *Scenarios for Ambient Intel-
    ligence 2010*, February. European Commission Community Research. Available as
    PDF: http://www.cordis.lu/ist/istag-reports.htm
14  Rheingold, H. (2002) *Smart Mobs: The Next Social Revolution*, p. 85. Cambridge:
    Perseus.
15  Rheingold, H. (2002) *Smart Mobs: The Next Social Revolution*, p. 86. Cambridge:
    Perseus.
16  Gow, G. A. and Ihnat, M. (2004) Prepaid Mobile Phone Service and the Anonymous
    Caller: Considering Wireless E9-1-1 in Canada, *Surveillance & Society*, 1(4): 555–72.
17  White, J. C. (2003) *People, Not Places: A Policy Framework for Analyzing Location Privacy
    Issues* (Masters Memo Prepared for the Electronic Privacy Information Center). Terry
    Sanford Institute of Public Policy, Duke University.
18  Rao, B. and Minakakis, L. (2003) Evolution of Mobile Location-based Services,
    *Communications of the ACM*, 46(12): 61–5.
19  Strayer, D., Drews, F., Albert, R. et al. (2002) Does cell phone conversation impair
    driving performance? US National Safety Council, 13 March. Retrieved September
    2005. Available at http://www.nsc.org/library/shelf/inincell.htm
20  *Textually.org* (2005) Text-messaging blamed for fatal road accident, 28 November.
    Retrieved November 2005. Available at http://www.textually.org/textually/archives/
    2005/11/010762.htm
21  Greenpeace (2005) Looming e-waste problems for Thailand and Philippines, 28
    September. Available at http://www.greenpeace.org/seasia/en/press/releases/toxic
    tech_sea
22  Krewski, D., Byus, C. V., Glickman, B. W. et al. (2004) Recent advances in research
    on radiofrequency fields and health: 2001–2003. The Royal Society of Canada.
    Available at http://www.rsc.ca/index.php?page=expert_panels_rf&lang_id=1&page_
    id=120
23  Terdiman, D. (2005) Putting flesh on phones, *Wired*, 8 April. Available at http://
    www.wired.com/news/wireless/0,1382,67165,00.html
24  Cellular Telecommunications Industry Association (2005) Wireless carriers announce
    wireless content guidelines, 8 November. Available at http://www.ctia.org/news_-
    media/press/body.cfm?record_id=1565
25  *The Register* (2004) Mobile porn is a 'time bomb', 10 June. Retrieved November 2005.
    Available at http://www.theregister.co.uk/2004/06/10/mobile_adult_content

26  Irish Cellular Industry Association (2005) *A Parent's Guide to Mobile Phones*. Available at http://www.icia.ie

27  Georgia Institute of Technology (2003) Mobility management in 4G wireless systems. Broadband and Wireless Networking Laboratory. Available at http://users.ece.gatech. edu/~jxie/4G/index.html

28  Knight, W. (2005) 4G prototypes reach blistering speeds, *New Scientist*, 2 September. Retrieved November 2005. Available at http://www.newscientist.com/article. ns?id=dn7943

29  For a helpful tutorial on SS7, see: International Engineering Consortium (2005) Signaling System 7 (SS7). Available at http://www.iec.org/online/tutorials/ss7/

30  Lu, W. (2005) 2006 4GMF Hong Kong Conference, 4–6 December. Retrieved December 2005. Available at http://www.delson.org/4g_hongkong/index.htm

31  *MobileTV News* (2005) Vodafone releases first mobile TV figures, 17 November. Retrieved November 2005. Available at http://www.mobiletv-news.com/content/ view/96/2/

32  MobiTV: Live Television. Anywhere. Anytime (2005) Retrieved November 2005. Available at http://www.mobitv.com/index.html

33  DVB-H: Global Mobile TV (2005) Retrieved November 2005. Available at http:// www.dvb-h-online.org/

34  Digital Terrestrial Television Action Group (DigiTAG) (2005) *Television on a Handheld Receiver: Broadcasting with DVB-H*, p. 14. Retrieved November 2005. Available at http://www.dvb-h-online.org/PDF/DigiTAG-DVB-H-Handbook.pdf

35  Japan Ministry of Internal Affairs and Communications (2005) u-Japan policy: Working toward realizing the ubiquitous network society by 2010. Retrieved December 2005. Available at http://www.soumu.go.jp/menu_02/ict/u-japan_en/ index2.html#

36  Wright, D., Vildjiounaite, E., Maghiros, I. et al. (2005) Safeguards in a World of Ambient Intelligence (SWAMI) – The brave new world of ambient intelligence: A state-of-the-art review, July: 14. European Commission Joint Research Centre – Institute for Prospective Technological Studies. Retrieved December 2005. Available at http://swami.jrc.es/

# Glossary

**1XEV-DO** 1XEvolution Data Optimized. Following 1XRTT, the next upgrade is to 1XEV-DO, recognized by the Telecommunications Industry Association as IS-856 and also referred to as the cdma2000 3G standard. 1XEV-DO (DO for packet data only).

**1XRTT** 1 eXtreme Radio Transmission Technology. The CDMA-based version of GPRS.

**3G** Third generation. An industry term used to describe the next generation of wireless applications beyond personal communications services. It represents a move from circuit-switched communications (where a device user dials into a network) to broadband, high-speed, packet-based wireless networks. 3G networks are able to transmit wireless data at 144Kbps at mobile user speeds, 384Kbps at pedestrian user speeds and 2Mbps in fixed locations.

**3GPP** See Third Generation Partnership Program.

**3GPP2** 3rd Generation Partnership Project for IS-41 (North American core network technology) and radio access via UTRA or cdma2000.

**Ad-hoc mode** A wireless network where devices communicate directly with each other without the need for a central infrastructure.

**Air-link** A cellular network can be described in three segments. The first segment is called the air-link, which refers to the radio transmissions that link the mobile phone to the base station.

**APT** Asia-Pacific Telecommunity (ITU Region 3).

**ARDIS** A wireless two-way slow speed data network jointly owned and operated by Motorola and IBM.

**Backhaul** In contingency networking, an alternative connection that is routed via a diversified path, e.g., an alternative frequency, satellite facility, cable, trunk or timeslot.

**Band plan** An allocation is an entry in the Table of Frequency Allocations of a service or services for use of a specific frequency band within a country.

**Band-clearing** The release of a licensed block of frequencies that allows a licence to be reissued.

**Bandwidth piracy** Intentional use of network bandwidth without authorization from the owner.

**Base-station controller (BSC)** A device and software associated with a base station that permits it to register mobile phones in the cell, assign control and traffic channels, perform hand-off and process call setup and termination.

**Block** Assignment of contiguous channels to form a block, which reduces the occurrence of adjacent channel interaction.

**Bluetooth** An open specification for short-range wireless personal area networking to connect devices within a radio bubble rather than over cable or infrared systems. The standard communicates over short-range, low power signals in the 2.4GHz ISM band.

**CDMA (Code Division Multiple Access).** A spread spectrum air interface technology used in some digital cellular, personal communications services and other wireless networks (CHIN, http://www.chin.gc.ca/English/Digital_Content/Tip_Sheets/ Wireless/ glossary.html).

**CDMA Development Group (CDG)** The consortium of companies supporting the 2G cdmaOne and 3G cdma2000 mobile network standards. Its equivalent for GSM is the GSM Association.

**cdma2000** Brand name for North American CDMA air interface standard aimed at Third Generation mobile requirements (see also 3G and IMT-2000). A rival to UMTS, cdma2000 includes a number of steps from cdmaOne to a full IMT-2000 3G specification. They include evolved narrowband CDMA schemes – 1X for higher capacity voice and data, 1xEV-DO (DO for packet data only) is asymmetric – claiming four times the speed for downlink vs. uplink and speeds of 300–700Kbps for mobile users, and as high as 2.4 Mbps for fixed users. Eventually cdma2000 will be a hybrid system with a wideband option in the uplink and multiple narrowband CDMA channels in the downlink. See also its ancestor cdmaOne and its industry body, CDG.

**CDPD (Cellular Digital Packet Data)** A packet-radio protocol that uses 30kHz AMPS radio channels to transmit packets of data on idle AMPS FDMA channels. Standardized by TIA/EIA/IS-732.

**Cellular network design** Conceived in Bell Labs in the late 1940s. Cellular networks are based on two principles: small radio coverage zones known as 'cells' and frequency re-use. Instead of placing a single high powered transceiver at the centre of a city to provide service for everyone, the cellular network design is based on many low powered transceivers that serve geographically small areas usually about 20 km in diameter and often much smaller. Because each cell provides coverage for a small area, the frequencies used for radio channels can be re-used in other cells that are located far enough away to prevent interference. In effect, this lets the network operator recycle a small number of frequencies and therefore provide service to more customers. In a large city there may be hundreds of cells that make up the network.

**CEPT** European Conference of Postal and Telecommunications Administrations.

**Circuit-switched** A networking method that establishes a dedicated channel between parties for the duration of a call.

**CITEL** Inter-American Telecommunication Commission is the international organization responsible for spectrum management within ITU Region 1, and operates under the auspices of the Organization of American States.

**Client/server model** A network system that has a central server with clients that access its resources (INTEL, http://support.intel.com/support/wireless/wlan/pro2200bg/userguide 81/glossary.htm).

**Compact HTML (C-HTML)** A derivative of HTML for mobile devices. Used in the iMode system (FBMC, http://homepages.nildram.co.uk/~jidlaw/pages/glossary/html#W).

**Comparative review** See 'Spectrum auction'.

**Compressional wave** In acoustics, a wave is an elastic medium which causes an element of the medium to change its volume without undergoing rotation (NASA).

**DataTAC** Motorola packet radio technology available in both private and public forms (FBMC, http://homepages.nildram.co.uk/~jidlaw/pages/glossary/html#W).

**Demodulation** The recovery, from a modulated carrier, of a signal having substantially the same characteristics as the original modulating signal (ATIS, http://www.atis.org/tg2k).

**Direct radio network** A network in which two or more radio transceivers are linked without the need for any intervening infrastructure. The Family Radio Service (FRS) two-way radio or Citizen Band (CB), are popular examples of this type of network design. The range of direct radio networks is often very small and limited by the output power of the radio transceivers. In some direct link radio networks a repeater may be used to extend its range across a wider geographical area.

**Direct Sequence Spread Spectrum (DSSS or DS-CDMA)** One of two types of spread spectrum radio, the other being frequency hopping spread spectrum. DSSS is a transmission technology used in LAWN transmissions where a data signal at the sending station is combined with a higher data rate bit sequence or chipping code that divides the user data according to a spreading ratio. The chipping code is a redundant bit pattern for each bit that is transmitted, which increases the signal's resistance to interference. If one or more bits in the pattern are damaged during transmission, the original data can be recovered due to the redundancy of the transmission. (Webopedia, http://webopedia.com/TERM/s/scatternet.html).

**Downlink** The transmission path from the base station down to the mobile station (cellglide, www.cellglide.com/glossaryb.5html).

**EDGE** Enhanced Data-rates for Global Evolution (formerly GSM Evolution). Use of new modulation schemes to increase data rates within the existing RF bandwidth for GSM. EDGE supports three bits per symbol. EDGE is also part of the evolution of US TDMA IS-136 standard networks towards UMTS and some US networks have already deployed it. As GPRS is regarded as '2.5 generation', EDGE can be '2.75 generation'. EDGE supports both more and better quality voice and faster GPRS, EGPRS. The RAN (radio access network) for EDGE is standardized by the GERAN group of 3GPP (FBMC, http://homepages.nildram.co.uk/~jidlaw/pages/glossary/html#W).

**Enhanced Messaging Service (EMS)** An extension of GSM SMS to support audio/music, simple graphics and pictures. Uses the SMS UDH (user data header) and SMS concatenation. EMS is a standardized way of delivering the logo and ring-tone download capabilities long supported by Nokia (the Nokia proprietary technology is called Smart Messaging) (FBMC, http://homepages.nildram.co.uk/~jidlaw/pages/glossary/html#W).

**ERO** European Radiocommunications Office.

**First come first served (FCFS)** Equivalent to FIFO (first in, first out): A policy that items are processed in order of arrival (NIST, www.nist.gov/clads/HTML/firstinfrstt.html).

**Fixed–mobile convergence** The removal of distinctions between fixed and wireless telecommunication networks that create seamless services using a combination of fixed broadband and local access wireless technologies (bitpipe, http://www.bitpipe.com/tlist)/Infrared-Data-Communications.html).

**FPLMTS** Future Public Land Mobile Telecommunications Systems. Now called IMT-2000 (FBMC, http://homepages.nildram.co.uk/~jidlaw/pages/glossary/html#W).

**Frequency** The number of cycles of a periodic motion in a unit of time. Period phenomena include sound, light, oscillating masses on springs and pendula. The SI unit of frequency is called hertz (Hz). One hertz corresponds to one cycle (or full oscillation) per second (About Physics, http://physics.about.com/cs/acoustics/g/frequency.htm).

**Frequency bands** A band of adjacent radio frequencies (e.g. assigned for transmitting radio or television signals). (Princeton)
Radio frequency band – a specified range of frequencies of electromagnetic waves (AMS, http://amsglossary.allenpress.com/glossary).

**Frequency Division Duplexing (FDD)** Separating transmit and receive (or uplink and downlink in the mobile context) channels by allocating different parts of the radio spectrum to them (FBMC, http://homepages.nildram.co.uk/~jidlaw/pages/glossary/html#W).

**Frequency hopping (FH-CDMA)** A simple form of spread spectrum where the transmitted signal is changed periodically in an pseudo-random pattern across a wide range of frequencies in the radio spectrum. One of the advantages of this is to produce frequency diversity. Where the baseband signal is modulated directly onto the carrier then this is direct sequence spread spectrum, as used in CDMA (code division multiple access) (FMBC, http://homepages.nildram.co.uk/~jidlaw/pages/glossary/html#W).

**Frequency sharing (frequency re-use)** The assignment to use the same radio frequency by two or more stations that are separated geographically or that use the frequency at different times (ATIS, http://www.atis.org/tg2k).

**Full duplex mode** In a communications system, the ability to simultaneously transmit and receive. A communications channel which transmits data in both directions at once (UNO, www.alt.uno.edu/glossary.html).

**Gateway** A device used to interconnect networks, subnets or other network devices. Gateways allow networks using different communications protocols to transfer information. Equivalent to a router, a gateway is an intelligent device used to connect two or more networks at the upper protocol layers of the Open Systems Interconnection (OSI) reference model (INTEL, http://support.intel.com/support/wireless/wlan/pro2200bg/userguide81/glossary.htm).

**GMSC** Gateway mobile switching centre. Provides an edge function within a PLMN (Public Land Mobile Network). It terminates the PSTN (Public Switched Telephone Network) signalling and traffic formats and converts it to protocols employed in mobile networks. For mobile terminated calls, it interacts with the HLR (Home Location Register) (mpirical, http://www.impirical.com/companion.html).

**GPRS** General Packet Radio Service. A standard for wireless communications that runs at speeds up to 115Kbps. GPRS, which supports a wide range of bandwidths, is an efficient use of limited bandwidth and is particularly suited for sending and receiving small bursts of data, such as email and web browsing, as well as large volumes of data (CHIN, http://www.chin.gc.ca/English/Digital_Content/Tip_Sheets/ Wireless/glossary.html).

**GSM** Global System for Mobile Communications. The mobile phone platform used in Europe and much of the rest of the world, though it is not yet mainstream in North America. Dual band phones are capable of operating on other bandwidths abroad (CHIN, http://www.chin.gc.ca/English/Digital_Content/Tip_Sheets/Wireless/glossary. html).

**Half duplex mode** A communications channel, which transmits data in either direction, but in only one direction at a time (UNO, www.alt.uno.edu/glossary.html).

**Handheld Device Markup Language (HDML)** Predecessor of WML, devised by Unwired Planet (which later became phone.com and then Openwave) (FBMC, http://homepages.nildram.co.uk/~jidlaw/pages/glossary/html#W).

**Hand-off** The process by which the Mobile Telephone Switching Office (MTSO) passes a wireless phone conversation from one radio frequency in one cell to another radio frequency in another cell. It is performed quickly enough that callers don't notice (discretewireless, http://discretewireless.com/products/glossary/glossary.asp).

**Hertz** The SI unit of frequency, equal to one cycle per second. Note: a periodic phenomenon that has a period of one second has a frequency of one hertz. 2. A unit of frequency, which is equivalent to one cycle per second (ATIS, http://www.atis.org/tg2k).

**High Speed Circuit Switched Data (HSCSD)** This service is based on a simple upgrade to GSM networks that gives customers up to four 14.4Kbps circuits at the same time, increasing the potential bandwidth to something like a 56K modem. In a real sense, HSCSD is like tying together two or more phone lines to increase the capacity for data transmission.

**Home Location Registry (HLR)** The main database of permanent subscriber information for a mobile network. The HLR is an integral component of code division multiple access (CDMA), time division multiple access (TDMA), and Global System for Mobile communications (GSM) networks (INTEL, http://support.intel.com/support/wireless/wlan/pro2200bg/userguide81/glossary.htm).

**Horizontal domain** In the horizontal domain, the system was envisioned as providing global roaming across terrestrial wide area cellular networks. To some extent, this objective has been achieved with GSM, as it is now possible to roam easily around much of the world using a tri-band GSM handset.

**Hotspot** An area in which an access point provides public wireless broadband network services to mobile users through a WLAN. Hotspots are often located in heavily populated places such as airports, hotels, coffee shops, libraries and convention centres (CHIN, http://www.chin.gc.ca/English/Digital_Content/Tip_Sheets/Wireless/glossary. html).

**IEEE 802.11** The IEEE standard for Wireless Local Area Networks (WLAN). It uses three different standards: 802.11a, 802.11b and 802.11g (CHIN, http://www.chin.gc.ca/English/Digital_Content/Tip_Sheets/Wireless/glossary.html).

**IMT-2000** International Mobile Telecommunications 2000. ITU umbrella requirement definition covering the various Third Generation Mobile Standards. See UMTS, 3GPP, 3GPP2 and cdma2000 (FBMC, http://homepages.nildram.co.uk/~jidlaw/pages/glossary/html#W).

**IMTS** Improved Mobile Telephone Service. Cellular telephone predecessor that uses a single central transmitter and receiver to service a region. A two-way mobile phone system that generally uses a single high-power transmitter to serve a given area and is automatically interconnected with a land line telephone system (mobileinfo, www.mobileinfo.com/Glossary/I_L.htm).

**Infrared device** An optical device that is limited to line of site data communication because it uses visible light or infrared beams for data transmission (bitpipe, http://

www.bitpipe.com/tlist)/Infrared-Data-Communications.html)
Infrared is 'The region of the electromagnetic spectrum bounded by the long-wave-length extreme of the visible spectrum and the shortest microwaves' (ATIS, http://www.atis.org/tg2k).

**Infrastructure mode**  A wireless network that requires all traffic to pass through a central wireless access point, which communicates by radio to the wireless cards in devices such as laptop computers or PDAs.

**Integrated circuit**  A microelectronic computer circuit incorporated into a chip or semiconductor; a whole system rather than a single component (Princeton, www.cogsci.princeton.edu/cgi-bin/webwn2.l).

**International Telecommunications Union (ITU)**  The International Tele-communications Union (ITU), under the auspices of the United Nations (UN) system headquartered in Geneva, is where the worldwide coordination of spectrum and the creation of radio regulations begins. The ITU is one of the oldest international orga-nizations, founded in 1865 by 20 European states initially to coordinate telegraph communications across national borders.

**LAN**  Local Area Network. A network of interconnected workstations sharing the resources of a single processor or server, typically within the area of an office building or other single location (CHIN, http://www.chin.gc.ca/English/Digital_Content/Tip_Sheets/Wireless/glossary.html).
A LAN is a group of computers and other devices connected by a communications link, allowing the devices to interact on the shared network (INTEL, http://support.intel.com/support/wireless/wlan/pro2200bg/userguide81/glossary.htm).

**Licence exempt status**  Members of the public can purchase and operate radio equipment that operates in these bands without applying to Industry Canada for an operator licence.

**Lottery**  A random selection process used to assign spectrum licences.

**Metropolitan Area Network (MAN)**  Covering larger areas than a LAN but less than a WAN (FBMC, http://homepages.nildram.co.uk/~jidlaw/pages/glossary/html#W).

**MMS**  Multimedia Messaging Service. Allows for non-real-time transmission of various kinds of multimedia contents, such as images, audio and video (CHIN, http://www.chin.gc.ca/English/Digital_Content/Tip_Sheets/Wireless/glossary.html).

**Mobile switching centre (MSC)**  In an automatic cellular mobile system, the interface between the radio system and the public-switched telephone network. The MSC per-forms all signalling functions that are necessary to establish calls to and from mobile stations (ATIS, http://www.atis.org/tg2k).

**Mobile Telephone Systems (MTS)**  Some of the earliest true mobile radiotelephone systems appeared in the United States just after World War Two in 1946. These services did provide interconnection with the public switched telephone network, thereby enabling telephone calls to be made from mobile radio (usually mounted in an auto-mobile). These systems were based on simple broadcast-type network design, with a large powerful antenna that provided blanket coverage across a wide area, usually an entire city.

**Mobile TV**  A combination of a television and a wireless telephone, which uses Digital Video Broadcast Handheld (DVB-H) technology to transmit multimedia.

**Mobitex**  Motorola packet radio technology available in both private and public forms (FBMC, http://homepages.nildram.co.uk/~jidlaw/pages/glossary/html#W).

**Modulation**  The process, or result of the process, of varying a characteristic of a carrier, in accordance with an information bearing signal (ATIS, http://www.atis.org/tg2k).

**Multiplexing**  Combining signals stemming from many sources into a single commu-nications path (UNO, www.alt.uno.edu/glossary.html).

**Packet-switching(-ed)**  When a packet is sent from one device to another by means of one or more intermediate device, the packet is received at each intermediate device in its entirety, stored there until the required output line is free, and then forwarded. Also known as a store and forward network (INTEL, http://support.intel.com/support/wireless/wlan/pro2200bg/userguide81/glossary.htm).

**PAN**  Personal area network. A networking scheme that enables computing devices such as PCs, laptop computers, handheld personal computers, printers and personal digital assistants (PDAs) to communicate with each other over short distances either with or without wires (INTEL, http://support.intel.com/support/wireless/wlan/pro2200bg/userguide81/glossary.htm).

A micronetwork that enables computing devices to communicate over short distances and is usually wireless. It usually provides connectivity for small devices that can be carried on the person (Bluetooth, http://www.bluetooth.org).

**Piconet** A network of devices that is formed when at least two devices connect in an ad-hoc manner using Bluetooth technology. While the devices are connected one device will control all of the others (Bluetooth, http://www.bluetooth.org).

**Point of interconnection** The third segment of a cellular network is known as the point of interconnection, which links the gateway mobile switching centre (GMSC) to the Public Switched Telephone Network (PSTN). The third segment is necessary to enable a mobile phone customer to connect with other customers operating on other networks, such as a landline telephone.

**Public switched telephone network (PSTN)** A domestic telecommunications network usually accessed by telephones, key telephone systems, private branch exchange trunks and data arrangements. Completion of the circuit between the call originator and call receiver in a PSTN requires network signalling in the form of dial pulses or multi-frequency tones (ATIS, http://www.atis.org/tg2k).

**Radio authorization** The exclusive right to operate on a specific frequency in a geographic area and under specified technical conditions.

**Radio bubble** The access range of a wireless access point, which creates a bubble of connectivity extending several metres or less. A device within the radio bubble can connect to the network.

**Radio channel** In wireless, a designated radio frequency available for use by the transmitter and receiver (audiotechnica, www.audiotechnica/com/glossary).

**Radio licence** Permits operation of specific type of radio equipment conforming to a set of standards and to operate within a specific geographic area.

**Radio spectrum** The complete range of frequencies or wave lengths of electromagnetic waves, specifically those used in radio and television (NASA, http://roland.lerc.nasa.gov/~dglover/dictionary//content.html).

**Scatternets** Two or more Bluetooth piconets that share at least one common device. The shared device communicates with both networks by swapping between frequency sequences (Bluetooth, http://www.bluetooth.org; Webopedia, http://webopedia. com/TERM /s/scatternet.html).

**Simple SMS messages** Limited to 160 bytes, which is roughly equivalent to 160 characters. Simple SMS can be used to not only send short text messages but also ring tones, advertising and SIM-card updates from the mobile operator.

**Simplex mode** Unidirectional; refers to a channel with one-way data transmission (UNO, www.alt.uno.edu/glossary.html)

**Single site radio networks** Networks in which two or more radio devices communicate with one fixed location transmitter and/or receiver. The fixed location transceiver might serve as a gateway between the radio devices and another network such as the public switched telephone network. Some radio paging systems use a single site radio network design, and the MTS radiotelephone systems (still available in certain parts of the United States and Canada) are based on a single site network design.

**SMS** Short Message Service. An integrated paging service which allows GSM users to send and receive text messages on their phones (CHIN, http://www.chin.gc.ca/English/Digital_Content/Tip_Sheets/Wireless/glossary.html).

**Spectral efficiency** How much value a wireless system can draw from a specific amount of bandwidth.

**Spectrum auction (or a comparative review)** A spectrum release plan based on a competitive process used where demand exceeds the available spectrum.

**Spectrum cap** A limit to the allocated spectrum designated for a specific service (MOBILEDIA, www.mobiledia.com/glossary)

The spectrum cap restricts the amount of bandwidth that any single operator is permitted to acquire or hold at any time. Since its first appearance, the spectrum cap has been modified to allow operators to expand their wireless networks but within a 'level playing field' intended to keep the marketplace competitive.

**Spectrum licence** Permits operation within a designated portion of the radio spectrum for a specific geographic area, with far less emphasis on the specific type of radio apparatus being used.

**Spectrum management** The international regulatory process of allocating specific frequency bands for specific uses and users. [UNOLS].

A spectrum is made up of the range of electromagnetic radio frequencies used in the transmission of radio, data, and video. [FCC].

The ITU formally recognizes 12 bands from 30Hz to 3000GHz. New bands from 3THz to 3000THz, are under active consideration for recognition (ATIS, http://www.atis.org/tg2k).

**spectrum scarcity** Radio spectrum is a natural resource that is finite when being used, but infinitely renewable over the course of time. It is possible to run out of usable frequencies in the spectrum because of congestion and interference from many users making demands for spectrum.

**Store and forward** The ability to transmit a message to an intermediate relay point and store it temporarily when the receiving device is unavailable (Discretewireless, http://discretewireless.com/products/glossary/glossary.asp).

**TDMA (Time Division Multiple Access)** A technique for multiplexing multiple users onto a single channel on a single carrier by splitting the carrier into timeslots and allocating these on an as needed basis (cellglide, www.cellglide.com/glossaryb.5html).

**Third Generation Partnership Program (3GPP)** International Mobile Telecommunications 2000. ITU umbrella requirement definition covering the various third generation mobile standards. See UMTS, 3GPP, 3GPP2 and cdma2000.

**Time Division Duplexing (TDD)** A technique in which a network, and the mobiles it supports, communicate by alternating transmit and receive in the same radio channel. TDD allows for unsymmetrical allocation of bandwidth, unlike FDD (Frequency Division Duplex) which has separate paired spectrum for the uplink and downlink (FBMC, http://homepages.nildram.co.uk/~jidlaw/pages/glossary/html#W).

**Time-Division Multiplexing (TDM)** A type of multiplexing where two or more channels of information are transmitted over the same link by allocating a different time interval ('slot' or 'slice') for the transmission of each channel (FOLDOC, http://foldoc.doc.ic.ac.uk/foldoc/index.html).

**Transistor** A semiconductor device capable of amplification (Princeton, www.cogsci.princeton.edu/cgi-bin/webwn2.l).

**Ultra High Frequency (UHF)** Radio frequencies exceeding 300MHz (National Weather Service, www.weather.gov/glossary/index/php).

**UMTS** Universal Mobile Telecommunications System. UMTS is a broadband wireless multimedia system that is predicted to allow users of mobile devices to undertake global roaming (CHIN, http://www.chin.gc.ca/English/Digital_Content/Tip_Sheets/Wireless/glossary.html).

**Uplink** The transmission path from the mobile station up to the base station (cellglide, www.cellglide.com/glossaryb.5html).

**vertical hand-off** A vertical hand-off refers to the capability of roaming between different types of networks, such as WAN to LAN, or terrestrial cellular to satellite.

**Virtual Private Network (VPN)** A data network that uses the public telecommunications infrastructure, but maintains privacy through the use of a tunnelling protocol and security procedures. A VPN gives a company the same capabilities as a system of owned or leased lines to which that company has exclusive access. However, costs are much lower because the VPN uses the shared public infrastructure rather than exclusive line access (INTEL, http://support.intel.com/support/wireless/wlan/pro2200bg/userguide81/glossary.htm).

**Visitors Location Registry (VLR)** A local database maintained by the cellular provider to track users who are roaming in the provider's home territory (INTEL, http://support.intel.com/support/wireless/wlan/pro2200bg/userguide81/glossary.htm).

**Voice Over Internet Protocol (VoIP)** A technology that allows users to make telephone calls using a broadband Internet connection instead of a regular (or analogue) phone line (FCC, http://www.fcc.gov/cib/handbook.html).

**WAN (Wide Area Network)** A voice, data or video network that provides connections from one or more computers or networks within a business to one or more computers or networks that are external to such business (INTEL, http://support.intel.com/support/ wireless/wlan/pro2200bg/userguide81/glossary.htm).

**WAP** Wireless Application Protocol. An open, global specification that gives users with wireless, mobile devices rapid access to information services. Designed to work with most wireless networks, WAP applications can be built on any operating system (CHIN, http://www.chin.gc.ca/English/Digital_Content/Tip_Sheets/ Wireless/glossary.html).

**War chalking** Fundamentally anarchic practice of graffiti indicating access to a wireless LAN, not necessarily with the network owners permission. Usually the LAN will be a 802.11b standard LAN supporting Wi-Fi interoperability (FBMC, http://home pages.nildram.co.uk/~jidlaw/pages/glossary/html#W).

**Wavelength** The distance between points of corresponding phase of two consecutive cycles of a wave (ATIS, http://www.atis.org/tg2k).

**Web clipping** Process of filtering HTML content to remove unnecessary formatting, gifs, etc., usually for display on a wireless device (FBMC, http://homepages.nildram.co.uk/ ~jidlaw/pages/glossary/html#W).

**Wideband CDMA (W-CDMA)** The multiplexing scheme for UMTS.

**Wi-Fi** Short for 'wireless fidelity' is denoted as 802.11b from the Institute of Electrical and Electronics Engineers, and is part of a series of wireless specifications together with 802.11, 802.11a, and 802.11g. All four standards use the Ethernet protocol and CSMA/ CA (carrier sense multiple access with collision avoidance) for path sharing. The future of Wi-Fi represents a newer type of higher frequency wireless local area network (WLAN) where it is anticipated that many companies may use Wi-Fi-enabled PDA technologies to form an alternative to a wired LAN (CHIN, http://www.chin.gc.ca/English/Digital_ Content/Tip_Sheets/ Wireless/glossary.html).

**WiMAX** A Standard Air Interface for Broadband Wireless Access. The IEEE 802.16 standard describes an interface for non-line-of-sight radio frequencies less than 11GHz and distances up to 30 km (WiMAX, http://www.wimaxforum.org/technology).

**Wireless access point** A device that connects to an existing wired network and communicates with wireless devices.

**Wireless Encryption Protocol (WEP)** WEP64 and WEP128: Wired Equivalent Privacy, 64 bit and 128 bit (64 bit is sometimes referred to as 40 bit) encryption protocol. This is a low-level encryption technique designed to give the user about the same amount of privacy that he or she would expect from a LAN (INTEL, http://support. intel.com/support/wireless/wlan/pro2200bg/userguide81/glossary.htm).

**WML** Wireless Markup Language.

**World Administrative Radio Conference (WRC)** Among its many activities, the ITU-R sponsors the World Administrative Radio Conference (WRC). The WRC is the place where spectrum management issues are addressed at an international level.

# Bibliography

Abbate, J. (1999) *Inventing the Internet*. Cambridge: MIT Press.

Agar, J. (2003) *Constant Touch: A Global History of the Mobile Phone*. Duxford: Icon Books.

Albrecht, K. (2002) RFID: Tracking everything, everywhere, *Consumers Against Supermarket Privacy Invasion and Numbering (CASPIAN)*. Available at http://www.nocards.org/AutoID/overview.shtml

Asia Pacific Telecommunity (2005) APT Conference Preparatory Group for WRC. Available at http://www.aptsec.org/Program/APG/papg.html

Baum, R. (2004) Text messages shape politics in Philippines, *Reuters*, 22 March. Available at http://www.reuters.com

Beck, J. C. and Wade, M. (2002) *DoCoMo – Japan's Wireless Tsunami: How One Mobile Telecom Created a New Market and Became a Global Force*. New York: AMACOM.

Benkler, Y. and Lessig, L. (1998) Net gains, *The New Republic*, 14 December. Available at http://www.thadk.net/ideas/lessigcopyright.html

Canadian Wireless Telecommunications Association (2003) Canadian and U.S. Wireless Service Providers Unify North American Text Message Markets, 23 January. Retrieved May 2005. Available at http://www.cwta.ca/CWTASite/english/pressreleases.html

Carlo, G.L. and Schram, M. (2003) *Cell Phones: Invisible Hazards in the Wireless Age*. Emeryville, CA: Avalon Travel Publishing.

Carpenter, D. (2005) First cell phone was a true 'brick', *ABC News*, 9 April. Retrieved May 2005. Available at http://abcnews.go.com/Technology/wireStory?id=656626

Cellular Telecommunications Industry Association (2002) CTIA demonstrates inter-carrier messaging, *CTIA Public Affairs*, 18 March. Retrieved May 2005. Available at http://www.ctia.org/news_media/press/body.cfm?record_id=1066

Cellular Telecommunications Industry Association (2003) U.S. wireless carriers to launch common short code capability, *CTIA Public Affairs*, 21 October. Retrieved May 2005. Available at http://www.ctia.org/news_media/press/body.cfm?record_id=1335

Cellular Telecommunications Industry Association (2005) Wireless carriers announce 'Wireless Content Guidelines', 8 November. Available at http://www.ctia.org/news_media/press/body.cfm?record_id=1565

Chodorowicz, D. and Sciadas, G. (1998) The cellular telephone industry: birth, evolution, and prospects, *Canadian Economic Observer*, August.

Coase, R. (1998) Comment on Thomas W. Hazlett, assigning property rights to radio spectrum users: why did FCC license auctions take 67 years? *Journal of Law and Economics*, 41: 577–80.

Commission of the European Communities (2001) *The Introduction of Third Generation Mobile Communications in the European Union: State of Play and the Way Forward*. Communication from the Commission to the Council, The European Parliament, the Economic and Social Committee and the Committee of the Regions.

Conklin, D. (1998) Spectrum allocation, *Adapting to New Realities: Canadian Telecommunications Policy Conference*. Ontario: University of Western Ontario, Richard Ivey School of Business.

Digital Terrestrial Television Action Group (DigiTAG) (2005) Television on a handheld receiver: broadcasting with DVB-H. Retrieved November 2005. Available at http://www.dvb-h-online.org/PDF/DigiTAG-DVB-H-Handbook.pdf

Dornan, A. (2002) *The Essential Guide to Wireless Communications*, 2nd edn. Upper Saddle River: Prentice Hall.

Ducatel, K., Bogdanowicz, M., Scapolo, F. et al. (2001) *Scenarios for Ambient Intelligence 2010*. Seville: Institute for Prospective Technological Studies, Directorate General Joint Research Centre, European Commission.

DVB-H: Global Mobile TV (2005) Retrieved November 2005. Available at http://www.dvb-h-online.org/

*Economist* (2001) The Internet untethered, 11 October. Retrieved June 2005. Available at http://www.economist.com/surveys/displaystory.cfm?story_id=811934

*Economist* (2000) The wireless gamble, 14 October. Retrieved June 2005. Available at http://www.economist.com/opinion/displayStory.cfm?Story_ID=392521

*Economist* (1999) *Cutting the cord*, 7 October. Available at http://www.economist.com/surveys/displayStory.cfm?Story_id=246152

*Economist* (1999) The world in your pocket, 7 October. Available at http://www.economist.com/surveys/displayStory.cfm?Story_id=246137

European Radiocommunications Office (2004) ERO information. Available at http://www.ero.dk/

*Eurotechnology.com*. (2005) 3G (wCDMA, CDMA-2000, UMTS, FOMA) in Japan FAQ. Available at http://www.eurotechnology.com/3G/index.html

Farley, T. (2004) Mobile telephone history, *Privateline.com*, pp. 6, 7, 9. Retrieved May 2005. Available at http://www.privateline.com/PCS/history.htm

Faulhaber, G. R. and Farber, D.J. (2002) Comments of Gerald R. Faulhaber and David J. Farber before the FCC Spectrum Policy Task Force, *FCC Spectrum Policy Task Force*, 18 July. Retrieved June 2005. Available at http://gullfoss2.fcc.gov/prod/ecfs/retrieve.cgi?native_or_pdf=pdf&id_document=6513282647

Flickenger, R. (2003) *Building Wireless Community Networks*, 2nd edn. Cambridge: O'Reilly Media.

Fransman, M. (2002) *Telecoms in the Internet Age: From Boom to Bust to . . . ?* Oxford: Oxford University Press.

*Freenetworks.org* (2003) What is a freenet? Retrieved April 2003. Available at http://www.freenetworks.org/

Georgia Institute of Technology (2003) Mobility management in 4G wireless systems, *Broadband and Wireless Networking Laboratory*. Available at http://users.ece.gatech.edu/~jxie/4G/index.html

Gow, G. A. and Ihnat, M. (2004) Prepaid mobile phone service and the anonymous caller: considering wireless E9-1-1 in Canada, *Surveillance & Society*, 1(4): 555–72.

Greenfield, A. (2006) *Everyware: The Dawning Age of Ubiquitous Computing*. Indianapolis: New Riders.

Greenpeace (2005) Looming e-waste problems for Thailand and Philippines, 28 September. Available at http://www.greenpeace.org/seasia/en/press/releases/toxictech_sea

*GSM World* (2005) Live GSM Networks. Available at http://www.gsmworld.com/news/statistics/networks.shtml

Guidry, M. (1995) Violence in the cosmos, *Department of Physics and Astronomy, University of Tennessee*. Retrieved April 2005. Available at http://csep10.phys.utk.edu/guidry/violence/lightspeed.html

Haines, L. (2005). Oz watchdog bans mobile porn, *The Register*, 5 July. Available at http://www.theregister.co.uk/2005/07/05/oz_mobile_smut_ban/

Hall, J. (2004) Mobile entertainment: the power of play, *The Feature*, 16 June. Available at http://www.thefeature.com/article?articleid=100764&ref=7960944

Hardin, G. (1968) The tragedy of the commons, *Science*, 13 December. Available at http://www.garretthardinsociety.org/articles/art_tragedy_of_the_commons.html

Hazlett, T. (2001) The wireless craze, the unlimited bandwidth myth, the spectrum auction faux pas, and the punchline to Ronald Coase's 'big joke': an essay on airwave allocation policy, *AEI Brookings Joint Center*, January. Available at http://www.aei.brookings.org/publications/index.php?tab=author&authorid=7

Hesseldahl, A. (2001a) Disaster of the day: Globalstar, *Forbes.com*, 17 January. Retrieved May 2005. Available at http://www.forbes.com/2001/01/17/0117disaster.html

Hesseldahl, A. (2001b) The winter of handset discontent, *Forbes.com*, 18 July. Retrieved May 2005. Available at http://www.forbes.com/2001/07/18/0718nokia.html

Hjelm, J. (2000) *Designing Wireless Information Services*. London: John Wiley & Sons.

Hoffman, J. (2003) *GPRS Demystified*. New York: McGraw-Hill.

Infrared Data Association (2004) What is infrared and Where is it used? Available at http://www.irda.org/

Inter-American Telecommunication Commission (2004) Permanent Consultative Committee II: Radiocommunication including Broadcasting. Retrieved December 2004. Available at http://www.citel.oas.org/ccp2-radio.asp

International Engineering Consortium (2005) Signaling System 7 (SS7). Available at http://www.iec.org/online/tutorials/ss7/

International Telecommunications Union (2000) Main results of WRC-2000 (Istanbul, Turkey, 8 May–2 June 2000). Available at http://www.itu.int/ITU-R/conferences/wrc/wrc-00/results/

International Telecommunications Union (2002) Internet for a mobile generation. Available at http://www.itu.int/osg/spu/publications/mobileinternet/index.html

International Telecommunications Union (2005) ITU Radiocommunication Sector Mission Statement. Available at http://www.itu.int/ITU-R/information/mission/index.html

Irish Cellular Industry Association (2005) A parent's guide to mobile phones. Available at http://www.icia.ie

Japan Ministry of Internal Affairs and Communications (2005) u-Japan policy: working toward realizing the ubiquitous network society by 2010. Retrieved December 2005. Available at http://www.soumu.go.jp/menu_02/ict/u-japan_en/index2.html#

*JiWire* (2005) Wi-Fi hotspot finder, product reviews, industry news. Available at http://www.jiwire.com/

Jones, R. V. (2004) About CDMA spread spectrum. Retrieved May 2005. Available at http://people.deas.harvard.edu/~jones/cscie129/nu_lectures/lecture7/hedy/lemarr.htm

Kamada, T. (1998) Compact HTML for small information appliances W3C NOTE, *World Wide Web Consortium (W3C)*, 9 February. Available at http://www.w3.org/TR/1998/NOTE-compactHTML-19980209/

Katz, J. E. and Aakhus, M. (eds) (2002) *Perpetual Contact: Mobile Communications, Private Talk, Public Performance*. Cambridge: Cambridge University Press.

King, B. (2005) Cannes demos the next fast thing, *The Register*, 16 February. Retrieved June 2005. Available at http://www.theregister.co.uk/2005/02/16/hsdpa_3g_demo/

King, P. and Hyland, T. (1997) Handheld device markup language specification, *W3C Note*, 9 May. Available at http://www.w3.org/TR/NOTE-Submission-HDML-spec.html

Klemperer, P. (2002) How (not) to run auctions: the European 3G telecom auctions. *European Economic Review*, 46: 829–45.

Knight, W. (2005) 4G prototypes reach blistering speeds, *New Scientist*, 2 September. Retrieved November 2005. Available at http://www.newscientist.com/article.ns?id=dn7943

Konkka, K. (2003) Indian needs: cultural end-user research in Mombai, in C. Lindholm, T. Keinonen and H. Kiljander (eds) *Mobile Usability: How Nokia Changed the Face of the Mobile Phone*, pp. 97–111. New York: McGraw-Hill.

Kopomaa, T. (2000) *The City in Your Pocket: Birth of the Mobile Information Society*. Helsinki: Gaudeamus.

Krewski, D., Byus, C. V., Glickman, B. W. et al. (2004) Recent advances in research on radiofrequency fields and health: 2001–2003, *The Royal Society of Canada*. Available at http://www.rsc.ca/index.php?page=expert_panels_rf&lang_id=1&page_id=120

Kwerel, E. and Williams, J. (2002) A proposal for a rapid transition to market allocation of spectrum: OPP Working Paper Series (No. 38), November. Federal Communications Commission, Office of Policy and Planning. Available at http://hraunfoss.fcc.gov/edocs_public/attachmatch/DOC-228552A1.pdf

*Lapp-Hancock Update* (2004) Anguilla's mobile solution, 11(3): 2–3.

Le Bodic, G. (2003) *Mobile Messaging: Technologies and Services*. London: John Wiley & Sons.

Le Maistre, R. (2002) Nokia extends handset lead, *Unstrung*, 26 November. Available at http://www.unstrung.com/

Lessig, L. (2002) *The Future of Ideas*. New York: Vintage.

Lie, E. (2004) *Radio Spectrum Management for a Converging World* (RSM/07). Geneva: International Telecommunications Union.

Lindholm, C., Keinonen, T. and Kiljander, H. (eds) (2003) *Mobile Usability: How Nokia Changed the Face of the Mobile Phone*. New York: McGraw-Hill.

Ling, R. (2004) *The Mobile Connection: The Cell Phone's Impact on Society*. Amsterdam: Elsevier.

Lundin, A. (2005) Intimidation at skateboard park, *The NOW Coquitlam, Port Coquitlam, Port Moody, Anmore and Belcarra*, 7 October: 15.

Mahan, A. (2003) Regulatory peripheries: using prepaid to extend the network, *info*, 5(4): 37–44.

Manktelow, N. (2000) One wireless viewpoint: WAP is crap, *ZDNet Australia*, 29 June. Retrieved September 2002. Available at http://zdnet.com

McGrath, M. (2000) *WAP in Easy Steps*. London: Computer Steps.

McMillan, J. (1995) Why auction the spectrum? *Telecommunications Policy*, 19(3): 191–9.

*MobileTV News* (2005) Vodafone releases first mobile TV figures, 17 November. Retrieved November 2005. Available at http://www.mobiletv-news.com/content/view/96/2/

MobiTV: live television. Anywhere. Anytime. (2005) Retrieved November 2005. Available at http://www.mobitv.com/index.html

Mock, D. (2005) *The Qualcomm Equation*. New York: AMACOM.

Murray, Jr., J. B. (2001) *Wireless Nation*. Cambridge: Perseus.

Myerson, G. (2001) *Heidegger, Habermas and the Mobile Phone*. Duxford: Icon Books.

Natsuno, T. (2003) *The i-mode Wireless Ecosystem*. London: John Wiley and Sons.

Nuechterlein, J. E. and Weiser, P. J. (2005) *Digital Crossroads: American Telecommunications Policy in the Internet Age*. Cambridge: MIT Press.

Nygard, M. (no date) A brief look at Java 2 micro edition, *Wireless Developer Network*. Available at http://www.wirelessdevnet.com/channels/java/features/j2me.html

Oates, J. (2005) Parents blame Vonage over girl's death, *The Register*, 10 May. Retrieved May 2005. Available at http://www.theregister.co.uk/2005/05/10/vonage_accused_over_911_death/

Ofcom (2004) Spectrum Framework Review, 23 November. Retrieved June 2005. Available at http://www.ofcom.org.uk/consult/condocs/sfr/sfr2/?a=87101

Orlowski, A. (2005) Smart phones boom – Symbian up, MS and Palm down, *The Register*, 26 April. Available at http://www.theregister.co.uk/2005/04/26/smartphones_q1_2005/

Pfanner, E. (2004) Text-messaging the revolution, *International Herald Tribune Online*, 22 March. Available at http://www.iht.com

Philips Research (2004) PHENOM: perceptive home environments. Retrieved November 2005. Available at http://www.research.philips.com/technologies/syst_softw/phenom/index.html

Ralph, D. and Graham, P. (2003) *Multi Media Messaging Service: Techologies, Usage and Business Models*. New York: John Wiley & Sons.

Rao, B. and Minakakis, L. (2003) Evolution of Mobile Location-based Services, *Communications of the ACM*, 46(12): 61–5.

Rheingold, H. (2002) *Smart Mobs: The Next Social Revolution*. Cambridge: Perseus.

Rheingold, H. (2004) Political texting: SMS and elections, *The Feature*, 12 April. Available at http://www.thefeature.com/

Rhodes, J. S. (2003) How warchalking died, *Webword.com*, 9 January. Retrieved May 2005. Available at http://webword.com/moving/warchalking.html

Rushkoff, D. (2004) Rock the (wireless) vote.com, *The Feature*, 22 March. Available at http://www.thefeature.com/

Schiller, J. (2003) *Mobile Communications*, 2nd edn. London: Addison-Wesley.

Seybold, A. and Samples, M. (1986) *Cellular Mobile Telephone Guide*. Indianapolis: Howard W. Sams & Co.

Shapiro, C. and Varian, H. (1998) *Information Rules: A Strategic Guide to the Network Economy*. Harvard Business School Press.

Specter, M. (2001) The phone guy, *The New Yorker*, 26 November: 62–72. Retrieved January 2006. Available at http://www.michaelspecter.com/ny/2001/2001_11_26_nokia.html

Staple, G. and Werbach, K. (2004) The end of spectrum scarcity, *IEEE Spectrum Online*, March. Available at http://www.spectrum.ieee.org/WEBONLY/publicfeature/mar04/0304scar.html

Steinbock, D. (2001) *The Nokia Revolution*. New York: AMACOM.

Steinbock, D. (2003) *Wireless Horizon: Strategy and Competition in the Worldwide Mobile Marketplace*. New York: AMACOM.

Steinbock, D. (2005) *The Mobile Revolution: The Making of Mobile Services Worldwide*. London: Kogan Page.

Strayer, D., Drews, F., Albert, R. et al. (2002) Does cell phone conversation impair driving performance? US National Safety Council, 13 March. Retrieved September 2005. Available at http://www.nsc.org/library/shelf/inincell.htm

Struzak, R. (1996) Spectrum management: key issues, *Pacific Telecommunications Review*, September.

Struzak, R. (1999a) Spectrum management (1/3), *ITU News*, 3: 27–34.

Struzak, R. (1999b) Spectrum management (2/3), *ITU News*, 5.

Struzak, R. (1999c) Spectrum management (3/3), *ITU News*, 6.

Struzak, R. (2000) Access to Spectrum: Orbit Resources and Principles of Spectrum Management. Retrieved January 2006. Available at http://www.ictp.trieste.it/~radio net/2000_school/lectures/struzak/AcceSpctrOrbICTP.htm

Sun Microsystems (2002) All IP wireless, all the time: building the 4th generation wireless system with open systems solutions, 28 January. Retrieved November 2005. Available at http://research.sun.com/features/4g_wireless/

Swartz, N. (2001) Waiting for GAIT, *Wireless Review*, 1 July. Retrieved April 2005. Available at http://industryclick.com/magazinearticle.asp?releaseid=6735&magazine articleid=111222&siteid=3&magazineid=9

TDMA: Time Division Multiple Access (2004) *3G Americas*. Retrieved May 2005. Available at http://www.uwcc.org/English/Technology%5FCenter/tdma.cfm

Telecommunications Industry Assocation (2001) Tom Carter inducted into RCR's wireless hall of fame, *Pulse Online*, August. Retrieved May 2005. Available at http://pulse.tiaonline.org/article.cfm?id=546

Terdiman, D. (2005) Putting flesh on phones, *Wired*, 8 April. Available at http://www.wired.com/news/wireless/0,1382,67165,00.html

*The Register* (2004) Mobile porn is a 'time bomb', 10 June. Retrieved November 2005. Available at http://www.theregister.co.uk/2004/06/10/mobile_adult_content

Trosby, F. (2004) SMS, the strange duckling of GSM, *Telektronikk*, 3: 187–94.

*UMTS Forum* (2003) 3G services examples. Retrieved June 2005. Available at http://www.umts-forum.org/servlet/dycon/ztumts/umts/Live/en/umts/3G_Services_example

Vincent, J. (2004) The social shaping of the mobile communications repertoire, *The Journal of the Communications Network* (January–March) 3: 1–5.

Weiser, M. (1991) The computer for the 21st century, *Scientific American*, September: 94–110.

Werbach, K. (2002) Open spectrum: the new wireless paradigm, *New America Foundation, Spectrum Policy Program*, October. Available at http://werbach.com/docs/new_wireless_paradigm.htm

White, J. C. (2003) *People, Not Places: A Policy Framework for Analyzing Location Privacy Issues*, Masters Memo Prepared for the Electronic Privacy Information Center. Terry Sanford Institute of Public Policy, Duke University.

Wi-Fi Alliance (2005) Certification programs. Available at http://www.wi-fi.org/Open-Section/certification_programs.asp?TID=2

*Wikipedia* (2005) Largest mobile phone companies, 9 May. Retrieved May 2005. Available at http://en.wikipedia.org/wiki/Largest_mobile_phone_companies#World

*Wireless Information Network* (2005) WAP push. Available at http://www.winplc.com/solutions/wap-push.aspx

Woolley, S. (2002) Dead air, *Forbes*, 25 November. Retrieved April 2003. Available at http://www.forbes.com/forbes/2002/1125/138_print.html

# Index